D0941304

LIBRARY
~~~~~ OF JUNIOR COLL~
5900 S~ ~~~~~ ~~~
LITTLETON, COLORADO

by Franz Schurmann and Orville Schell

THE CHINA READER

★ IMPERIAL CHINA: *The Decline of the Last Dynasty and the Origins of Modern China The 18th and 19th Centuries*

★★ REPUBLICAN CHINA: *Nationalism, War, and the Rise of Communism 1911–1949*

★★★ COMMUNIST CHINA: *Revolutionary Reconstruction and International Confrontation 1949 to the Present*

by Franz Schurmann

IDEOLOGY AND ORGANIZATION IN COMMUNIST CHINA

Imperial China:
The Decline of the Last Dynasty and the Origins of Modern China
The 18th and 19th Centuries

1 The China Reader

Edited, annotated,
and with introductions
by FRANZ SCHURMANN
and ORVILLE SCHELL

Imperial China
The Decline of the Last Dynasty and the Origins of Modern China
The 18th and 19th Centuries

RANDOM HOUSE, New York

First Printing

© Copyright, 1967, by Franz Schurmann and Orville Schell
All rights reserved under International and Pan-American Copyright
Conventions. Published in New York by Random House, Inc., and
simultaneously in Toronto, Canada, by Random House of Canada Limited.

Library of Congress Catalog Card Number: 66–21489

Manufactured in the United States of America,
by The Colonial Press Inc., Clinton, Massachusetts

The authors wish to thank the following for permission to reprint:

The American Geographical Society for *China: Land of Famine* by Walter H. Mallory (1926).

Harvard University Press for *China's Response to the West* by Ssu-yü Teng and John K. Fairbank, © Copyright, 1954, 1960, by the President and Fellows of Harvard College; *In Search of Wealth and Power* by Benjamin Schwartz, © Copyright, 1964, by the President and Fellows of Harvard College; *Studies on the Population of China* by Ping-ti Ho, © Copyright, 1959, by the President and Fellows of Harvard College; *The United States and China* by John K. Fairbank, © Copyright, 1959, by the President and Fellows of Harvard College.

Lewis A. Maverick for *China, A Model for Europe* (1946).

R. Oldenbourg Verlag for *Das Jahrhundert der Chinesischen Revolution 1851-1949* by Wolfgang Franke (1958).

Stanford University Press for *The Last Stand of Chinese Conservatism* by Mary C. Wright. © Copyright, 1957, by the Board of Trustees of the Leland Stanford Junior University.

University of California Press for *Confucian China and Its Modern Fate* by Joseph R. Levenson (1958); *Religion in Chinese Society* by C. K. Yang (1961).

To the Faculty Peace Committee

F.S.

To my parents

O.S.

"*It is of great importance that we try to learn something more about the strange and fascinating Chinese nation, about its past and its present, about the aims of its leaders and the aspirations of its people. Before we can make wise political—and perhaps military—decisions pertaining to China, there are many questions to be asked and, hopefully, answered: What kind of people are the Chinese? To what extent are they motivated by national feeling? To what extent by ideology? Why are the Chinese Communist leaders so hostile to the United States and why do they advocate violent revolution against most of the world's governments? To what extent is their view of the world distorted by isolation and the memory of ancient grievances? And to what extent, and with what effect on their government, do the Chinese people share with us and with all other peoples what Aldous Huxley has called the 'simple human preference for life and peace'? We need to ask these questions because China and America may be heading toward war with each other and it is essential that we do all that can be done to prevent that calamity, starting with a concerted effort to understand the Chinese people and their leaders.*"

—J. WILLIAM FULBRIGHT

Preface

When Random House approached us early in 1966 to do a reader on China for fall publication, our first thoughts were that it could not be done, and in any case there were already many books on China available. But the worsening situation in Eastern Asia made us feel that a well-thought-out reader could help answer some of the serious questions concerning China. The great quantity of literature on China is, ironically, one of the main obstacles to understanding. At John J. Simon's urging we decided that a reader which distilled down some of these materials and provided some commentary would be a contribution.

Our reader's three volumes cover China's past and present. Nevertheless they form a whole: the first two volumes are not the chronological predecessors of the third but, rather, provide material elucidating China's present state of mind. History is more than background or ultimate cause: it is the framework of the present.

We have taken material from scholars, journalists, literary men, and political leaders. Our criteria for selection have been relevance and readability. We have abridged some selections, while trying not to change the sense of the original. Generally we have used existing translations, but have made our own in a few cases. Footnotes have been removed, since most of them are of interest only to the specialist. We wish to express our gratitude to all who have given permission to include their writings.

Each selection or set of selections has an introduction which guides the reader into the material and analyzes the problems dealt with. Some of our selections reflect points of view and approaches with which we do not fully agree, but we have felt it important to present a broad spectrum of thinking on a subject so complex as China. People may disagree with some of our analysis, but at least we hope to have provided some ideas with which one can disagree. There is a wealth of descriptive material on China; what is lacking is interpretation. We welcome all dialogues that may ensue from the ideas we present.

Each section has an introduction which sketches out the main trends and characteristics of the period in question. Here we go beyond analysis and make judgments and evaluations. We hope that this will help the reader get a sense of the period as a whole.

Each volume has a general introduction which states our convictions about China. The tragic events of the last few years have made us realize that the scholar has a duty to do more than analyze material and act as a technical expert for those who make decisions. He must take a rational and moral position on issues. As Sinologists we are involved with the country and people of China. As citizens we are members of a country which one day may be at war with China. Such a war would be a tragedy for the American and the Chinese peoples. In our general introductions we express our personal opinions on the meaning of China's past and present. We fear that America's and China's role in the world is leading to ever more hostile confrontation. We do not believe that earnest words about better relations between the two countries are going to eradicate the dangers. Our readers will see numerous instances where the Chinese have talked one way and acted another. We are now beginning to realize that our government does the same.

China is a strange and fascinating nation, but it is understandable. Understanding may not have much effect on political action, but it will help reason and moral judgment, to which we hope this reader will contribute.

Franz Schurmann
Orville Schell
Berkeley, California, 1966

Contents

Introduction

China is a country and a civilization distant from our own Western traditions. Over three thousand years ago she began to develop her own civilization, at times borrowing from neighboring cultures, notably Buddhism from India. But unlike the lands of Europe which for centuries looked to each other, China just sent her pilgrims to India to bring back what was desirable. When Buddhism took root in China and became a great Chinese religion, the Chinese forgot about India, and from the Sung Dynasty to recent times India was as remote from China as was Europe. The Chinese traditionally regarded themselves as at the center of the universe, and the outer galaxies, except when they bothered China, were of no concern to her.

The Chinese believed they had devised man's most perfect system of government and society. If they were not always perfect in practice, that was just because man could not live up to his ideals. They regarded the universe as made up of harmonious balances; thus if man understood the laws of the universe, and the learned man were given authority, then there was no reason for everything not to be in harmony: individual, family, empire. In no civilization did education hold so central a place nor did learned men enjoy such political authority as in China.

Enlightenment, however, was not accessible to all. Human society was forever divided into "gentlemen" and "small men." Some of the latter, through hard work and study, might attain the rank of the gentlemen, but the great mass of small men would forever remain where they were. It was the gentleman's duty to exercise benevolent rule over the small men: emperor over his subjects, magistrate over the people, husband over wife and children. If all men accepted the wisdom of the *Tao* (the Way), then peace would prevail. The old Chinese conception of peace was expressed through the word "flat": no disturbances in the realm, the village, or the home, no passion in the life of man, serenity in old age where death calmly supplanted life.

Old China was destroyed by internal revolution and external humiliation. The foundations of society were undermined when Confucianism's human ideals failed the challenges of the modern world. Those ideals were ignorant of reason, disdainful of passion. China, as Joseph Needham has shown, had a magnificent tradition of philosophy, of protoscience, of logical and mathematical reasoning. But the eighteenth-century educated men of China were not philosophers but plodding academics, laboriously compiling huge encyclopedias of much information but little thought. Except for a few intellectual critics, the Chinese literati—calm patient men, of the type portrayed by the fables of Lin Yutang—forgot what reason was. But if passionate love and hatred were absent among the gentlemen, they were there for the small men, as we can see in China's great traditional novels—naturally despised by the Confucians—and in the emotions of China's many revolts. The favorite traditional expression for the suppression of revolt was "to flatten."

Reason and passion came to old China from two directions: the West and the small men of China.

Toward the end of the nineteenth century the Chinese were finally convinced that there was a universe beyond China's confines. For decades the Chinese had had contacts with Westerners, but regarded them as little more than modern versions of the ancient nomadic invaders. But then, as had been the case with Indian Buddhism fifteen hundred years earlier, they began to realize that peoples outside of China had discovered secrets about man, society, and cosmos of which the Chinese were entirely unaware. Both the Chinese discovery of India and of the West came during times of breakdown in China, but there was an important difference. Buddhism's Indian missionaries went quietly to China, set up monasteries, and translated scriptures. Westerners who went to China in the nineteenth century subjected the Chinese to humiliation of the deepest sort, branding them an inferior race, beating them militarily, reviling them as heathen whose souls had to be transformed before they could become fully human. What made the humiliation even harder to bear was the realization that the Westerners' spiritual horizons were broader than any the Chinese had ever known, and that they experienced a world of emotions which the Chinese denied themselves in the interests of Confucian harmony.

China's material suffering of the nineteenth and twentieth centuries is well known to the West, but we must also realize the depths of China's spiritual pain that remain to this day. Confucianism taught the Chinese how to live in harmony with the world, and Buddhism taught them the secrets of the soul. By the beginning of the twentieth century, however, the Chinese saw themselves alone in a hostile and unknown world without the means either of rearranging it or fitting into it.

The Chinese reluctantly began to learn reason from the West, and so began China's intellectual revolution.

Humiliation from the West was accompanied by the degeneration of Chinese society itself. The rebellious currents of the late eighteenth century led from the Taiping Rebellion, to the Boxers, to the Kuomintang, and finally to the Communists. The small men of China—peasants, merchants, workers, women, and the young—burst forth in murderous hatred of their rulers. One has only to compare the Taipings' proclamations with the official documents of the Imperial suppressors of revolution to see the gulf separating new and old. The Taipings, with their millenarian beliefs, projected a world of love, joy, and hatred: the enemies of the people would be smashed, all men would be made equal, the wealth would be shared, and a good society would come into being. The Imperial documents are detailed battle reports about "bandit suppression," proposals about improving conditions, and schemes for restoring harmony. The Imperial bandit-suppressor Tseng Kuo-fan never understood the

Taipings' passion, nor did Chiang Kai-shek, who thoroughly admired Tseng, understand Communism's emotional substance.

As we read the bland Confucian maxims with which Chiang
Kai-shek tried to supplant the ideology of Communism, let us
remember that during the last hundred years China has experienced internal violence on a scale unsurpassed in any other nation. Every revolt was bloodily put down, with the traditional
authority figures—landlords, officials, village teachers—hasten-
ing to resume their old positions. Revolution and counter-revolution brutalized the country, with the effect, over the century
of its duration, of creating more revolutionaries and making
the revolution's ultimate triumph inevitable.

Revolution began in inland China, but in the second decade
of this century revolutionary currents arose in the cities as well.
The May Fourth Movement of 1919, whose anniversary is still
celebrated today by Chinese of different political convictions,
marked the intellectuals' revolt against the old order. During the
1920s a revolutionary movement, Chinese Communism, began
in the cities as the ideology and the movement of revolutionary
intellectuals and workers. Reason and passion met in the form
of Marxism, which, as the science of socialism, claimed all the
products of reason that bourgeois society had created and that
the revolutionary classes would now take as their own. As the
ideology of revolution it gave men's revolutionary passions purpose, goals, and historical justification.

City and village drifted apart in early-twentieth-century
China. The cities became Westernized and a part of the world
market system which foreign imperialism had created. Shanghai,
for example, became more a European than a Chinese city. The
village, though affected by the new cities, retained its traditional
heritage. The Chinese Communists speak of pre-1949 China as
"semi-feudal and semi-colonial," thus attesting to the gap between modern city and traditional village. The Chinese Communist Party bridged that gap, bringing to the village a modern,
international, urban ideology, but one able to tap the peasants'
revolutionary energies.

It has become commonplace today for some writers to see

Communist China as little more than a reincarnation of its Imperial past. That this view is often held out of sympathy for China—to show, for example, that China is more interested in her own problems than expanding into the outside world—does not demonstrate its validity. China is no longer a self-contained universe, even though time and time again she has shown ethnocentric tendencies. The millions of men who lead Chinese society today are very different from the long-gowned gentry officials of times past. From what the Chinese Communists say, two types of leaders have emerged: the reds and the experts. The phrase "red and expert" is used again and again in China, indicating two human ideals which the Communists want to join but which they have not yet been able to do.

Since the introduction of modern education, a new type of intellectual has emerged in China, turning, as in most developing countries, toward science and technology. The best students in China today are in the sciences. Even in America, one sees thousands of Chinese scientists and technicians, often brilliant leaders in their fields, who are the heirs to the tradition of Western reason, first brought to China by Englishmen and Americans and then by Russian and Chinese Marxists. They worship science much as nineteenth-century Westerners did. No matter how much they may be attacked for "egotism," they know that science is a supreme value, assured by Marxist ideology and the international canons of reason.

We in the West understand these people. They are the products of the modern Chinese cities. They speak our language and, in fact, are a part of the international community. They read the international journals of science, plentifully represented even in remote Chinese libraries. Though China is no longer a part of the world market system, her intellectual links to the Western world, forged by science, technology, and trade, remain strong. As China enters more deeply into the international political community, these links will become even stronger.

Who are the reds? In essence, they are the political cadres drawn from the young and the poor, from those groups of the population who made the Chinese Revolution. They are the heirs to China's revolutionary passion. They dominate the Party committees of the villages, factories, and offices. They are the preferred candidates for military service and officer training. They are given preferential treatment in the country's higher schools. Mao Tse-tung, who is their prophet, knows well that every bureaucracy tends, in time, to become middle-aged and routinized, that there is the danger that the figure of the old official can reappear. He is determined that this shall not happen before China has been fully transformed—and that time still is decades away. For Mao the hope of the revolution lies in the young and the poor, in short, the oppressed classes of traditional Chinese society.

China's poor are mainly her peasants. Mao Tse-tung's great dream is that the peasantry's inland world will someday be brought into modern civilization. His unconcern with the cities appears to reflect a confidence that the cities will continue to industrialize and modernize, as is the case with many other developing countries. But Mao is one of the few important leaders today who believes that the modernization of even the poorest peasant regions is essential to China's future. In neighboring Japan the modern world has spread over city and village alike, and standards of living approximate those of Europe. Mao is determined that China shall achieve this too. Japan never completely cut her ties with the past, nor has China. But what counted for Japan were the new values of modernization and industrialization. And so they count for China, for what matters today is that which is new.

China, like every other nation-state, has her own culture, language, and problems. To label her uniqueness "ethnocentrism" is to fall victim to long-dead Confucian ideas which often seem to have more persistence outside of China than within. *Chung-kuo* means "country of the middle," but no modern Chinese has seriously suggested that it means the center of the world. In the past, Chinese ethnocentrism was reflected in disdain for foreign writings, natural for someone living in his own sealed universe. Today, for example, no one can read the documents of the Sino-Soviet dispute without seeing that the Chinese take absolutely seriously every idea put forth by the Russians, if only to refute them with international Marxist argumentation. Thousands of foreign works have been translated into Chinese and have become a part of the modern Chinese cultural heritage.

Nationalism has made every modern people assert its cultural identity, and China is no exception. The Chinese are a proud people with much to be proud of. But unlike many peoples, the Chinese today again and again reaffirm their commitment to "internationalism," which means that they see themselves as a part of the world community.

This participation in the world community takes two forms. One, essentially rational and practical, may be termed "expert." China is within the international scientific and academic tradition, and with some notable exceptions such as the social sciences, participates readily. Chinese diplomatic and commercial relations span the world, as with other modern nations. On the other hand, participation also takes a "red" form. Despite the Sino-Soviet split, China still regards herself as a member of the socialist camp of nations. But, perhaps more importantly, she sees herself as the greatest nation of the third world. The leaders of China, as Marxists, have a view of world history. They believe that throughout the world the poor will rise against the rich, the young against the old, the village against the cities, and the natives against the foreigners. This world view is, of course, a generalization of their own revolutionary experiences in China, and of their Marxist beliefs that there are scientific laws of historical development. But it is also an expression of their conviction that China is a great nation of the world and not just a universe unto herself.

Nothing has so aroused American fears as this "red" Chinese view of the world. Twenty years ago America accepted the Soviet view of the trends of world history, and created a defensive system of awesome power against the Soviet Union. Today she has accepted the Chinese view and acts to prevent "national liberation movements" from arising or succeeding in different parts of the world. The tragic war in Vietnam is be-

ing fought to prove that America has the capability of halting
"Communist aggression," regardless of its form. The long-range
American aim appears to be to frustrate the "red" side of
Chinese internationalism so that in time the "expert" side will
emerge and a rational, practical China will take its place in the
world community.

Since the end of World War II both ideological and practical approaches have characterized the foreign policies of countries. Ideological approaches—whose principal justification has
been war and revolution—have tended to polarize the world
between Communist and anti-Communist forces, with the neu-
tralists maintaining a precarious balance in between. In China's
recent history we can see a peculiar dialectic between war and
revolution: the more the process of violence and counter-vio-
lence grew (after the general strike of May 30, 1925, after the
"white terror" of April 1927, after Chiang's "bandit extermination" campaigns in the early 1930s, after the outbreak of the
Sino-Japanese War in 1937, after the beginning of the Civil War
in 1946, after the beginning of the Korean War in 1950), the
greater became the Communists' ideological and organizational
power. No one can say that Mao Tse-tung is wrong when he
predicts that a world-wide process of violence and counter-
violence will ultimately end in the triumph of revolutionary
movements and in the collapse of world imperialism and capitalism. In short, Mao is confident that the ideologization of world
politics will help world revolution succeed.

On the other hand, where practical approaches have dominated foreign policies, the trend has been away from polarization. Trade relations, one of the most practical forms of relations
between countries, have already led to crisscrossing of ideological dividing lines. A look at China's non-ideological relations
with other countries reveals a variegated pattern dictated largely
by China's concrete self-interest. Two of the most practical
countries today, West Germany and Japan, have made international business into chief interests of their foreign policies,
have relations with practically every country in the world, and
are thriving economically.

Red and expert are said to be in contradiction within China, and so they may be said to be on the international scene. America and China are the two great powers of the modern world most committed to ideological approaches. Thus it is not coincidental that the most dangerous war and revolution of the mid-1960s, Vietnam, is being fought on China's borders. Both countries seem to be collaborating to force the world back into an ideological polarization from which it appeared to have been escaping after the beginnings of the Soviet-American détente.

In no country of the world save Japan has so much been written on China as in America, and in no country is the linguistic and technical expertise on China as great as in America. We hope the material presented in the three volumes of this *China Reader* will further our rational understanding of China. There is nothing exotic or mysterious about China, unless we choose to make it so. The Chinese are a common-sense people and Confucianism is easily understandable to any American familiar with Benjamin Franklin. Chinese Communism appears wild and jargonistic at first glance, but careful study makes it understandable, as is evident in the writings of dozens of American scholars professionally concerned with that country. If we accept Marxism as part of the Western heritage, then we share a world of reason with the Chinese. If we remember that before Marxism reached China her major cities had long been a part of the Western world's economic and cultural system, then the kinship of reason is even closer.

We should, however, do well to remember that there is a realm we do not share with the Chinese: the historical legacy of empire, humiliation, and revolution. Every nation lives with its past, even if unaware. The Chinese are acutely conscious of their history: they remember with pride when they were respected as a great civilization; they remember with agony when they were despised as an inferior race; they remember the revolution. Few Americans can share these feelings, but should not be surprised when many people outside of America, in circumstances similar to those of pre-1949 China, show sympathy to Mao's China.

Americans have generally been sympathetic to traditional China, and so the idea of Imperial reincarnation is popular. Judging from American delight in discovering Soviet "embourgeoisement," it is predictable that a similar reaction would occur if China's "expert" side were to meet its American counterpart. Many Americans would like to believe that underneath the ideology, there is not "red and expert" but Confucian and Western, even though such a wish ignores the legacy of China's past and the extent to which the Communists have transformed that past. China is "red," but we might do well to remember that America's distrust of her "redness" is part of a larger fear of world revolution. America's fear of Soviet Communism has abated out of growing conviction that its power to spread to other parts of the world has declined and that its revolutionary appeal has waned. But the possibilities of radical revolutionary movements erupting in countries of the third world have not disappeared. The Chinese have said that their revolution is the prototype for these potential revolutions, and American hostility to China can be accounted for to a large extent by the fear that the Chinese may be correct.

Americans who hope that a new and practical "second generation" will emerge in China are saying, in effect, that they hope the revolutionary pressures within China and within the world as a whole will subside. In the summer of 1966 we note swings to the right in many different countries of the third world. A good example is Indonesia, where a powerful Communist Party, with roots deep in society, has been virtually annihilated in a massive army-instigated bloodletting. Indonesia, like many countries in Asia, Africa, and Latin America, today is ruled by a military dictatorship. That these dictatorships can maintain control for a period of time seems beyond doubt. But whether they can resolve the problems which create revolutionary discontent is doubtful. If they cannot, then new radical movements can be expected to arise, committed this time to protracted armed struggle against the military regimes.

The relationship between America and China is governed partly by practical issues, notably Taiwan and Vietnam. If ways could be found to initiate a resolution of these issues, some form of peaceful coexistence between the two countries is conceivable. But the relationship is also governed by ideological views of the world which are not just the products of misconceptions or paranoiac fantasies, but are their respective understandings of the long-term trends of world history. Different men may come to power in Washington and Peking; they may be willing to modify those views or to let the practical supersede the ideological. Yet those views will ultimately be determined by real situations: the relationship between the Soviet Union and the United States, the political and economic stability of the free world and the socialist camp, and the revolutionary situation in the poor countries.

In this introduction we have ranged beyond the eighteenth and nineteenth centuries to the problems of the present. We believe that China as she was in these two centuries is part of the present-day consciousness of her leaders and people. Their response to challenges is determined not only by the requisites of the immediate situation but by their historical legacy. Thus we urge that the materials presented in this and the following two volumes be read, not as background to the present, but as part of the present itself.

I. Empire and Splendor:
The Eighteenth Century

In the eighteenth century China was the greatest empire on earth. Her domain extended from the Siberian forests of the Amur region three thousand miles westward, deep into the plains of Central Asia and fifteen hundred miles southward into the tropical mountains of Southeast Asia. Surrounding China were countries—Japan, Korea, Annam, Burma, Nepal, and the sheikhdoms of Central Asia—which acknowledged her suzerainty by sending tribute. Russian expansion had come to China's borders, but two treaties had stabilized relations and a Russian diplomatic and spiritual mission resided quietly in Peking. Spain, Portugal, Holland, and England had been warring on the southern seas off the Chinese coast, but by the eighteenth century tranquility had returned. Only the Portuguese maintained a foothold in Macao, where the Chinese Empire tolerated them as a contact point between East and West. Peking, located far to the north on the Mongol borderlands, was the Empire's resplendent capital, ruling its great domains in confidence that empire and splendor would last forever.

By the end of the nineteenth century Chinese and foreigners alike held the dynasty in contempt. Peking had been occupied by foreign troops in 1860 and in 1900, and the new Western empires had wrested privileges and territorial concessions from China. Emergent Japan had badly beaten the ostensibly superior Chinese forces. A great rebellion had torn the Empire apart. By the turn of the century the proud Chinese lay at the nadir of their two-thousand-year history, sandwiched between foreign servitude and their Manchu rulers, who retreated into obscurantism as internal decay and external pressure slowly weakened them.

The Chinese Empire was the product of centuries of development. In the third century B.C. disciplined soldiers from the northwest unified the country and established the first Imperial dynasty, the Ch'in, from which the word China derives. China's first emperor, Ch'in Shih huang-ti, created a monarcho-bureaucratic system which, with brief interludes of discontinuity, was to hold China together for two thousand years. The Han Dynasty, which succeeded the short-lived Ch'in, ruled eastern Eurasia as Rome ruled western Eurasia, and Chinese armies held almost all the territories which China controls today. Empire brought social expansion and cultural unification. Chinese migrated into the Yangtze River Valley and further southward into what today are Fukien and Kwangtung provinces. Foreigners were assimilated, forming the world's largest body of culturally unified people. Despite its many spoken dialects, the written language throughout the greater part of China is uniform. China progressed rapidly in the sciences and arts, and developed political, social, and economic institutions which, as they became known to other civilizations, were greatly admired. Though its unity was threatened time and time again by external invasion of powerful nomadic tribes and by internal upheavals caused by political and social unrest, the Empire endured. From the founding of the Sung Dynasty in A.D. 960 until the 1911 Revolution, China remained unified. Dynasties changed and foreigners took over the country temporarily (the Liao, Ch'in, Yuan, and Ch'ing dynasties were foreign), but the fabric of state and society remained intact.

The Manchus were the last foreign people to rule over China, and their dynasty was China's last. Originally a tribal people hunting and farming in the Manchurian forests, by the late sixteenth century, under the leadership of Nurhachi, one of those great tribal leaders who periodically appeared in the history of the borderland peoples, they succeeded in creating a small-scale replica of the Chinese Empire in Manchuria. In 1644 they conquered the Ming Dynasty and set up their rule in Peking. Under the leadership of the three greatest Manchu emperors—K'ang-hsi, Yung-cheng, and Ch'ien-lung—Imperial armies conquered Sinkiang and Tibet and so created China's present borders.

The Manchus ruled over a country with hundreds of years of institutional stability by putting their own people into commanding military and bureaucratic positions or by setting them alongside Chinese officials. But the bureaucracy remained Chinese in form and membership; the local magistrates were Chinese, as they had been for centuries. Despite resistance from some intellectuals and peasants during the foreign dynasty's early years, most Chinese accepted it and served it well. Anti-Manchu feeling intensified later in the nineteenth century, but in the seventeenth century both the literati officials and the peasantry were resigned to the fact that the monarch and his armies were foreign.

The Manchus imposed and maintained their rule by means of the traditional legitimate forms of power. They accepted Confucianism, China's traditional ethos, becoming more Confucian than the Chinese. They kept their own language and ethnic identity, but learned Chinese so well that even today the Manchus' descendants speak the purest Mandarin and are known for their devotion to the traditional arts. While not reluctant to use force, they nevertheless maintained efficient political and military organization, which commanded respect from the population. But most important, they knew that to rule China, they had to gain the cooperation of her elite, the traditional educated gentry, who constituted the leading families of the local communities and furnished officials to the national bureaucracy.

What marks the eighteenth century is the sense, shared by Manchus and Chinese alike, that China had reached an apogee from which descent was inconceivable. Since China was the world's greatest civilization, in her own as well as in foreigners' eyes, her achievements seemed to represent the highest possible attainment of humanity. No country granted its people such durable peace; no country had so high a standard of living; none could match China's institutional stability; none had comparable art and literature. This sense of perfection is visible in the detailed carvings, the exquisite landscapes of the period, in the literary compilations of the past's rich legacy. Life was pleasant, for intellectuals as well as for most of the common people.

Now, two centuries later, we know that China's rulers were living on a gently sloping mountain soon to turn into a volcano. Abbé Huc, writing in the mid-nineteenth century, describes China's political system with admiration, yet laments: "It is impossible, however, to disguise from one's self that the Chinese do appear at present to have arrived at one of those epochs in which the evil has gained the ascendant over the good. Morality, arts, industry, all seem to be on the decline, and poverty and destitution are making rapid progress." The volcano had already begun to erupt.

What were the causes of this unexpected decline? Subsequently we present selections on internal rebellion. Yet rebellion was the product of a decay already inherent in the social fabric of the eighteenth century. Ping-ti Ho speaks of the technological stagnation marking the Chinese economy of the Ch'ing period, and Joseph R. Levenson discusses the exhaustion of the amateur ideal, which had contributed so much to the humanity of Chinese civilization. If a picture be worth a thousand words, let us note John K. Fairbank's description of the typical gentry home: ". . . big high-walled compounds enclosing many courtyards, replete with servants"; the anonymous Chinese author of the description of Europe notes that European homes have no surrounding walls and no inner courtyards. The description of the traditional gentry mansion suggests that the scholar-gentry were in large part responsible for the stagnation and exhaustion of Chinese civilization and the poverty and unrest which arose later. The gentry lived in towns and cities, distant from the peasant population from which they derived their incomes. High walls with small, tightly guarded gates faced dusty streets, much like the houses one sees today in Latin Europe and South America. But inside there were gardens, luxurious rooms, quarters for a small army of wives, children, and servants. Chinese have always valued the private life, and the gentry valued it particularly. Yet in pursuing the private life, they lost contact with the peasantry, failed to perceive its needs, and, faced with trouble, either resorted to force or withdrew still further into their isolation.

Technological stagnation and population increase sowed the seeds of the popular disaffection which broke out in the nineteenth century, but paired with this was an endemic corruption of the ruling political elites. Fairbank notes that "the bureaucracy lived by what we today would call systematized corruption which sometimes became extortion." In the eighteenth century, when prosperity reigned, corruption was regarded as legitimate wastage in a general situation of affluence. But as the century came to an end, the court was forced to crack down, as in the famous case of the talented courtier Ho-shen, who usurped power and squandered the Empire's resources. During the nineteenth century the Taiping rebels justified their cry of *"ta-kuan"*—"smash the officials"—on the grounds that corruption had become a part of the system.

As the gentry became a decadent, inept class, so also did the Manchu rulers recede from reality. The anonymous Chinese author's brief description of Europe indicates a state of mind incapable of grasping external realities, and, worse, not even interested. The Ch'ien-lung Emperor's letter to King George III has an imperial magnificence but betrays the blindness which China's rulers displayed to a growing external threat. Centuries of Confucian education and unchallenged pre-eminence imbued the Chinese scholar-official class with a way of thinking that precluded new ideas. Thus it was inevitable that revolution, when it finally came, necessitated the destruction of traditional Chinese thought and the class that upheld it.

As China was blind to Europe, so Europeans looked at China with a distorted perspective. The *philosophes* wrote about China with considerable knowledge, yet not to enlighten their countrymen about a nation with which they must deal but to argue principles of just and unjust government. China was a model for Europe, not as reality but as an abstraction. Europe, distant from China, saw only its exotic products, which it wanted more than the Chinese wanted the products of Europe. But in some *philosophes* we see that mode of thinking which was only later to affect China so profoundly: systematic and rational analysis, in short, the scientific mode of thought. By the eighteenth century, Europe had already undergone centuries of experimentation and innovation: a quest for truth and action. But isolated China felt that she already knew truth, and continued to allow the cumulative experience of the past to dictate action.

1. CHINA—STATE AND SOCIETY
𝕏 The Humanist Ethos of Traditional China

ALL CIVILIZATIONS in the past have held conscious beliefs
about the nature of man and the cosmos from which they have
derived moral and ethical imperatives or values. These beliefs
and values are the ethos of a civilization. Traditionally, the
Chinese called their ethos "the way of Confucius." Way—*Tao*
—meant the principles governing the nature of man and the
cosmos. Confucius and his disciples explained the Way, translating it into moral and ethical imperatives.

For two millennia learning was the basis of civilized life
in China. Even the modern word for culture, *wen-hua,* means
"to be transformed through writing." Learning began with the
reading of the classics, phrases from which have gone deep into
the Chinese language and can frequently be heard even in the
speech of common people. The "Way of Confucius" was the
most sacred spiritual possession of the Chinese people, enduring as such throughout Chinese history, until the twentieth
century, as the basis of Chinese culture.

In later sections of this reader we shall meet the modern
word "ideology," and as we come closer to Chinese Communism that word will dominate our discussions and selections. "Ideology" has the sense of a driving force, a pushing
toward some future goal. The opposite characterized "the Way
of Confucius." As Confucius looked back into the past, so
learned men for two millennia looked back to him. His quiet
philosophy told men to search within themselves. One finds
none of Christianity's torment in his teachings. When the Chi-

nese began to sense pain within their souls, they turned to different philosophies, like Taoism and Buddhism.

Confucius lived when the ancient moral order had begun to collapse. Mencius, who lived almost two hundred years later, taught at a time of complete disunity. As princes fought each other and dictators arose in the "warring states," polemical philosophers propounded conflicting doctrines of moral and political salvation. Despite the brilliance of these men and the logical elegance of their philosophies, in the end it was the simple and conservative teachings of Confucius and Mencius which became Imperial China's official ethos. By the time of the Sung Dynasty, fifteen hundred years later, Confucian philosophy had been formulated into a unified and consistent philosophical system. Chu Hsi, the last and greatest of the Neo-Confucianists, gave China a rational system which explained everything—the traditional Chinese view of man and cosmos became fixed.

Mencius, like Confucius, taught that human nature is good and disputed Kao Tzu's idea "that human nature is neither good nor bad." When Mencius speaks of the "four beginnings," he reveals what he means by the goodness of human nature: man is basically a social being, and if true to his nature, will love his fellow men. But love is concrete and must have a beginning, namely in love for one's parents. An old saying goes: first reform yourself, then arrange your family, and so pacify the world. Herein was expressed a moral sociology: human society can be built only from the bottom up, through good men, stable families, contented villages, and, finally, humane empires. During the time of the "warring states" the political leaders sought the opposite: defeat the enemy, take his capital, and then extend control downward.

Though all men possessed the same human nature, neither Confucius nor Mencius taught that all men are equal. When men acquire virtue, they also gain authority, the basis of political rule. The five cardinal human relations were between ruler-subject, father-son, elder brother-younger brother, husband-wife, and friend-friend; except for the last all these relations imply the superiority of one over another. Much of Mencius' writing deals with the proper conduct of kings. Humane rule is the true source of power: "the people turn to a humane ruler as water flows downward or beasts take to wilderness." Build from the bottom up, and the empire will be secure. Hundreds of years later Chinese pointed to the powerful but short-lived Ch'in Empire as proof of the correctness of Mencius' teachings.

Mencius was suspicious, and rightly so, of the powerful rulers of the time. He warned: "when the ruler regards his ministers as dust and grass, the ministers regard their ruler as a brigand or foe." He stated: "[In the constitution of a state] the people rank highest, the spirits of land and grain come next, and the ruler counts least." If we remember that "people," somewhat like the Italian Renaissance word *popolo,* meant not the peasants in the fields but the notables whose services the king needed, then we can understand Mencius' prescription for a stable government: the ruler must surround himself with humane officials who themselves are good fathers to their people.

Here we can see why the Way of Confucius became the ethos of the later scholar-official class. It proclaimed the importance of the local community in the function of the state; it gave pre-eminence to the scholar-official; and it warned the despot to avoid the fallacy of absolutism.

The scholar-officials of later times fulfilled the Mencian ideal in many ways: educated men, they concerned themselves with the country's economy, raised large families, ruled paternally over their peasants, and were the teachers of the people. If the teachings of Confucius, however, avoided the torment of supernatural religion, China could not. Men were not satisfied with the bland, confident teachings on human nature, and sought to penetrate deeper into the mysteries of the soul. In time Taoism and Buddhism developed as powerful faiths, attracting many through their promise of salvation and release from the world. The limited "right of revolution" allowed by the sages was not enough. As early as the Eastern Han Dynasty, great rebellions broke out, armed with millennial beliefs initially of Taoist and later of Buddhist origin.

The simple humanity of Confucius survives deeply in the

Chinese people to this day. Yet as an ethos it was tied too closely to the scholar-official class, and when China began to turn against that class, she also turned on "Confucianism." The May Fourth Movement of 1919, with its iconoclastic anti-Confucianism, sounded the death knell of the class and of its ethos. The modern young intellectuals of China saw behind the pious teachings a conservative philosophy that looked to the past, could not conceive of anything new, and used its humanism to cloak nepotism, corruption, and cliquism.

Yet in the eighteenth century, a time of empire and splendor the "Way of Confucius" was so firmly rooted that no one in China questioned its claim to monopoly over truth. The philosophical disputes between Confucianism, Buddhism, and Taoism lay in the distant past. The conquering Manchus not only accepted the Chinese political system in its entirety but became more Confucian than the Chinese. The political critics of the early Ch'ing all stated their attacks within the orthodox framework of Confucianism. Even the Jesuits, a century or so earlier, had begun to succumb to the self-evident truth of Confucius' teachings, and sought to explain Catholicism with Confucian terminology.

The world sees the Chinese as a race of philosophers. One of the traits of philosophical thinking is the confidence that one has the rational tools for explaining everything, tools deriving from a correct and efficient theory about man, society, and the universe. To the Chinese in the eighteenth century there appeared to be nothing that was inexplicable. That era's vast compendia and encyclopedias testify to this supreme Confucian philosophical confidence. The theory was simple yet magnificent, ancient yet timeless; above all, it worked.

MENCIUS *
From *The Book of Mencius*

HUMAN NATURE

Kao Tzu said: "The nature of man may be likened to the willow tree, whereas righteousness may be likened to wooden cups and wicker baskets. To turn man's nature into humanity and righteousness is like turning a willow tree into cups and baskets."

Mencius replied: "Sir, can you follow the nature of the willow tree, and make the cups and baskets? Or must you violate its nature to make the cups and baskets? If you must violate the nature of the willow tree to turn it into cups and baskets, then don't you mean you must also violate the nature of man to turn it into humanity and righteousness? Your words, alas, would incite everyone in the world to regard humanity and righteousness as a curse!"

Kao Tzu said: "The nature of man may be likened to a swift current of water: you lead it eastward and it will flow to the east; you lead it westward and it will flow to the west. Human nature is neither disposed to good nor to evil, just as water is neither disposed to east nor west." Mencius replied: "It is true that water is neither disposed to east nor west, but is it neither disposed to flowing upward nor downward? The tendency of human nature to do good is like that of water to flow downward. There is no man who does not tend to do good; there is no water that does not flow downward. Now

* Mencius in William T. de Bary, Wing-tsit Chan, and Burton Watson, comps., *Sources of Chinese Tradition* (New York: Columbia University Press, 1960), pp. 102–112.

you may strike water and make it splash over your forehead, or you may even force it up the hills. But is this in the nature of water? It is of course due to the force of circumstances. Similarly, man may be brought to do evil, and that is because the same is done to his nature."

Kao Tzu said: "Nature is what is born in us." Mencius asked: " 'Nature is what is born in us'—is it not the same as saying white is white?" "Yes," said Kao Tzu. Mencius asked: "Then the whiteness of a white feather is the same as the whiteness of white snow, and the whiteness of white snow the same as the whiteness of white jade?" "Yes," Kao Tzu replied. Mencius asked: "Well, then, the nature of a dog is the same as the nature of a cow, and the nature of a cow the same as the nature of a man, is it not?"

Kao Tzu said: "The appetite for food and sex is part of our nature. Humanity comes from within and not from without, whereas righteousness comes from without and not from within." Mencius asked: "What do you mean when you say that humanity comes from within while righteousness comes from without?" Kao Tzu replied: "When I see anyone who is old I regard him as old. This regard for age is not a part of me. Just as when I see anyone who is white I regard him as white, because I can observe the whiteness externally. For this reason I say righteousness comes from without." Mencius said: "Granted there is no difference between regarding the white horse as white and the white man as white. But is there no difference between one's regard for age in an old horse and one's regard for age in an old man, I wonder? Moreover, is it old age itself or our respectful regard for old age that constitutes a point of righteousness?" Kao Tzu persisted: "My own brother I love; the brother of a man of Ch'in I do not love. Here the sanction for the feeling rests in me, and therefore I call it [i.e., humanity] internal. An old man of Ch'u I regard as old, just as an old man among my own people I regard as old. Here the sanction for the feeling lies in old age, and therefore I call it [i.e., righteousness] external." Mencius answered him: "We love the Ch'in people's roast as much as we love our own roast. Here we have a similar situation with respect to things. Would you say, then, that this love of roast is also something external?"

The disciple Kung-tu Tzu said: "Kao Tzu says that human nature is neither good nor bad. Some say that human nature can be turned to be good or bad. Thus when [sage-kings] Wen and Wu were in power the people loved virtue; when [wicked kings] Yu and Li were in power the people indulged in violence. Some say that some natures are good and some are bad. Thus even while [the sage] Yao was sovereign there was the bad man Hsiang, even a bad father like Ku-sou had a good son like [the sage-king] Shun, and even with [the wicked] Chou for nephew and king there were the men of virtue Ch'i, the Viscount of Wei, and the Prince Pi-kan. Now, you say that human nature is good. Are the others then all wrong?" Mencius replied: "When left to follow its natural feelings human nature will do good. This is why I say it is good. If it becomes evil, it is not the fault of man's original capability. The sense of mercy is found in all men; the sense of shame is found in all men; the sense of respect is found in all men; the sense of right and wrong is found in all men. The sense of mercy constitutes humanity, the sense of shame constitutes righteousness; the sense of respect constitutes decorum (*li*); the sense of right and wrong constitutes wisdom. Humanity, righteousness, decorum, and wisdom are not something instilled into us from without; they are inherent in our nature. Only we give them no thought. Therefore it is said: 'Seek and you will find them, neglect and you will lose them.' Some have these virtues to a much greater degree than others—twice, five times, and incalculably more—and that is because those others have not developed to the fullest extent their original capability. It is said in the *Book of Odes:*

> Heaven so produced the teeming multitudes that
> For everything there is its principle.
> The people will keep to the constant principles,
> And all will love a beautiful character.

Confucius said, regarding this poem: 'The writer of this poem understands indeed the nature of the Way! For wherever there are things and affairs there must be their principles. As the people keep to the constant principles, they will come to love a beautiful character.' "

Mencius said: "All men have a sense of commiseration. The ancient kings had this commiserating heart and hence a commiserating government. When a commiserating government is conducted from a commiserating heart, one can rule the whole empire as if one were turning it on one's palm. Why I say all men have a sense of commiseration is this: Here is a man who suddenly notices a child about to fall into a well. Invariably he will feel a sense of alarm and compassion. And this is not for the purpose of gaining the favor of the child's parents, or seeking the approbation of his neighbors and friends, or for fear of blame should he fail to rescue it. Thus we see that no man is without a sense of compassion, or a sense of shame, or a sense of courtesy, or a sense of right and wrong. The sense of compassion is the beginning of humanity; the sense of shame is the beginning of righteousness; the sense of courtesy is the beginning of decorum; the sense of right and wrong is the beginning of wisdom. Every man has within himself these four beginnings, just as he has four limbs. Since everyone has these four beginnings within him, the man who considers himself incapable of exercising them is destroying himself. If he considers his sovereign incapable of exercising them, he is likewise destroying his sovereign. Let every man but attend to expanding and developing these four beginnings that are in our very being, and they will issue forth like a conflagration being kindled and a spring being opened up. If they can be fully developed, these virtues are capable of safeguarding all within the four seas; if allowed to remain undeveloped, they will not suffice even for serving one's parents."

Mencius said: "Man's innate ability is the ability possessed by him that is not acquired through learning. Man's innate knowledge is the knowledge possessed by him that is not the result of reflective thinking. Every child knows enough to love his parents, and when he is grown up he knows enough to respect his elder brothers. The love for one's parents is really humanity and the respect for one's elders is really righteousness

—all that is necessary is to have these natural feelings applied
to all men."

HUMANE GOVERNMENT

Mencius went to see King Hui of Liang. The king said: "You
have not considered a thousand *li* too far to come, and must
therefore have something of profit to offer my kingdom?"
Mencius replied: "Why must you speak of profit? What I have
to offer is humanity and righteousness, nothing more. If a king
says, 'What will profit my kingdom?' the high officials will say,
'What will profit our families?' and the lower officials and com-
moners will say, 'What will profit ourselves?' Superiors and inferiors will try to seize profit one from another, and the state
will be endangered. . . . Let your Majesty speak only of
humanity and righteousness. Why must you speak of profit?"

Mencius said: "It was by virtue of humanity that the Three
Dynasties won the empire, and by virtue of the want of humanity that they lost it. States rise and fall for the same reason.
Devoid of humanity, the emperor would be unable to safeguard
the four seas, a feudal lord would be unable to safeguard the
altars of land and grain [i.e., his state], a minister would be
unable to safeguard the ancestral temple [i.e., his clan-family],
and the individual would be unable to safeguard his four limbs.
Now people hate destruction and yet indulge in want of humanity—this is as if one hates to get drunk and yet forces oneself to drink wine."

Mencius said: "An overlord is he who employs force
under a cloak of humanity. To be an overlord one has to be
in possession of a large state. A king, on the other hand, is he
who gives expression to his humanity through virtuous conduct.
To be a true king, one does not have to have a large state.
T'ang [founder of the Shang dynasty] had only a territory of
seventy *li* and King Wen [founder of the Chou] only a hundred.
When men are subdued by force, it is not that they submit
from their hearts but only that their strength is unavailing.

When men are won by virtue, then their hearts are gladdened and their submission is sincere, as the seventy disciples were won by the Master, Confucius. This is what is meant in the *Book of Odes* when it says:

> From east and west,
> From north and south,
> Came none who thought of disobedience."

Mencius said: "States have been won by men without humanity, but the world, never."

Mencius said: "It was because Chieh and Chou lost the people that they lost the empire, and it was because they lost the hearts of the people that they lost the people. Here is the way to win the empire: win the people and you win the empire. Here is the way to win the people: win their hearts and you win the people. Here is the way to win their hearts: give them and share with them what they like, and do not do to them what they do not like. The people turn to a humane ruler as water flows downward or beasts take to wilderness.". . .

IMPORTANCE OF THE PEOPLE AND THE RIGHT OF REVOLUTION

[Mencius' disciple] Wan Chang asked: "Is it true that Yao gave the empire to Shun?" Mencius replied: "No. The emperor cannot give the empire to another." Wan Chang asked: "Who then gave it to him, when Shun had the empire?" Mencius said: "Heaven gave it to him." Wan Chang asked: "You say Heaven gave it to him—did Heaven do it with an explicit charge?" Mencius said: "No. Heaven does not speak. It simply signified its will through his conduct and handling of affairs." Wan Chang asked: "How was this done?" Mencius said: . . . "Of old, Yao recommended Shun to Heaven and Heaven accepted him. He presented him to the people and the people accepted him. This is why I said that Heaven does not speak but simply signified its will through Shun's conduct and handling of affairs." Wan Chang said: "May I venture to ask, how was this acceptance by Heaven and the people indicated?" Mencius said: "He was appointed to preside over the sacrifices, and all the spirits were pleased with them: that indicated his acceptance by Heaven. He was placed in charge of public affairs, and they were well administered and the people were at peace: that indicated his acceptance by the people. Heaven thus gave him the empire; the people thus gave him the empire. That is why I said, the emperor cannot give the empire to another. . . . This is what is meant in the Great Declaration [in the *Book of History*] where it is said: 'Heaven sees as my people see, Heaven hears as my people hear.' "

Mencius said: "Men are in the habit of speaking of the world, the state. As a matter of fact, the foundation of the world lies in the state, the foundation of the state lies in the family, and the foundation of the family lies in the individual."

Mencius said: "[In the constitution of a state] the people rank the highest, the spirits of land and grain come next, and the ruler counts the least."

Mencius said: "There are three things that a feudal lord should treasure—land, people, and the administration of the government. If he should treasure pearls and jades instead, calamity is sure to befall him."

Mencius said: "It is not so important to censure the men appointed to office; it is not so important to criticize the measures adopted in government. The truly great is he who is capable of rectifying what is wrong with the ruler's heart."

Mencius said to King Hsüan of Ch'i: "When the ruler regards his ministers as his hands and feet, the ministers regard their ruler as their heart and bowels. When the ruler regards his ministers as his dogs and horses, the ministers regard their ruler as a stranger. When the ruler regards his ministers as dust and grass, the ministers regard their ruler as a brigand or foe."

King Hsüan of Ch'i asked: "Is it not true that T'ang banished Chieh and that King Wu smote Chou?" Mencius replied: "It is so stated in the records." The king asked: "May a subject, then, slay his sovereign?" Mencius replied: "He who outrages humanity is a scoundrel; he who outrages righteousness is a scourge. A scourge or a scoundrel is a despised creature [and no longer a king]. I have heard that a despised creature called Chou was put to death, but I have not heard anything about the murdering of a sovereign."

The men of Ch'i made war on Yen and took it. The other feudal lords began plotting to liberate Yen. King Hsüan [of Ch'i] asked: "The feudal lords of many states are plotting war against me; how shall I deal with them?" Mencius replied: "I have heard of one who, with a territory of only seventy *li,* extended his rule to the whole empire. That was T'ang. But never have I heard of the lord of a thousand *li* having to stand in fear of others. It is said in the *Book of History:* 'T'ang launched his punitive expedition, first against Ko. The whole empire had faith in him. When he carried his campaign to the east, the tribes in the west grumbled. When he carried his campaign to the south, the tribes in the north grumbled, saying: "Why should we be last?" ' [Announcement of Chung-hui]. People looked for his coming as they would look for the rain clouds in time of great drought. Those going to the market were not stopped; those tilling the land were not interrupted. He put their rulers to death and he consoled the people. His visit was like the falling of rain in season, and the people were overjoyed. Thus it is said in the *Book of History:* 'We have been waiting for our lord. When he comes, we shall have a new life.' . . ."

MENCIUS' DEFENSE OF FILIAL PIETY

. . . Now that sage-kings are no longer with us, the feudal lords yield to their lusts and idle scholars indulge in senseless disputation. The words of Yang Chu and Mo Ti fill the land, and the talk of the land is either Yang Chu or Mo Ti. Yang is for individualism, which does not recognize the sovereign; Mo is for universal love, which does not recognize parents. To be without sovereign or parent is to be a beast.

Mencius said: "Of services which is the greatest? The

service of parents is the greatest. Of charges which is the greatest? The charge of oneself is the greatest. Not failing to keep oneself and thus being able to serve one's parents—this I have heard of. Failing to keep oneself and yet being able to serve one's parents—this I have not heard of."

Mencius said: "There are three things which are unfilial, and the greatest of them is to have no posterity."

Mencius said: "The substance of humanity is to serve one's parents; the basis of righteousness is to obey one's elder brothers.". . .

❧ Government, Society, and Man in Imperial China: A European Traveler's Description

THE ABBÉ Régis-Evariste Huc, missionary apostolic in China from 1839 to 1851, was one of the great travelers of the nineteenth century. He started his missionary work in Hopei, where he learned Chinese, and subsequently moved into the Mongol borderlands, where he acquired equal fluency in Mongolian. From there his travels took him into the Tibetan regions of Chinghai province, and finally to Lhasa itself, from where, however, he was ejected by the Lamaist theocracy. He left China in 1851 and died in France in 1860. He wrote two excellent books on China: *Souvenirs d'un voyage dans la Tartarie, le Thibet, et la Chine,* and *L'empire chinois.* The following selection is taken from an English translation of the latter.

Huc was one of the last European travelers of literary skill to have seen Imperial China before the Taiping onslaught, and though famine, poverty, and institutional atrophy were already visible, the greatness of China was still the overriding impression left with him. Europeans, struggling out of feudalism, had been preoccupied for centuries with the problems of government, which China appeared to have solved long ago. Despite the accusation of despotism which Montesquieu aimed at China, Abbé Huc notes ". . . absolute as the government is, it is not on that account tyrannical. If it were, it would have probably long since ceased to exist."

We have chosen the label "Imperial China" for eighteenth-century China. In the last decade the term "Traditional China" has come into vogue, but there is an unstated conceptual difference between these two appellations. "Imperial China" stresses China's political institutions, its state power, while "Traditional China" directs attention to the constitution of Chinese society. Scholars have long argued about whether state or society was more important as a foundation for the millennial existence of the Chinese Empire. Thus, in the polemics about the role of the gentry, some have maintained that gentry power arose from official position in the state bureaucracy, but others have countered that landownership and position in the local community were the decisive factors in gentry power.

To Abbé Huc the contemporary polemic would not have made much sense, since both state and society were powerful in the China he saw. He states, "the sovereign power . . . is a strong and vast system of centralization," but also, "the communal organization is perhaps nowhere else as perfect as in China." China, with millennial experience, knew that man was both a political and a social being, who demanded and needed a system of authority, as well as a community in which to live with his fellow men. What Abbé Huc observed was a system of state and society in which these basic human needs had been resolved on a scale achieved by no other civilization.

ABBÉ HUC *
From *The Chinese Empire*

From the thirteenth century, when the first notions of China were brought into Europe by the celebrated Venetian, Marco Polo, up to our own days, all parties seem to have agreed in regarding the Chinese as a very singular people—a people unlike all others. But if we except this one opinion, which is universally received, we scarcely find in what has been written

* Régis-Evariste Huc, *The Chinese Empire* (London: Longman Brown, Green, and Longmans, 1855), Vol. I, pp. 83–89, 96–97; Vol. II, pp. 101–103, 255–257, 321–323.

concerning the Chinese, anything but contradictions. Some are in perpetual ecstasy with them; others are constantly heaping upon them abuse and ridicule.

Voltaire has drawn for us an enchanting picture of China, its patriarchal manners, its paternal government, its institutions based on filial piety, and its wise administration always entrusted to the most learned and virtuous men. Montesquieu, on the contrary, has used the darkest colors, and painted them as a miserable abject race, crouching under a brutal despotism, and driven, like a vile herd, by the will of the Emperor.

These two portraits, drawn by the authors of *L'Esprit des Lois,* and *L'Essai sur les Mœurs,* have very little resemblance to the original. There is gross exaggeration on both sides, and the truth is certainly to be sought for between them.

In China, as everywhere else, there is a mixture of what is good and bad, of vice and virtue, that may give occasion to satire or panegyric as the attention is fixed on one or the other. It is easy to find among a people whatever you desire to see in them, if you set out with a preconceived opinion and the resolution to preserve it intact. Thus Voltaire was dreaming of a nation whose annals should be in contradiction with Biblical tradition, a people rationalistic, anti-religious, and whose days nevertheless flowed on in uninterrupted peace and prosperity. In China he thought he had found this model nation, and he did not fail to recommend it to the admiration of Europe.

Montesquieu, on the other hand, was putting forth his theory of despotic government, and wanted some example to illustrate it. He took the Chinese for this purpose; and showed them trembling under the iron rod of a tyrant, and crushed beneath a pitiless system of legislation.

We intend to enter into some details concerning Chinese institutions and the mechanism of this government, which assuredly does not merit either the invectives that have been poured out on its despotism, or the pompous eulogies that have been pronounced on its antique and patriarchal wisdom. In developing the Chinese governmental system, we shall see that practice is often in contradiction to theory; and that the fine laws found in the books are not quite so often seen in application.

The idea of the family is the grand principle that serves as the basis of society in China. Filial piety, the constant subject of dissertation to moralists and philosophers, and continually recommended in the proclamations of Emperors and the speeches of Mandarins, has become the fundamental root of all other virtues.

All means are made use of to exalt this sentiment, so as to make of it an absolute passion; it assumes all forms, mingles in all actions, and serves as the moral pivot of public life. Every crime, every attempt against the authority, property, or life of individuals, is treated as filial disobedience; whilst on the other hand, all acts of virtue, devotion, compassion towards the unfortunate, commercial probity, or even valor in battle, are referred to filial piety; to be a good or a bad citizen, is to be a good or bad son.

The Emperor is the personification of this grand principle, which dominates and penetrates more or less deeply all the strata of society, in this immense agglomeration of three hundred millions of individuals. In the Chinese language he is called *Huang-ti,* August Sovereign . . . ; but his name *par excellence* is *T'ien-tzu,* Son of Heaven.

According to the ideas of Confucius and his disciples, the great movements and revolutions of the Empire are under the direct guidance of Heaven; and it is the will of Heaven only, that overthrows some dynasties and substitutes others. Heaven is the true and only master of the Empire, it chooses whom it pleases as its representative, and communicates to him its absolute authority over the people. The sovereignty is a celestial mandate, a holy mission entrusted to an individual for the sake of the community, and withdrawn from him as soon as he shows himself forgetful of his duty and unworthy of his high office. It follows from this political fatalism, that in epochs of revolution the struggles are terrible, until some decided success and evident superiority have become, for the people, a sign of the will of Heaven. Then they rally at once round the new power, and submit to it for a long time without any hesitation.

Heaven, they imagine, had a representative, an adopted son; but it has abandoned him, and withdrawn its credentials; it has chosen another, and he of course is the one to be obeyed.—This is the whole system.

The Emperor being the Son of Heaven, and consequently, according to the Chinese expression, Father and Mother of the Empire, has a right to the respect, the veneration, the worship even of his children. His authority is absolute; it is he who makes and who abolishes the laws, who grants privileges to Mandarins or degrades them, to whom alone belongs the power over life and death, who is the source of all administrative and judicial authority, who has at his disposal the whole power and revenues of the Empire; in one word, the state is the Emperor. His omnipotence, indeed, extends even farther, for he can transmit this enormous power to whom he pleases, and choose his successor among his children, without any law of inheritance imposing a restraint upon him in his choice.

The sovereign power in China is, then, in all respects absolute; but it is not, as has been supposed, for that reason despotic. It is a strong and vast system of centralization. The Emperor is the head of an immense family; and the absolute authority that belongs to him is not absorbed, but delegated to his ministers, who in their turn transmit their powers to the inferior officers of their administrative governments. The subdivisions of authority thus extend gradually downwards to groups of families, of which the fathers are the natural chiefs, and just as absolute within their sphere as any other. It may well be supposed that this absolute power, being thus infinitely divisible, is no longer equally dangerous; and besides, public opinion is always ready to check any excesses on the part of the Emperor, who would not without exciting general indignation, dare to violate the rights of any of his subjects. He has also his private and general councils, the members of which have the right of expressing their opinions, and even remonstrating with him on matters both of public and private concern. One may read in the annals of China, how the censors have often acquitted themselves of their duty, with a freedom and vigor worthy of all praise. Finally, these potentates, the objects of so much homage during their lives, are often after death, like the ancient kings of Egypt, subjected to a trial, the verdict from which is attached to their name and descends to posterity. By these posthumous names only do they become known to history; and as they are always either eulogistic or satirical, they serve to give a brief estimate of the character of their reign.

The greatest counterpoise of the Imperial power consists of the literary aristocracy, or corporation of men of letters; an ancient institution which has been established on a solid basis, and the origin of which is at least as early as the eleventh century before our era. It may be said that the administration receives all its real and direct influence from this sort of literary oligarchy.

The Emperor can only choose his civil agents among the lettered class, and in conformity with established arrangements. Every Chinese may present himself for the examination for the third literary degree; and those who obtain this, may then become candidates for the second, which opens the way to official employment. To fill the higher offices the prize must be obtained in the competition for the first degree.

It seems, doubtless, a magnificent thing to organize the government of a great Empire by literary qualification; but though it may be a subject of admiration, it is not to be regarded as a model for imitation in all countries.

The Emperor is recognized by the laws as the sole proprietor of the soil of the Empire; but this is a mere theory, and it does not hinder the property in land from being really as firmly established as it is in Europe. The government, in fact, only possesses the right over it in case of non-payment of the tax, or of confiscation for state crimes.

The villages are collectively responsible to the Exchequer

for the discharge of all fiscal impositions, and they have at their head a mayor called *Hsiang-yüeh,* who is chosen by universal suffrage.

The communal organization is perhaps nowhere else as perfect as in China; and these mayors are chosen by the people, without the Mandarins presenting any candidates or seeking in any way to influence the votes.

Every man is both elector and eligible for this office; but it is usual to choose one of advanced age, who both by his character and fortune occupies a high position in the village. We have known many of the Chinese mayors, and we can affirm that in general they are worthy of the suffrages with which they have been honored by their fellow citizens. The time for which they are elected varies in the different localities; they are charged with the police duties, and serve also as mediators between the Mandarins and the people, in matters beyond their own competence. We shall have occasion to return to this salutary institution which agrees very ill with the ideas we commonly entertain of the heavy despotism which is supposed to weigh on the Chinese nation.

The corporation of lettered men, recruited every year by the method of examination, constitutes a privileged class, almost the only nobility recognized in China, and it may be considered as the chief strength and nerve of the Empire. Hereditary titles only exist for the Imperial family, and for the descendants of Confucius, who are still very numerous in the province of Shantung. . . .

In ordinary times, and when they are not under the influence of any revolutionary movement, the Chinese are not at all inclined to meddle with affairs of government: they are a delightfully quiet people to deal with. In 1851, at the period of the death of the Emperor Tao-kuang, we were traveling on the road from Peking, and one day, when we had been taking tea at an inn in company with some Chinese citizens, we tried to get up a little political discussion.

We spoke of the recent death of the Emperor, an important event which, of course, must have interested everybody. We expressed our anxiety on the subject of the succession to the Imperial throne, the heir to which was not yet publicly declared. "Who knows," said we, "which of the three sons of the Emperor will have been appointed to succeed him? If it should be the eldest, will he pursue the same system of government? If the younger, he is still very young; and it is said there are contrary influences, two opposing parties, at court— to which will he lean?" We put forward, in short, all kinds of hypotheses, in order to stimulate these good citizens to make some observation. But they hardly listened to us. We came back again and again to the charge, in order to elicit some opinion or other, on questions that really appeared to us of great importance. But to all our piquant suggestions, they replied only by shaking their heads, puffing out whiffs of smoke, and taking great gulps of tea.

This apathy was really beginning to provoke us, when one of these worthy Chinese, getting up from his seat, came and laid his two hands on our shoulders in a manner quite paternal, and said, smiling rather ironically, "Listen to me, my friend! Why should you trouble your heart and fatigue your head by all these vain surmises? The Mandarins have to attend to affairs of State; they are paid for it. Let them earn their money, then. But don't let us torment ourselves about what does not concern us. We should be great fools to want to do political business for nothing."

"This is very conformable to reason," cried the rest of the company; and thereupon they pointed out to us that our tea was getting cold and our pipes were out. . . .

The province of Kiangsi is regarded as one of the most populous in China, and we were therefore greatly surprised to observe on our route vast plains without cultivation, and without inhabitants, the wild and dreary aspect of which reminded us of the steppes and deserts of Mongolia. It is not uncommon in China to meet with desolate tracts of this kind, whether on account of the barrenness of the soil, or from the thoughtless carelessness of the people of the locality, who prefer seeking a more precarious subsistence from the chances of trade and navigation, to trusting to the peaceful labors of the field. These fallow grounds are most common in the neighborhood of the great lakes, and on the banks of rivers. The inhabitants leave the land when they can, and go and pass their lives in the boats, so that it has often been thought that notwithstanding the encouragement given to agriculture, China could yet supply more completely the wants of her inhabitants, or support a greater number of them.

It is certain that the Chinese government does not know how to turn to account all the elements of abundance and riches that are met with in this magnificent country. An intelligent administration, zealous for the public good, by guiding judiciously this patient and industrious population, might develop prodigiously the immense resources of the Empire, and procure for the masses a much larger share of prosperity and comfort.

We will not venture to say it is easier in China than elsewhere completely to extinguish pauperism. In all the great centers of population, there will always be, unfortunately, many extremely poor, and the class of the necessitous will be always considerable. But the number of these might certainly be diminished; and we have noticed during our residence in China, that it is every year on the increase. This circumstance may, perhaps, help to explain the astonishing facility and rapid progress of the formidable insurrection that is threatening at this moment totally to overthrow this colossal Empire.

At all epochs, and in the most flourishing and best governed countries, there always have been, and there always will be, poor; but unquestionably there can be found in no other country such a depth of disastrous poverty as in the Celestial Empire. Not a year passes in which a terrific number of persons do not perish of famine in some part or other of China; and the multitude of those who live merely from day to day is incalculable. Let a drought, an inundation, or any accident whatever, occur to injure the harvest in a single province, and two thirds of the population are immediately reduced to a state of starvation. You see them then forming themselves into numerous bands—perfect armies of beggars—and proceeding together, men, women, and children, to seek in the towns and villages for some little nourishment wherewith to sustain, for a brief interval, their miserable existence. Many fall down fainting by the wayside, and die before they can reach the place where they had hoped to find help. You see their bodies lying in the fields, and at the roadside, and you pass without taking much notice of them—so familiar is the horrid spectacle. . . .

Chinese civilization originates in an antiquity so remote that we vainly endeavor to discover its commencement. There are no traces of the state of infancy among this people. This is a very peculiar fact respecting China. We are accustomed in the history of nations to find some well-defined point of departure, and the historic documents, traditions, and monuments that remain to us generally permit us to follow, almost step by step, the progress of civilization, to be present at its birth, to watch its development, its onward march, and, in many cases, its subsequent decay and fall. But it is not thus with the Chinese. They seem to have been always living in the same stage of advancement as in the present day; and the data of antiquity are such as to confirm that opinion.

It would not be then very rash to conjecture that some mysterious event of the highest importance must have brought the Chinese suddenly to the point at which we find them, and this fact must have left a profound impression on the imagination of the people. Thence may proceed the respect, the veneration, the gratitude felt for the first founders of their ancient monarchy, who conducted them in so rapid a manner to a certain state of enlightenment. Thence the worship of ancestors, of all ancient things, of those who hold towards the state the place that the father and mother occupy in the family. The Chinese have in fact always attached the idea of something holy and mysterious to whatever is antique, to all that has existed for ages, and this respect generalized has taken the name of filial piety.

This sentiment, carried to excess, had the necessary consequence of cherishing a sort of exclusive spirit, and a contempt for foreigners, who were regarded as barbarians; and in the second place, a stationary condition of civilization, which seems to have remained pretty nearly what it was in the beginning.

These reflections enable us to assign to the laws relative to filial piety, political and social, their true importance. As the style is the man, so legislation, which is the style of nations, reflects faithfully the manners, habits, and instincts of the people for and by whom it has been created, and we may say of Chinese legislation, that it represents very accurately the Chinese people.

The inhabitants of the Celestial Empire, being wanting in religious faith, and living from day to day without troubling themselves either about the past or the future, profoundly skeptical, and totally indifferent to what touches only the moral nature of man, having no energy for anything but the amassing of sapeks, cannot, as may easily be supposed, be well induced to obey the laws from a sentiment of duty. The official worship of China does not in fact possess any of the characteristics of what can properly be called a religion, and is, consequently, unable to communicate to the people those moral ideas that do more for the observance of the laws, than the most terrible penal sanctions. It is, therefore, quite natural that the bamboo should be the necessary and indispensable accessory of every legal prescription; and the Chinese law will consequently always assume a penal character, even when it has in view objects purely civil. . . .

From this slight sketch of the political system of the Empire, it will readily be perceived, that, absolute as the government is, it is not on that account necessarily tyrannical. If it were, it would probably long since have ceased to exist; for it is not easy to conceive that three hundred millions of men could be ruled arbitrarily and despotically for many successive centuries, let them be ever so apathetic and brutalized—and assuredly the Chinese are neither the one nor the other.

To maintain order amidst these terrific masses of people, nothing less was needed than that powerful system of centralization which was invented by the founders of the Chinese monarchy, and which the numerous revolutions by which it has been agitated have only modified, without ever disturbing from the foundations.

Under shelter of these strong, energetic, and, one may say, learnedly combined institutions, the Chinese have been able to live in peace, and enjoy some tolerable sort of happiness, which, after all, is perhaps the most that man in this world can reasonably pretend to.

The annals of China resemble those of most other nations; they contain a mixture of good and evil—an alternation of peaceable and happy periods, with others that were agitated and miserable; governments probably will never be found perfect, till the day when men shall be born free from faults.

It is impossible, however, to disguise from one's self, that the Chinese do appear at present to have arrived at one of those epochs in which the evil has gained the ascendant over the good. Morality, arts, industry, all seem to be on the decline, and poverty and destitution are making rapid progress.

We have seen the most frightful corruption penetrating the whole mass of society—magistrates selling justice to the highest bidder; Mandarins of every degree, instead of protecting the people, oppressing and pillaging them by every means in their power.

But ought these disorders and abuses that have glided into the exercise of power, to be attributed to the form of the Chinese government? One can hardly think that. These abuses depend mostly on causes that we shall have occasion to point out in the course of our narrative; but however that may be, it cannot be disputed, that the mechanism of the Chinese government deserves to be studied carefully, and without prejudice, by the politicians of Europe.

We must not wholly despise the Chinese; there may be even much that is admirable and instructive in their ancient and curious institutions, based upon literary qualification, by which it has been found possible to grant, in the communes, universal suffrage to three hundred millions of men, and to render every distinction accessible to all classes. . . .

۞ Chinese Society: the Confucian Pattern and the Political Tradition

THE GREAT eighteenth-century European philosophical writings on China were followed by a nineteenth-century Sinology fascinated by the details of China's ancient civilization. The picture of China as an entity began to dissolve kaleidoscopically, each part brilliant in itself but no longer fitting together. More recent historians have again turned their attention to the whole picture, and have tried to discern the fundamental patterns of pre-modern Chinese civilization. Foremost among the scholars of Imperial China is John King Fairbank, Professor of History at Harvard University and Director of the East Asian Research Center, who has probably written more and done more than any man in America to encourage interest in China and her transition into the modern world. The following are selections from Fairbank's classic work *The United States and China,* which, in concise manner, sketches out the main patterns of state and society in Imperial China.

Fairbank notes that Chinese society was divided into two main parts: the scholar-gentry-official stratum and the vast mass of peasants. The educated gentry class played a dual role, combining the economic power of landholding with the political power of officeholding. Above them was the government, with its powerful monarchy and great bureaucracy; below them the peasantry, with its deep-rooted traditions of kinship, family, and village organization.

Fairbank examines the role of Confucianism in stabilizing the whole political and social structure. The emphasis on moral behavior and right conduct led to an ideal of "government by goodness." The important concept of the Mandate of Heaven was at once a source of ethical sanction for benevolent and effective government and a source of legitimation for rebellion against bad government. Fairbank concludes that this subtle combination of stability and the right to rebel was China's strength and was indeed "a great political invention."

China had the most imposing bureaucratic structure in the pre-modern world, which many modern Western scholars, notably Max Weber, have studied in detail. The monarchy could not rule without the bureaucracy, yet built into the bureaucratic structure was a unique system of checks and balances which helped avoid misgovernment and keep ambitious officials—and, on occasion, overpowering despots—in line. On the other hand, the system also depended on recourse to personal relations and "organized corruption" to keep the administrative wheels turning.

The Imperial government drew its officials from the scholar class through an examination system based on the Confucian classics, which not only provided the government with able administrators, but served as an important avenue of social mobility. Chinese society was clearly stratified, but it was possible to rise from bottom to top. Achievement rather than birth determined a man's position. Fairbank concludes, "the structure was flexible, automatically self-perpetuating and very stable."

JOHN K. FAIRBANK *
The Nature of Chinese Society

SOCIAL STRUCTURE

Since ancient times there have been two Chinas—the myriad
agricultural communities of the peasantry in the countryside,
where each tree-clad village and farm household persists stati-
cally upon the soil; and the superstructure of walled towns and
cities peopled by the landlords, scholars, merchants, and officials
—the families of property and position. There has been no
caste system, and the chance to rise from peasant status has
not been lacking. Yet China has always remained a country
of farmers, four fifths of the people living on the soil they till.
The chief social division has therefore been that between town
and countryside, between the 80 per cent or more of the population who have stayed put upon the land and the 10 or 20
per cent of the population who have formed a mobile upper
class. This bifurcation still underlies the Chinese political scene
and makes it difficult to spread the control of the state from
the few to the many.

If we look more closely at this inherited class structure,
we note that the upper levels have included really several classes
—the landowning gentry, the scholar-literati, and the officials,
as well as the merchants, the militarists and their hangers-on.
This composite upper stratum has been the active carrier of
Chinese culture in its many aspects. Within this minority segment
of the Chinese people have been developed and maintained all
the literature and most of the fine arts, all the higher philosophy,

* John K. Fairbank, *The United States and China* (Cambridge, Mass.:
Harvard University Press, 1959), pp. 28–42, 52–58, 87–94.

ethics, and political ideology of the state, the sanctions of power, and much of the wealth that accompanied them. Culture has filtered down to the masses.

The Peasant: Family and Village. The Chinese people are still mostly peasants tilling the soil, living mainly in villages, in houses of brown sun-dried brick, bamboo, or whitewashed wattle, or sometimes stone, with earth floors, oil lamps, if any, and paper, not glass, in the windows. At least half and sometimes two thirds to three quarters of their meager material income is used for food. The other necessaries of life, including rent, heat, light, clothing, and any possible luxuries, come from the tiny remainder. They lack even the luxury of space. Peasant dwellings have usually about four small room-sections for every three persons. Sometimes family members of both sexes and two or three generations must all sleep on the same brick bed. There is little or no meat in the diet, and so simple a thing as iron is scarce for tools or for building. Even today the per capita consumption of steel in the United States is several hundred times that in China. Manpower takes the place of the machine for most purposes. In this toilsome, earthbound existence the hazards of life from malnutrition and disease until recently have given the average baby in China, as in India, little more than twenty-six years of life expectancy. Human life compared with the other factors of production is abundant and therefore cheap.

To an American with his higher material standard of living the amazing thing about the Chinese peasantry is their ability to maintain life in these poor conditions.

The answer lies in their social institutions which have carried the individuals of each family through the phases and vicissitudes of human existence according to deeply ingrained patterns of social behavior. These institutions and behavior patterns have been the oldest and most persistent social phenomena in the world. China has been the stronghold of the family system and has derived both strength and inertia from it.

The Chinese family has been a microcosm, the state in miniature. The family, not the individual, has been the social

unit and the responsible element in the political life of its locality. The filial piety and obedience inculcated in family life
have been the training ground for loyalty to the ruler and
obedience to constituted authority in the state.

This function of the family to raise filial sons who would
become loyal subjects can be seen by a glance at the pattern of
authority within the traditional family group. The father was a
supreme autocrat, with control over the use of all family property and income and a decisive voice in arranging the marriages
of the children. The mixed love, fear, and awe of children for
their father was strengthened by the great respect paid to age.
An old man's loss of vigor was more than offset by his growth
in wisdom. As long as he lived in possession of his faculties the
patriarch possessed every sanction to enable him to dominate
the family scene. He could even sell his children into slavery.
In fact, of course, parents were also bound by a reciprocal code
of responsibility for their children as family members. But law
and custom provided little check on parental tyranny if they
chose to exercise it.

The domination of age over youth within the old-style
family was matched by the domination of male over female.
Chinese baby girls in the old days were more likely than baby
boys to suffer infanticide. A girl's marriage was, of course, ar-
ranged and not for love. The trembling bride became at once
a daughter-in-law under the tyranny of her husband's mother.
In a well-to-do family she might see secondary wives or concubines brought into the household, particularly if she did not
bear a male heir. She could be repudiated by her husband for
various reasons. If he died she could not easily remarry. All this
reflected the fact that a woman had no economic independence.
Her labor was absorbed in household tasks and brought her no
income. Peasant women were universally illiterate. They had
few or no property rights. Until the present century their sub-
jection was demonstrated and reinforced by the custom of foot-
binding. This crippling practice by which a young girl's feet
were tightly wrapped to prevent normal development seems to
have begun about the tenth century A.D. The "lily feet" which it

produced through the suffering of hundreds of millions of young girls acquired great aesthetic and erotic value. In practice bound feet kept womankind from venturing far abroad.

The inferiority of women imposed upon them by social custom was merely one manifestation of the hierarchic nature of a society of status. It exemplified an entire social code and cosmology. Philosophically, ancient China had seen the world as the product of two interacting complementary elements, yin and yang. Yin was the attribute of all things female, dark, weak, and passive. Yang was the attribute of things male, bright, strong, and active. While male and female were both necessary and complementary, one was by nature passive toward the other. Building on such ideological foundations, an endless succession of Chinese male moralists worked out the behavior pattern of obedience and passivity which was to be expected of women. These patterns subordinated girls to boys from their infancy and kept the wife subordinate to her husband and the mother to her son. Forceful women, whom China has never lacked, controlled their families by indirection, not by fiat.

Status within the family was codified in the famous "five relationships," a doctrine emphasized by the Confucian philosophers. These five relationships were those between ruler and subject (prince and minister), father and son, elder brother and younger brother, husband and wife, and friend and friend. To an egalitarian Westerner the most striking thing about this doctrine is that three of the five relations were within the family, and four of the five were between superior and subordinate. The relationship of mother and son, which in Western life often allows matriarchal domination, was not stressed in theory, though naturally important in fact.

Within the family every child from birth was involved in a highly ordered system of kinship relations with elder brothers, sisters, maternal elder brother's wives, and other kinds of aunts, uncles, and cousins, grandparents, and in-laws too numerous for a Westerner to keep in mind. These relationships were not only more clearly named and differentiated than in the West but also carried with them more compelling rights and duties dependent upon status. A first son, for example, could not long remain unaware of the Confucian teaching as to his duties toward the family line and his precedence over his younger brothers and his sisters.

Chinese well habituated to the family system have been prepared to accept similar patterns of status in other institutions, including the official hierarchy of the government. One advantage of a system of status (as opposed to our individualist system of contractual relations) is that a man knows automatically where he stands in his family or society. He can have security in the knowledge that if he does his prescribed part he may expect reciprocal action from others in the system. It has often been observed that a Chinese community overseas tends to organize its activities and meet new situations in a hierarchic fashion.

The life cycle of the individual in a peasant family is inextricably interwoven with the seasonal cycle of intensive agriculture upon the land. The life and death of the people follow a rhythm which interpenetrates the growing and harvesting of the crops. The peasant village which still forms the bedrock of Chinese society is built out of family units; village, family, and individual follow the rhythm of seasons and crops, of birth, marriage, and death.

Socially, the Chinese in the village are organized primarily in their kinship system and only secondarily as a neighborhood community. The village has ordinarily consisted of a group of family or kinship units (clans) which are permanently settled from one generation to the next and continuously dependent upon the use of certain landholdings. Each family household is both a social and an economic unit. Its members derive their sustenance from working its fields and their social status from membership in it.

The Chinese kinship system is patrilineal, the family headship passing in the male line from father to eldest son. Thus the men stay in the family while the girls marry outside of it into other family households, in neither case following the life pattern which Western individuals take as a matter of course. Until recently a Chinese boy and girl did not choose each other as life mates, nor did they set up an independent household together after marriage. Instead, they entered the husband's father's household and assumed responsibilities for its maintenance, subordinating married life to family life in a way that modern Americans would consider insupportable.

From the time of the first imperial unification, before Christ, the Chinese abandoned the institution of primogeniture by which the eldest son would have retained all the father's property while the younger sons sought their fortunes elsewhere. The enormous significance of this institutional change can be seen by comparison with a country like England or Japan where younger sons who have not shared their father's estate have provided the personnel for government, business, and empire. By the abolition of primogeniture the Chinese created a system of equal division of the land among the sons of the family. They left the eldest son only certain ceremonial duties, to acknowledge his position, and sometimes an extra share of property; otherwise the land was divided. This constant parcelization of the land has tended to destroy the continuity of family landholding, forestall the growth of landed particularism among great officials, and keep peasant families on the margin of subsistence. Under this system the prime duty of each married couple has been to produce a son who can maintain the family line, and yet the birth of more than one son may mean impoverishment.

Contrary to a common myth, a large family with several children has not been the peasant norm. The scarcity of land, as well as disease and famine, has set a limit to the number of people likely to survive in each family unit. The large joint family of several married sons with many children all within one compound, which has usually been regarded as typical of China, appears to have been the ideal exception, a luxury which only the well-to-do could afford. The average peasant family was limited to four, five, or six persons. Division of the land among the sons has constantly checked the accumulation of property and savings and the typical family has had little opportunity to rise in the social scale. The peasantry have been bound to the soil not by law and custom so much as by their own numbers.

THE GENTRY CLASS

This group dominated Chinese life, so much so that sociologists have called China a "gentry state" and even ordinary people may speak of the "scholar gentry" as a class. But do not let yourself be reminded of the landed gentry with their roast beef and fox hunts in merry England, for "gentry" in the case of China is a technical term with two principal meanings and an inner ambiguity. It requires special handling.

Non-Marxists generally agree, first of all, that the gentry were not a mere "feudal landlord" class, because Chinese society was not organized in any system that can be called "feudalism," except possibly before 221 B.C. While "feudal" may still be a useful swear word, it has little value as a Western term applied to China. For instance, an essential characteristic of feudalism, as the word has been used with reference to medieval Europe and Japan, has been the inalienability of the land. The medieval serf was bound to the land and could not himself either leave it or dispose of it, whereas the Chinese peasant both in law and in fact has been free to sell and, if he had the means, to purchase land. His bondage has resulted from a press of many circumstances but not from a legal institution similar to European feudalism. Nor has it been maintained by the domination of a professional warrior caste. Avoidance of the term feudal to describe the Chinese peasant's situation in life by no means signifies that it has been less miserable. But if the word feudal is to retain a valid meaning for European and other institutions to which it was originally applied, it cannot be very meaningful in a general Chinese context.

The Chinese gentry can be understood only in a dual, economic-and-political sense, as connected both with landholding and with officeholding. The narrow definition, following the traditional Chinese term *shen-shih,* confines gentry status to those *individuals* who held official degrees gained normally by passing examinations, or sometimes by recommendation or purchase. This has the merit of being concrete and even quantifiable —the gentry in this narrow sense were degree-holders, as officially listed, and not dependent for their status on economic resources, particularly landowning, which is so hard to quantify from the historical record.

Yet in an agrarian society one can hardly ignore the importance of landholding as one source of upper-class strength, much as one may wish to avoid the Marxist exaggeration of the role of economic relations. The main point about the gentry as individuals was that they were public functionaries, playing political and administrative roles, in addition to any connection with the landlord class. Yet, being Chinese, they were also enmeshed in family relations, on which they could rely for material sustenance. This political-economic dualism has led many writers to define the term gentry more broadly, as a group of *families* rather than of individual degree-holders only. Both the narrow and the broad definitions must be kept in mind.

Looked at descriptively, the gentry families lived chiefly in the walled towns rather than in the villages. They constituted a stratum of families based on landed property which intervened between the earth-bound masses of the peasantry, on the one hand, and the officials and merchants who formed a fluid matrix of over-all administrative and commercial activity, on the other. They were the local elite, who carried on certain functions connected with the peasantry below and certain others connected with the officials above.

For the peasant community they included the big landowners, the lowest economic rung of the great ruling class. Their big high-walled compounds enclosing many courtyards, replete with servants and hoarded supplies and proof against bandits, still dominate the old market towns. This is the type of "big house" celebrated in both Chinese and Western novels of China. As a local ruling class the gentry managed the system of customary and legal rights to the use of the land. These ordinarily were so incredibly diverse and complicated that decided managerial ability was required to keep them straight. The varied tenant relationships, loans, mortgages, customary payments and obligations on both sides formed such a complex within the community that many peasants could hardly say whether they were themselves mainly small landowners or mainly tenants. In general, a peasant's loss of title to his land was more likely to make him a tenant and decrease his share of its product than to make him a displaced and homeless wanderer. Peasant poverty was reflected sometimes in the increase of landless laborers in the villages, but it was marked chiefly by the increased payment of land rent.

In the 1930s it was estimated that perhaps three fifths (or possibly only half) of the Chinese peasants owned their own land, about one fifth were part owners and part tenants, and one fifth outright tenants. Tenantry was more frequent in South China and was increasing. Tenants paid between half and two thirds (sometimes three fourths) of their crop in rent. If a farmer owned his land, he still had to pay the land tax.

More significant than the proportion of tenants was the high proportion of land and capital in landlord hands. As in all farming, the seasonal need of capital permitted usurious interest on loans, which ran as high as 12 per cent a month, depending on what the traffic would bear. Since capital was accumulated from the surplus product of the land, landowners were moneylenders. The gentry families thus rested in part upon property rights and money power, as well as social prestige. In the early twentieth century, they still dominated the back country in most provinces. Modern developments like absentee landlordism strengthened rather than weakened their position, by stressing economic claims untempered by personal relations.

For the officials of the old China the gentry families were one medium through whom tax collections were effected. By this same token they were for the peasantry intermediaries who could palliate official oppression. They influenced official policy in the process of carrying it out. Conditions of flood or famine or incipient rebellion and the multitude of minor criminal cases and projects for public works were dealt with by the local officials through the help of the gentry community. It was the buffer between populace and officialdom.

The economic role of the gentry families was no more than half the story, for they had very important political-administrative functions in the Chinese state which made them unlike any group in Western history. Here we meet a problem of historical interpretation, created by the ambivalence of the term "gentry," which in the present literature on China may refer either to landowning families or to degree-holding individuals. Unfortunately for the clarity of the term, the latter group was not entirely included within the former. Peasants without landlord-family backing could and did rise through the examination system to become degree-holders and officials. Thus a poor man, by his educational qualifications alone, could become a member of the gentry in the narrow sense used above, even though he was not connected with a gentry family in the broad sense used above. This fact makes the term "gentry" ambiguous and therefore subject to dispute.

The view taken here is that the degree-holding individuals were in most cases connected with landowning families, and the latter in most cases had degree-holding members. Until the subject is clarified by further research we can only proceed on the assumption that, in general and for the most part, the gentry families were the out-of-office reservoir of the degree-holders and the bureaucracy. The big families were the seedbed in which officeholders were nurtured and the haven to which dismissed or worn-out bureaucrats could return.

If we turn to the narrower and more concrete, political-administrative definition of the gentry, we find that in each local community the gentry as individuals, in the basic sense of literati or degree-holders, had many important public functions. They raised funds for and supervised public works—the building and upkeep of irrigation and communication facilities such as canals, dikes, dams, roads, bridges, ferries. They supported Confucian institutions and morals—establishing and maintaining schools, shrines and local temples of Confucius, publishing books, especially local histories or gazetteers, and issuing moral homilies

and exhortations to the populace. In time of peace they set the
tone of public life. In time of disorder they organized and commanded militia defense forces. From day to day they arbitrated
disputes informally, in place of the continual litigation which
goes on in any American town. The gentry also set up charities
and handled trust funds to help the community, and made contributions at official request to help the state, especially in time
of war, flood, or famine. So useful were these contributions that
most dynasties got revenue by selling the lowest literary degrees,
thus admitting many persons to degree-holding status without
examination. While this abused the system, it also let men of
wealth rise for a price into the upper class and share the gentry
privileges, such as contact with the officials and immunity from
corporal punishment.

The position of the gentry families as the reservoir from
which most of the individual scholar-officials emerged may explain why officialdom did not penetrate lower down into Chinese
society. The imperial government remained a superstructure
which did not directly enter the villages because it rested upon
the gentry as its foundation. The many public functions of the
local degree-holders made a platform under the imperial bureaucracy and let the officials move about with remarkable
fluidity and seeming independence of local roots. Actually, the
Emperor's appointee to any magistracy could administer it only
with the cooperation of the gentry in that area. All in all, in a
country of over four hundred million people, a century ago,
there were less than twenty thousand regular imperial officials but roughly one and a quarter million scholarly degree-
holders.

Continued domination of the gentry families over the peasantry was assured not only by landowning but also by the fact
that the gentry mainly produced the scholar class from which
officials were chosen. This near-monopoly of scholarship was
made possible in turn by the nature of the Chinese language.

The Scholar. The scholar class produced by mastery of the
characters was closely integrated with both the gentry families
beneath it and the official system above. When successful as a

degree-holder and perhaps an official, the scholar found his channel of expression and achievement through the established structure of government. He could become an official, however, only by mastering the official ideology of the state as set down in the canonical works of the Chinese classics. These texts were part of a system of ideas and ritual practices in which the scholar-official learned and applied the Confucian rules and attitudes on the plane of verbal conduct while participating in the personal relationships, political cliques, organized perquisites, and systematic squeeze which distinguished the official class on the plane of practical action.

For the scholar who did not rise into official life there was always the alternative of the family system from which he had sprung. His status as a degree-holder gave him contact with the lower fringes of official power and through this personal contact he could serve his family by representing its interests. This function again called for the use of Confucian ideas in verbal and literary expression. In this way the scholar, whether in official life or out of it, was wedded to the established order of family and state. His living depended upon them and in practice he served them both. As a cultivated gentleman incapable of manual labor or trade and trained to be the bearer of the family-state ideology, he had no alternative.

It was the security of the individual boy in the gentry family which made it possible for him to take the risk involved in the investment of his time in scholarship. His preparation for the examinations and for official life required many years of study. Yet the examinations were a gamble and talented youths could be fed into the system only from sources which had means. The risk and mobility of official life contrasted with the security and stability of the landed gentry. The point of balance between them was the examination system. In a society which seems to us remarkable for its emphasis upon personal relations, the Chinese examinations appear to have been amazingly impersonal and universalistic. When the system was functioning effectively at the height of a dynasty, every effort was made to eliminate personal favoritism. Candidates were locked in their cubicles, several thousand of which in long rows covered a broad area at each provincial capital. Papers were marked with the writer's number only. Such precautions were, of course, necessary for the maintenance of any rational and objective standards in the selection of candidates for office. They expressed the Chinese ruler's genuine need of talented personnel to maintain an efficient administration. Once the best talent of the land had been chosen by this impersonal institution, however, it was then perfectly consistent that the officials should conduct a highly personal administration of the government, following a "virtue ethic" which attached importance to the qualities of individual personality rather than a "command ethic" which laid emphasis upon an impersonal and higher law.

The fact and the myth of social mobility in the Chinese state are still matters of debate. Most dynasties which supported the examination system as a mechanism for the selection of talent gave extensive lip service to the myth that all might enter high position, depending only upon ability. Western writers for long assumed that the Chinese examinations were a really democratic institution, providing opportunity for the intelligent peasant to rise in the world. In fact, however, this seems to have happened rather seldom. The many years of assiduous study required for the examinations were a barrier which no ordinary peasant could surmount. The legend of the villagers who clubbed together to support the studies of the local peasant genius has been an inspiring tradition. But it was not an everyday occurrence.

Of the various avenues open to the common peasant, advancement could not be sought through the use of new land or founding of new enterprises, nor, except rarely, through increased agricultural production and the accumulation of profits and savings. This fact has given Chinese life a character far different from our own and makes the American doctrine of individualism and free enterprise, when transplanted to China, an almost incomprehensible and rather dubious jumble of slogans. In Chinese circumstances, advancement for the common man has lain in the direction of connections with the bureaucracy. Entrance into the official class or into the penumbra of money handlers and fixers which surrounded it was a goal to be achieved through personal contacts and personal services. But this route on the whole led through the gentry and not around them.

Thus landlords, scholars, and officials were all parts of a composite ruling class. Landowning families, having some agricultural surplus, could give their sons leisure for study to become scholars. Scholars, with a mastery of classical learning, could pass examinations and become officials. Officials, with the perquisites and profits of bureaucratic government, could protect and increase their family landholdings. The structure was flexible, automatically self-perpetuating, and very stable. . . .

The Confucian Pattern

Superficial Western observers, looking only at the texts of the Confucian classics, have been impressed with their agnostic this-worldliness and their ethical emphasis upon proper conduct in personal relations. In its larger sense as a philosophy of life, we have generally associated with Confucianism those quiet virtues so artfully described in Lin Yutang's *My Country and My People*—patience, pacifism and compromise, the golden mean, conservatism and contentment, reverence for the ancestors, the aged, and the learned, and, above all, a mellow humanism—taking man, not God, as the center of the universe.

All this need not be denied. But if we take this Confucian view of life in its social and political context, we will see that its esteem for age over youth, for the past over the present, for established authority over innovation, has in fact provided one of the great historic answers to the problem of social stability. It has been the most successful of all systems of conservatism. For most of two thousand years the Confucian ideology was made the chief subject of study in the world's largest state. Nowhere else have the sanctions of government power been based for so many centuries upon a single consistent pattern of ideas attributed to one ancient sage.

Naturally, in the course of two thousand years many

changes have occurred within the broad limits of what we call Confucianism—periods of decline and revival, repeated movements for reform, new emphases and even innovations within the inherited tradition. The range of variety may be less broad than among the multiple facets of Christianity but it is certainly comparable. Consequently the term Confucianism means many things and must be used with care.

As a code of personal conduct Confucianism tried to make each individual a moral being, ready to act on ideal grounds, to uphold virtue against human error, especially against evil rulers. There were many Confucian scholars of moral grandeur, uncompromising foes of tyranny. But their reforming zeal, the dynamics of their creed, aimed to reaffirm and conserve the traditional polity, not to change its fundamental premises.

That Confucian ideas persist in the minds of Chinese politicians today should not surprise us. Confucianism began as a means of bringing social order out of the chaos of a period of warring states. It has been a philosophy of status and obedience according to status, and consequently a ready tool for autocracy and bureaucracy whenever they have flourished. Unifiers of China have been irresistibly attracted to it, for reasons that are not hard to see.

When Chiang Kai-shek on Christmas day 1936 was released by the mutinous subordinates who had forcibly held him at Sian, he returned to Nanking amid unprecedented national rejoicing. Yet four days later he submitted his resignation.

> Since I am leading the military forces of the country, I should set a good example for my fellow servicemen. It is apparent that my work failed to command the obedience of my followers; for otherwise the mutiny . . . would not have occurred . . . I sincerely hope that the central executive committee will censure me for my negligence of duties. After the Sian incident, it is no longer fit for me to continue in office.

Nine years later in his famous wartime book, *China's Destiny,* Chiang Kai-shek said:

To cultivate the moral qualities necessary to our national salvation . . . we must revive and extend our traditional ethical principles. The most important task is to develop our people's sense of propriety, righteousness, integrity, and honor. These qualities are based upon the Four Cardinal Principles and the Eight Virtues, which in turn are based on Loyalty and Filial Piety . . .

These two examples could be multiplied. They demonstrate the degree to which China down to recent decades remained a Confucian state. In the first case no one wanted Chiang to resign, nor did he intend to do so, and his resignation was elaborately declined. In the second case no one expected that China's national salvation in the midst of Japanese aggression, blockade, and inflation could be achieved through moral qualities alone, nor did Chiang think so. But in both cases his words delineated the traditional Confucian way.

Countless Chinese leaders before Chiang Kai-shek have quoted Confucius while fighting off rivals or alien invaders, who, like the Japanese, have invoked the Sage on their part while trying to take over China. Peking today sings a different tune, but there are Confucian overtones in the Marxist orchestration. The crucial role of ideology under Communism lends particular interest to China's ideological past.

CONFUCIAN PRINCIPLES

The principles of Confucian government, which still lie somewhere below the surface of Chinese politics, were worked out before the time of Christ. Modifications made in later centuries, though extensive, have not been fundamental.

First of all, from the beginning of Chinese history in the Shang and Chou periods (from prehistoric times before 1400 B.C. to the third century B.C.) there was a marked stratification into the classes of the officials and nobility on the one hand, and the common people on the other. Thus the term "hundred

names" (*pai-hsing*) referred originally to the clans of the officials who were in a category quite different from the common
people (*min*). It was not until much later that the modern term
"old hundred names" (*lao-pai-hsing*) became transferred to the
populace. This difference between the ancient ruling class and
the common people gave rise to a particular type of aristocratic
tradition which has been preserved and transmitted through
Confucianism down to the present. The Confucian aristocrat
has been the scholar-official.

In the second place, Confucianism has been the ideology
of the bureaucrat. The bureaucratic ruling class came into its
own after the decentralized feudalism of ancient China gave
way to an imperial government. The unification of 221 B.C., in
which one of the warring states (Ch'in) swallowed the others,
required violent dictatorial methods and a philosophy of absolutism (that of the so-called "Legalist" philosophers). But
after the short-lived Ch'in Dynasty was succeeded by the Han
in 202 B.C., a less tyrannical system of administration evolved.
The Emperors came to rely upon a new class of administrators
who superintended the great public works—dikes and ditches,
walls, palaces, and granaries—and who drafted peasant labor
and collected the land tax to support them. These administrators
supplanted the hereditary nobility of feudal times and became
the backbone of the imperial regime.

In the two centuries before Christ the early Han rulers
firmly established certain principles. First, that the political
authority in the state was centralized in the one man at the top
who ruled as Emperor. Second, the Emperor's authority in the
conduct of the administration was exercised on his behalf by
his chief ministers, who stood at the top of a graded bureaucracy
and who were responsible to him for the success or failure of
their administration. Third, this bureaucracy was centralized in
the vast palace at the capital where the Emperor exercised the
power of appointment to office. His chief task became the selection of civil servants, with an eye to the maintenance of his
power and his dynasty. For this reason the appointment of
relatives, particularly from the maternal side, became an early

practice. (Maternal relatives were the one group of persons completely dependent upon the ruler's favor as well as tied to him by family bonds, in contrast to paternal relatives who might compete for the succession.) Fourth, the early Han rulers developed the institution of inspection which later became the censorate, whereby an official in the provinces was checked upon by another official of lower rank, who was sent independently and was not responsible for the acts of his superior. In this and in many other ways the central problem of the imperial administration became that of selecting and controlling bureaucrats. It was here that Confucianism played its central role.

This ideology did not, of course, begin with Confucius (551–479? B.C.). The interesting concept of the Mandate of Heaven, for example, went back to the early Chou period (ca. 1000–771 B.C.). According to the classic *Book of History,* the wickedness of the last ruler of the preceding dynasty of Shang, who was a tyrant, caused Heaven to give a mandate to the Chou to destroy him and supplant his dynasty, inasmuch as the Shang people themselves had failed to overthrow the tyrant. As later amplified this ancient idea became the famous "right of rebellion," the last resort of the populace against tyrannical government. It emphasized the good conduct or virtue of the ruler as the ethical sanction for preserving his dynasty. Bad conduct on his part destroyed the sanction, Heaven withdrew its Mandate, and the people were justified in deposing the dynasty, if they could. Consequently any successful rebellion was justified and a new rule sanctioned, by the very fact of its success. "Heaven decides as the people decide." The Chinese literati have censored bad government and rebels have risen against it in terms of this theory. It has also reinforced the belief that the ruler should be advised by learned men in order to ensure his right conduct.

Government by Moral Prestige. Confucius and his fellow philosophers achieved their position by being teachers who advised rulers as to their right conduct, in an age when feudal princes were competing for hegemony. Confucius was an aristocrat and maintained at his home a school for the elucidation and transmission of the moral principles of conduct and princely rule. Here he taught the upper class how to behave. He emphasized court etiquette, state ceremonies, and proper conduct toward one's ancestors and in the famous five degrees of relationship. One of the central principles of this code was expressed in the idea of "proper behavior according to status" (*li*). The Confucian gentleman or *chün-tzu* ("the superior man," "the princely man") was guided by *li,* the precepts of which were written in the classics.

It is important to note that this code which came to guide the conduct of the scholar-official did not originally apply to the common people, whose conduct was to be regulated by rewards and punishments rather than moral principles.

This complex system of abstruse rules which the Confucians became experts at applying stemmed from the relationship of Chinese man to nature, which has already been mentioned. This relation had early been expressed in a primitive animism in which the spirits of land, wind, and water were thought to play an active part in human affairs. The idea is still prevalent in the practice of Chinese geomancy or *feng-shui* (lit., "wind and water"), which sees to it that buildings in China are properly placed in their natural surroundings. Temples, for example, commonly face south with protecting hills behind them and a watercourse nearby. In its more rationalized form this idea of the close relation between human and natural phenomena led to the conception that human conduct is reflected in acts of nature. To put it another way, man is so much a part of the natural order that improper conduct on his part will throw the whole of nature out of joint. Therefore man's conduct must be made to harmonize with the unseen forces of nature, lest calamity ensue.

This was the rationale of the Confucian emphasis on right conduct on the part of the ruler, for the ruler was thought to intervene between mankind and the forces of nature. As the Son of Heaven he stood between Heaven above and the people below. He maintained the universal harmony of man and nature by doing the right thing at the right time. It was, therefore, logical to assume that when natural calamity came, it was the ruler's fault. It was for this reason that the Confucian scholar became so important. Only he, by his knowledge of the rules of right conduct, could properly advise the ruler in his cosmic role.

The main point of this theory of "government by goodness," by which Confucianism achieved an emphasis so different from anything in the West, was the idea of the virtue which was attached to right conduct. To conduct oneself according to the rules of propriety or *li* in itself gave one a moral status or prestige. This moral prestige in turn gave one influence over the people. "The people (are) like grass, the ruler like the wind"; as the wind blew, so the grass was inclined. Right conduct gave the ruler power.

On this basis the Confucian scholars established themselves as an essential part of the government, specially competent to maintain its moral nature and so retain the Mandate of Heaven. Where the Legalist philosophers of the Ch'in unification had had ruthlessly efficient methods of government but no moral justification for them, the Confucianists offered an ideological basis. They finally eclipsed the many other ancient schools of philosophy. As interpreters of the *li,* they became technical experts, whose explanations of natural portents and calamities and of the implications of the rulers' actions could be denied or rejected only on the basis of the classical doctrines of which they were themselves the masters. This gave them a strategic position from which to influence government policy. In return they provided the regime with a rational and ethical sanction for the exercise of its authority, at a time when most rulers of empires relied mainly upon religious sanctions. This was a great political invention. . . .

The Political Tradition

BUREAUCRACY

One key to the understanding of the Communist administration
in China is the fact that the old Imperial government was a
bureaucracy of the most thoroughly developed and sophisticated
sort. To the American who has confronted the problems of
bureaucracy only recently, the effort of modern Chinese to
escape from the evils and capitalize upon the good points of
their own bureaucratic tradition is a matter of absorbing interest.

The Capital. The old government centered in the capital.
Without question the vast symmetrical plan of Peking makes it
the most magnificent of all capital cities. Paris and London,
Washington and Moscow are creations of yesterday and do not
attest, in the balance of gate against gate and avenue against
avenue, the omnipotence of Oriental despots who created their
capital city as an outer cover to their palace. Peking centers
upon the moats and red walls of the Forbidden City. Within it
the yellow-roofed throne halls rising from their marble platforms
form the main axis of the whole metropolis. Behind them a
great manmade hill of earth protects them from the north. Before them, broad avenues and today the Red Square lead south
to the Front Gate of the city. No Western capital is so plainly
a symbol of centralized and absolute monarchy.

At Peking, for the greater part of thirteen centuries the
civil administration of China was divided among the famous
Six Ministries (or Boards), namely those of civil office (appointment of officials), revenue, ceremonies, war, punishments,
and public works (such as flood control). This structure, adum-
brated in the first imperial system of the Ch'in and Han, had
been formally established under the T'ang. In addition to the
Six Ministries there were two other independent hierarchies of
administration—the military establishment and the Censorate,

as well as a number of minor offices—the imperial academy of literature, a court to review criminal cases, a historiographer's office, the imperial stud, and offices in charge of banquets and sacrificial worship. At the apex of everything the Ming had created the Grand Secretariat, in which high officials assisted the Emperor in his personal administration of affairs. One of the few Manchu innovations was to add in 1729 a less formal body, the Grand Council, which handled military and other important matters and so became the real top of the administration.

The Provinces. Spread out over the eighteen provinces of China under the Manchu dynasty was a network of territorial divisions. Each province was divided into several circuits (*tao*) and below them into prefectures, departments, and *hsien* (districts or counties) in descending order. The mandarins in charge of these divisions with their ubiquitous assistants and subordinates formed the main body of the territorial magistracy. Like civil servants trained in the classics at Oxford, they were supposedly omnicompetent, responsible for the collection of revenue, maintenance of order, dispensing of justice, conduct of literary examinations, superintendence of the postal service, and in general for all public events within their areas. Theoretically, they stood *in loco parentis* to the people and were called, or rather called themselves, the "father and mother officials."

The imperial civil service was divided into nine ranks, each of which was divided into upper and lower grades. Each rank was entitled to a particular and very fine costume, including a colored button on the cap and insignia such as "mandarin squares" embroidered on the front and back of the gown. Prerogatives, titles, and dignities were minutely set forth in the statutes. High officials might be rewarded with the right to wear a peacock feather or bear the title of "Junior Guardian of the Heir Apparent."

Intervening between the hierarchy of local officials and the government at the capital stood the higher administration in each province. This consisted of a governor-general who was in most cases responsible for two provinces and, as his junior colleague, a governor responsible for a single province. These two officials were of course so placed as to check each other, for they were expected to act and report jointly on important matters. Under the Ch'ing (Manchu) Dynasty, frequently the governor-general was a Manchu and the governor Chinese. Beneath them were four provincial officers who exercised province-wide functions—a treasurer, judge, salt comptroller, and grain intendant (who supervised the collection of grain for the capital).

Official business over the far-flung Chinese empire was conducted as in all bureaucracies by a flow of documents of many kinds. In their special forms and designations these multifarious communications mirrored the elaborate proliferation of red tape. A governor addressed his imperial master in certain prescribed forms and addressed his subordinates in others. Every communication began with a clear indication of its nature as a document to a superior, an equal, or a subordinate. Similarly there were special forms for memorials submitted to the Emperor and edicts issued from him. Each document also went through a certain procedure of preparation, transmission, and reception. Hundreds of thousands of brush-wielding scriveners were kept busy year in and year out transcribing, recording, and processing official communications. In the imperial archives in the Peking palace are more than one hundred different types of documents which were in common use.

The flow of paperwork was maintained by an official post which reached to all corners of the empire but was limited to the transportation of official mail, official shipments (as of funds), and persons traveling on official business. This postal system was made up of some two thousand stations stretched out along five main and many subsidiary routes which ran into Manchuria, across Mongolia, westward to Turkestan and Tibet, southeastward through the coastal provinces, and southward through the interior of Central China. Couriers and travelers on these routes were provided with official tallies entitling them to the use of the transportation facilities, which in different areas might be horses, camels, donkeys, chairs (palanquins), or boats. In time of crisis couriers could cover 250 miles a day.

Such speed was achieved by the use of horses in relays, a system which the Mongols had developed to cover the distances of Central Asia. In the early nineteenth century this pony express regularly transmitted messages from Canton to Peking in less than three weeks and from Shanghai to Peking in one week.

Central Controls. Given this network of officials, connected by a flow of documents and persons along the postal routes, it was the problem of the capital to stimulate the local bureaucrats to perform their functions and yet prevent them from getting out of hand. This control was achieved by the application of techniques common to bureaucracies everywhere, in addition to the special measures (noted above) whereby the Manchus sought to preserve their dynasty.

Among these techniques the first was the appointment of all officers down to the rank of district magistrate by the Emperor himself. This made them all aware of their dependence upon the Son of Heaven and their duty of personal loyalty to him. Circulation in office was another device. No official was left in one post for more than three years or at most six years. Ordinarily when moving from one post to another the official passed through the capital and participated in an imperial audience to renew his contact with the ruler.

Thus Chinese officialdom was a mobile body which circulated through all parts of the empire without taking root in any one place. In this it was aided by its reliance upon the Mandarin (Peking) dialect as a lingua franca of universal currency in official circles. Frequently an official would arrive at his new post to find himself quite incapable of understanding the local dialect and therefore the more closely confined to his official level.

One means to prevent officials taking local root was the "law of avoidance" according to which no mandarin could be appointed to office in his native province, where the claims of family loyalty might impair devotion to the imperial regime.

Another custom, which interrupted an official's rise to

power, was the rule of three years' mourning (actually some twenty-five months) after the death of his father, during which an official retired to a life of quiet abstention from worldly activities. As Arthur Waley says, this was "a sort of 'sabbatical' occurring as a rule toward the middle of a man's official career. It gave him a period for study and reflection, for writing at last the book that he had planned . . . , for repairing a life ravaged by official banqueting, a constitution exhausted by the joint claims of concubinage and matrimony."

In general the bureaucratic principle was to set one official to check upon another. This was done particularly through the system of joint responsibility. The Six Ministries each had two presidents, one Manchu and one Chinese, who watched each other. It was common to appoint one man after he had gained prominence to several offices so that he was not able to master any one of them, and at the same time to appoint many men to perform one job so that no one of them could completely control it. Indeed many offices were sometimes created to carry on the same function, checking each other through their duplication of activity. The result of this duplication of offices and mutual responsibility was to hedge each official about with a multiplicity of commitments in each of which others were concerned. It was something like the unlimited liability of a partnership in which there were dozens of partners. Over and above all these immediate checks created by the involvement of many officials in a common responsibility, there was the system of the Censorate. Under it some fifty-six censors selected for their loyalty and uprightness were stationed in fifteen circuits through the provinces with the duty of keeping the Emperor informed upon all matters concerning the welfare of the people and the dynasty.

The evils inherent in bureaucracy were all too evident. All business was in form originated at the bottom and passed upward to the Emperor for decision at the top, memorials from the provinces being addressed to the Emperor at the capital. The higher authority was thus left to choose alternatives of action proposed, and yet the proposal of novel or unprecedented action was both difficult and dangerous for the lower official. The greater safety of conformity tended to kill initiative at the bottom. On the other hand the efficiency of the one man at the top was constantly impaired by his becoming a bottleneck. All business of importance was expected to receive his approval. All legislation and precedent were established by his edict. Modern China still suffers from this tradition.

In view of the complete and arbitrary power which the imperial bureaucracy asserted over the whole of Chinese life, it is amazing how few and how scattered the officials were in number. The total of civil officials for whom posts were statutorily available, both at the capital and in the provinces, was hardly more than nine thousand. The military officials were supposed to number only about seventy-five hundred. It is true, of course, that there were a great many supernumerary or "expectant" officials who might be assigned to various functions without receiving substantive appointments. There was also the vast body of clerks and factota necessary for the copying, recording, negotiating, and going and coming in each Chinese official's establishment or "yamen." Down to the gatemen, runners, and chair-bearers, these human elements in the official machine no doubt totaled millions. But if we look for the men of genuine official status who could take official action and report it in the hierarchy as representatives of his imperial majesty, we find them few and thinly spread, totaling at a rough estimate hardly more than thirty or forty thousand "officials" at most, ruling over a country of about two hundred million which grew to perhaps four hundred million by the middle of the nineteenth century. Of the nine ranks, for example, the seventh rank near the bottom of the scale began with the district magistrate who was responsible for a population on the order of 250,000 persons. This relative smallness of the imperial administration no doubt reflects the fact that it depended upon the gentry class to lead and dominate the peasantry in the villages. . . .

Government as Organized "Corruption." Another anomaly of the bureaucracy was its low salaries. According to the official

redbook, a governor-general in charge of two provinces as big
as European countries received from his imperial master a salary
equivalent in our terms to only $300 a year. To this nominal
sum was added a larger payment drawn from the provincial
rather than the imperial treasury. For the governor-general in
question this supplementary salary (*yang-lien,* lit., "to nourish
honesty"), would be equivalent to some $41,000 a year. But
still, when added together from all sources, such salaries could
not begin to meet the needs of an officer who had to employ a
great retinue of private secretaries and special assistants.

The imperial officials were held responsible for all public
events within their jurisdiction but not for all public funds.
Budgeting and accounting procedures were rudimentary. The
bureaucracy lived by what we today would call systematized
corruption which sometimes became extortion. This was a necessary concomitant of the system of intricate personal relationships that each official had to maintain with his superiors, colleagues, and subordinates.

Among the bureaucracies of history, the Chinese has been
distinguished by the way in which the twin institutions of
"squeeze" and nepotism reinforced each other. The former
operated through forms of politeness rather than secrecy. Junior
officials in the course of their duties gave their superiors customary "gifts." But like all prices in old China, the amount of
such a gift resulted from the working out of a personal relationship. The "squeeze" system was no more cut and dried than
any other part of the man-to-man bargaining which pervaded
Chinese life. The extralegal sums which passed between officials
were larger but no different in kind from the small commissions
extracted until only recently from every money transaction by
underpaid houseboys.

Nepotism supported the "squeeze" or "leakage" system by
giving an added sanction for personal arrangements contrary to
the public interest. Even classic texts extolled duty to family,
and particularly filial piety, as superior to any duty to the state.
Thus the interest of the imperial administration at the capital,
which needed the sustenance of revenue from the provinces,

was constantly in conflict with the multifarious private interests of all the officials, each of whom had to provide for his relatives and his further career. High office commonly meant riches. The favorite minister of the Ch'ien-lung Emperor, when tried for corruption and other crimes by that Emperor's successor in 1799, was found to have an estate worth in our terms of that period more than one billion dollars—probably an all-time record. Another high Manchu, who fell into disfavor at the time of the Opium War in 1841, was found to have an estate of some 425,000 acres of land, $30,000,000 worth of gold, silver, and precious stones, and shares in 90 banks and pawnshops. I would not suggest that Westerners have been backward or less adept in the art of graft. But in China corruption remained longer into modern times an accepted institution, unashamed and unafraid.

Communist China's vast new bureaucratism must be seen against the tradition sketched above. Today's totalitarianism, though utterly unprecedented in its total effect, has certain ancient foundations to build on. It also faces the age-old problem—how to keep the bureaucrats energetic, efficient, and honest. . . .

The Chinese Written Language

Chinese writing is not only different to look at, it is based on utterly different principles from the phonetically written tongues of western Asia and Europe, many of which look to us just as baffling as Chinese but are in fact closely similar to our own language. Even Siamese children, for example, when they study Thai in school go through a process very similar to American children, learning the sounds to associate with a number of otherwise meaningless symbols, or alphabet. As far as their mode of thought and study is concerned, they could just as well learn the English alphabet (with various adjustments to convey Thai sounds) and then proceed to write down words heard in everyday life and develop their vocabularies and powers of self-expression. With a Chinese child it is different. He learns symbols which have meaning because of their appearance, and which exist like pictures or like the figure 5, apart from any sounds.

The earliest Chinese characters have been found at the archaeological site of the ancient Shang Dynasty capital of Anyang, which is in Honan province north of the Yellow River. It appears that the ancient kings' diviners took the auspices by applying a hot point to flat slips of bone, producing cracks which could be interpreted as the advice of the ancestors. Characters were scratched on these "oracle bones" and the results were recorded there. This written language was both pictographic and symbolic, in either case ideographic rather than phonetic.

The Chinese language today consists of well over forty thousand characters in the biggest dictionary. But these boil down to about seven thousand necessary for a newspaper font, including about three thousand that one needs to know in order to be really literate. The form of these characters has hardly changed since the early Christian era. Until a generation ago the Chinese were still getting along with a written language comparable in age to ancient Greek and Latin, so terse that it usually had to be seen to be understood—the sound alone being inadequate. This was one factor helping to keep China, down to the twentieth century, in its archaic Confucian mold. The language inhibited easy contact with alien societies, whose students of Chinese found it even harder then than now.

A Note on Chinese Writing. Chinese characters began as pictures or symbols. The ancient character ☉ (later written 日) was the sun, and ☽ (later 月) the moon. Sun and moon together 明 meant bright, illustrious, clear. 木 meant a tree, two trees 林 meant a forest, and three 森 a dense growth. The symbols 一 二 三 are certainly easier than "one, two, three." 囗 indicates an enclosure or "to surround," while a smaller square 口 is the sign for the mouth and by extension means a hole, a pass, a harbor, and the like.

In its early growth the Chinese written language could not expand on a purely pictographic basis (like the joining of "sun" and "moon" to make "bright," noted above). A phonetic element crept into it. As a result most Chinese characters are combinations of other simple characters. One part of the combination usually indicates the root meaning, while the other part indicates something about the sound.

For example, take the character for east, 東, which in the Peking dialect has had the sound "tung" (pronounced like "doong," as in Mao Tse-tung's name). Since a Chinese character is read aloud as a single syllable and since spoken Chinese is also rather short of sounds (there are only about four hundred different syllables in the whole language), it has been plagued with homophones, words that sound like other words, like "soul" and "sole" or "all" and "awl" in English. It happened that the spoken word meaning freeze had the sound "tung." So did a spoken word meaning a roof beam. When the Chinese went to write down the character for freeze, they took the character for east and put beside it the symbol for ice 冫, which makes the character 凍 ("tung," to freeze). To write down the word sounding "tung" which meant roof beam, they wrote the character east and put before it the symbol for wood 木 making 棟 ("tung," a roof beam).

These are simple examples. Indeed any part of the Chinese language is simple in itself. It becomes difficult because there is so much of it, so many meanings and allusions, to be remembered. When the lexicographers wanted to arrange thousands of Chinese characters in a dictionary, for instance, the best they could do in the absence of an alphabet was to work out a list of 214 classifiers, one of which was sure to be in each character in the language. These 214 classifiers, for dictionary purposes, correspond to the 26 letters of our alphabet, but are more ambiguous and less efficient.

In spite of its cumbersomeness the Chinese written language was used to produce a greater volume of recorded literature than any other language before modern times. One sober estimate is that until 1750 there had been more books published in Chinese than in all the other languages in the world put together.

Perhaps enough has been said to indicate why written Chinese became a monopoly of the scribes. The Chinese language had the character of an institution, rather than a tool, of society. Men worshiped it, and devoted long lives to mastering even parts of its literature, which was a world of its own, into which one might gain admittance only by strenuous effort. The Chinese writing system was not a convenient device lying ready at hand for every schoolboy to pick up and use as he prepared to meet life's problems. It was itself one of life's problems. If little Lao-san could not find the time for long-continued study of it, he was forever debarred from social advancement. Thus the Chinese written language, rather than an open door through which China's peasantry could find truth and light, was a heavy barrier pressing against any upward advance and requiring real effort to overcome—a hindrance, not a help to learning.

Consequently much of Chinese learning stopped with the language and the classical literature. Students were exhausted merely by the mastery of them. In the old days a boy needed ten years of leisure in which to master the myriad literary allusions to be found in the classics. Only a gentry family could normally afford it. . . .

⊛ Wealth, Power, and the Seeds of Decline in the Economy of Imperial China

DESPITE WIDESPREAD poverty in many parts of the country during much of the Ch'ing Dynasty, China was one of the wealthiest and most productive countries in the world. In the following selection Ping-ti Ho, Professor of History at the University of Chicago, describes the vast commercial networks which developed in China at this time. As he points out, China shared in the benefits of the commercial revolution which had occurred in other parts of the world, but commercial progress had its roots inside China as well as abroad. Despite accumulating wealth, however, China could do no more than expand within the traditional limits of her economy, and was unable to create a new economy, as England and Continental Europe did from the late eighteenth century onward. As Ho writes: "[China] was capable of small gains but incapable of innovations in either the institutional or technological sense." In the eighteenth century China did not yet feel the need for a new economy, for while the population started to increase, it had not yet reached the gigantic nineteenth- and twentieth-century proportions. Peking lived in splendor—and in slumber. Chinese novels of the period testify to the *dolce vita* enjoyed by the privileged classes. For the merchant commerce was the surest road to success and a rise on the social scale, for himself or his sons. Ho points out that wealth was often the first rung on the ladder of social mobility. During the Ch'ing Dynasty commerce did produce wealth for some, but it could not increase the productive capacity of the economy as a whole. As the nineteenth century progressed China began to feel the strain of a stagnant economy: living standards dropped, leading to upheaval and finally contributing to the greatest rebellion of all: the Taiping Rebellion.

PING-TI HO *
From *The Population of China*

Not only were increased means of livelihood provided by a vastly expanding and more intensive agriculture; the employment opportunities offered by an immense domestic trade, by a highly lucrative if somewhat limited foreign commerce, and by some newly rising industries and crafts throughout the later Ming and early Ch'ing were also considerable. Ever since the latter half of the eighth century the influence of money had been increasingly felt, at least in the Yangtze regions, which, thanks to an incomparable network of rivers, lakes, and canals, constituted a vast single trading area. The economic development of the Yangtze area was further stimulated by the continual influx of silver from the Europeans and the Japanese after the early sixteenth century. True, the Yangtze area and the southeast coast were not representative of the whole country. But when the southeast coast was brought into the sphere of a worldwide commercial revolution, the effects reached far into inland China. The commutation of labor services, which by 1600 had become nationwide, is one of the eloquent testimonials to the increasing influence of money. Although the majority of the people were engaged in subsistence farming, as they still are today, there were relatively few localities that did not depend to some extent on the supply of goods and products of neighboring or distant regions.

Whatever the institutional and ethical checks on the growth

* Ping-ti Ho, *Studies on the Population of China* (Cambridge, Mass.: Harvard University Press, 1959), pp. 196–206.

of capital, the late Ming period witnessed the rise of great merchants. The unusually observant Hsieh Chao-che, *chin-shih* of 1602, later governor of Kwangsi and author of the famous cyclopedia *Wu-tsa-tsu,* gives the following account:

> The rich men of the empire in the regions south of the Yangtze are from Hui-chou (southern Anhwei), in the regions north of the river from Shansi. The great merchants of Hui-chou take fisheries and salt as their occupation and have amassed fortunes amounting to one million taels of silver. Others with a fortune of two or three hundred thousands can only rank as middle merchants. The Shansi merchants are engaged in salt, or silk, or reselling, or grain. Their wealth even exceeds that of the former.

In fact, many regions in later Ming times boasted resourceful long-distance merchants. People of the congested islands in the Tung-t'ing Lake in the heart of the lower Yangtze delta, for example, were driven by economic necessity to trade in practically every part of the country and for a time vied with the Hui-chou merchants in wealth. Merchants of the central Shensi area, while active in trading almost everywhere, specialized in transporting and selling grains to garrisons along the Great Wall, in the salt trade in the Huai River region, in the cotton cloth trade in southern Kiangsu, and in the tea trade with various vassal peoples along the thousand-mile western frontier stretching from Kokonor to the Szechwan-Tibet border. The southern Fukien ports, Ch'üan-chou and Chang-chou, which handled the bulk of the Sino-Portuguese trade in the sixteenth century, probably produced some of the largest individual fortunes.

As interregional merchants became more numerous, they gradually established guildhalls in commercial centers. In the early Ch'ing period there were guildhalls in Peking established by moneylenders from Shao-hsing in Chekiang, wholesale dye merchants from P'ing-yao in Shansi, large tobacco dealers from Chi-shan, Chiang-hsien, and Wen-hsi in Shansi, grain and vegetable-oil merchants from Lin-hsiang and Lin-fen in Shansi, silk merchants from Nanking, and Cantonese merchants who specialized in various exotic and subtropical products. From the late seventeenth century the accounts in local histories of guild-halls established by distant merchants became more and more common, which indicated the continual development of the interregional trade.

The dimensions of individual and aggregate merchant fortunes were growing along with the volume of interregional trade. It has been estimated that some of the Hui-chou salt merchants of the eighteenth century had individual fortunes exceeding 10,000,000 taels and that the aggregate profit reaped by some three hundred salt merchant families of the Yang-chou area in the period 1750–1800 was in the neighborhood of 250,000,000 taels. It was known to the Western merchant community in Canton during the early nineteenth century that the Wu family, under the leadership and management of the famous Howqua, had built up through foreign trade a fortune of 26,000,000 Mexican dollars. Commercial capital had made giant strides since China's first contacts with the Europeans.

A sampling of the biographies in the histories of Hui-chou prefecture reveals that the Hui-chou merchants, though their headquarters were in the cities along the lower Yangtze, carried on trade with various parts of north and central China, Yunnan, Kweichow, Szechwan, and even the remote aboriginal districts and Indochina. In the national capital alone there were 187 tea stores in 1789–1791 and 200 in 1801 which were owned and operated by merchants of She-hsien, the capital city of Hui-chou prefecture. So ubiquitous were the Hui-chou merchants that there was a common saying: "No market is without people of Hui-chou." The radius of the trading activities of these and other comparable merchant bodies is one indication of the increasingly mobile character of the national economy. The fact that it was trade as well as agriculture that sustained the local population and made its multiplication possible is well attested by various local histories, particularly those of the active trading areas, such as Hui-chou, a number of counties in Shansi, Shensi, and Kansu, the lower Yangtze counties, the Ningpo and Shao-hsing areas in Chekiang, Chang-chou and Ch'üan-chou in southern Fukien, and the Canton area. Even people of the poor and backward western Hupei highlands depended to a substantial degree on trading with Szechwan as a means of livelihood.

The interregional and local trade consisted of an exchange of a few staple commodities, like grains, salt, fish, drugs, timber, hardwares, potteries, and cloths, and of a number of luxury and artistic goods of quality for the consumption of the ruling classes. The quantity of internal trade in late Ming and early Ch'ing China, although not unusual according to modern Western standards, certainly left a profound impression upon the Jesuits of the seventeenth and eighteenth centuries. In fact, few modern scholars are in a better position to compare the dimensions of the domestic trade of early Ch'ing China with that of early modern Europe than were the Jesuits, who, knowing both about equally well, measured the Chinese economy with the standards of pre-industrial Europe.

Du Halde, whose famous description of China may well be regarded as the synthesis of seventeenth- and early eighteenth-century Jesuit works on China, said of Chinese commerce:

> The riches peculiar to each province, and the facility of conveying merchandise, by means of rivers and canals, have rendered the domestic trade of the empire always very flourishing. . . . The inland trade of China is so great that the commerce of all Europe is not to be compared therewith; the provinces being like so many kingdoms, which communicate to each other their respective productions. This tends to unite the several inhabitants among themselves, and makes plenty reign in all cities.

This generalization probably referred only to the vast Yangtze area, but it can nevertheless be applied to many other parts of China. The trade of mountainous Fukien during the late sixteenth century was described by the educational commissioner Wang Shih-mao:

There is not a single day that the silk fabrics of
Fu-chou, the gauze of Chang-chou, the indigo of Ch'üan-
chou, the ironwares of Fu-chou and Yen-p'ing, the oranges
of Fu-chou and Chang-chou, the lichee nuts of Fu-chou
and Hsing-hua, the cane sugar of Ch'üan-chou and Chang-
chou, and the paper products of Shun-ch'ang are not
shipped along the watershed of P'u-ch'eng and Hsiao-kuan
to Kiangsu and Chekiang like running water. The quantity
of these things shipped by seafaring junks is still harder
to reckon.

Wang's description of the large quantities of commodities
shipped along the difficult mountain pass of northern Fukien
is borne out by the later Jesuit testimony that in the watershed
at P'u-ch'eng there were "eight or ten thousand porters attending to the barks, who get their livelihood by going continually
backwards and forwards across these mountains." Wang's comment on the large coastal trade between Fukien ports and the
lower Yangtze area is also corroborated by other sources. The
demand of remote markets for Fukien sugar was so great that
by the late sixteenth century a considerable percentage of the
rice paddies in the Ch'üan-chou area had been turned into
sugar-cane fields. Throughout the late Ming and early Ch'ing
annually "hundreds and thousands of junks" discharged sugar
in Shanghai and went back to southern Fukien ports with full
loads of raw cotton which were made into cotton cloth locally.
Even in landlocked north China the interregional trade
was very lively. Despite the lack of cheap water transportation
in many northern areas, daily necessities as well as luxury goods
from distant regions were carried by wheelbarrows, carts, mules,
and asses. "The prodigious multitudes of people" and "astonishing multitudes of asses and mules" engaged in the shipping of
commodities in north China never failed to impress those
Jesuits commissioned by the K'ang-hsi Emperor as Imperial
cartographers. Silk and cotton fabrics of various kinds and
luxury goods from the lower Yangtze region and Chekiang
were to be found in practically every northern provincial town,

including the late Ming military posts along the Great Wall. Generally speaking, it was the technologically advanced southeast that supplied the inland Yangtze and northern provinces with finished products, for which the recipients paid in rice, cotton, and other raw materials. Even in westernmost Yunnan bordering Burma, trade in precious and common metals, ivory, precious stones and jades, silk and cotton fabrics was constantly going on during the late Ming. In fact, so great was the volume of China's interregional trade that for centuries it consistently impressed the Europeans.

This growing internal trade stimulated industries and crafts and made possible regional specialization in commercial crops. In the late Ming and early Ch'ing, rural industries and crafts of regional importance were so numerous that it is possible here to mention only a few outstanding ones. The pottery or porcelain industry of Ching-te-chen in northern Kiangsi expanded greatly during the sixteenth century, thanks to increasing government demand for high-quality porcelains and the investment of the Hui-chou merchants in privately owned kilns. By the K'ang-hsi period (1662–1722), when Chinese porcelain "had materially altered" the artistic tastes of the English aristocracy, the Ching-te borough had about five hundred porcelain furnaces working day and night to meet the national and foreign demand. At night, with its flame and smoke, this township, which stretched one and a half leagues along a river, looked like "a great city all on fire, or a vast furnace with a great many vent-holes." Since all the provisions and fuel had to be supplied by the surrounding districts, the cost of living in this industrial town was high. Yet, in the words of a contemporary Jesuit and longtime resident, "it is the refuge of an infinite number of poor families, who . . . find employment here for youths and weakly persons; there are none, even to the lame and blind, but get their living here by grinding colours."

Another outstanding industry was cotton textiles, in the Sung-chiang area, of which Shanghai was a rising city. Thanks to an early start and to its moist climate, Sung-chiang was the

Lancashire of early modern China. Although an enormous quantity of cotton was grown locally, Sung-chiang in the seventeenth and eighteenth centuries depended on remote northern provinces like Honan and western Shantung for the supply of raw cotton. The Jesuits reckoned that in the late seventeenth century there were in the Shanghai area alone "200,000 weavers of calicoes." Since at least three spinners were needed to supply the yarn for one weaver, the total number of spinners must have been several times larger. Cloth of many grades and designs was made to meet the varied demands of the people of Shansi, Shensi, the Peking area, Hupei, Hunan, Kiangsi, Kwangtung, and Kwangsi. Contemporaries remarked that Sung-chiang clothed and capped the whole nation. The Su-chou area was also an important textile center, supplying much of western Shantung with its finished products.

The area around Nanking, from which the name of the famous cotton fabric nankeen was derived, produced cloth of high quality which was exported to the West from Canton. Exports increased constantly until over one million pieces were being exported annually to Great Britain and the United States during the early nineteenth century. H. B. Morse, a New Englander and the famous historian of the Chinese Customs, said:

> Cotton manufactures in 1905 constituted 44 per cent of the value (excluding opium) of all [China's] foreign imports, but in this industry the West could compete with cheap Asiatic labor only after the development springing from the inventions of Richard Arkwright and Eli Whitney, and in the eighteenth and early nineteenth centuries the movement of cotton cloth was from China to the West, in the shape of nankeens to provide small-clothes for our grandfathers.

From the late sixteenth century Sung-chiang was subject to increasing competition from the rising cotton textile centers in north China. The low plain area of north China could produce cotton at lower cost and in larger quantity than the densely populated lower Yangtze region. This increased production of raw cotton in turn stimulated spinning and weaving, which were becoming very important rural industries in north China. The rapid development of the cotton industry in southern Pei-chihli, or modern Hopei, greatly impressed the Christian prime minister Hsü Kuang-ch'i (1562–1633), a native of Shanghai, who estimated that the cotton cloth produced by Su-ning county alone amounted to one tenth of the cloth produced by the entire Sung-chiang prefecture. In the course of the seventeenth century many northern districts became regionally famous for their finished cotton products, although few could vie with Sung-chiang in skill and quality. Toward the end of the seventeenth century the Hankow area had already deprived Sung-chiang of much of its old market in the northwest and the southwest.

Cotton cultivation, which had been extensive in the Ming period, further expanded under the repeated exhortations of the early Ch'ing emperors. Many counties in southern and western Chihli, western Shantung, Honan, the Wei River valley in Shensi, the Fen River valley in Shansi, the Hupei lowlands, and central Szechwan derived a major portion of their incomes from cotton. Cotton spinning and weaving became a common rural industry even in Yunnan and Kweichow. A great many people must have made their living partly or entirely on the growing of cotton or cotton spinning and weaving. . . .

A well-traveled European during the 1840s commented on the general state of commerce:

> One excellent reason why the Chinese care little about foreign commerce is that their internal trade is so extensive. . . . This trade consists principally in the exchange of grain, salt, metal, and other natural and artificial production of various provinces. . . . China is a country so vast, so rich, so varied, that its internal trade alone would suffice abundantly to occupy that part of the nation which can be devoted to mercantile operations. There are in all great towns important commercial estab-

lishments, into which, as into reservoirs, the merchandise of all the provinces discharges itself. To these vast store-houses people flock from all parts of the Empire, and there is a constant bustle going on about them—a feverish activity that would scarcely be seen in the most important cities of Europe.

From this and earlier Jesuit comments it becomes clear that the early Ch'ing economy, if somewhat less variegated than that of Europe, was reasonably complex and able to meet both the basic and the more sophisticated demands of the nation.

However, even during the period of steady economic growth there were inherent weaknesses in the traditional Chinese economy. It was capable of small gains but incapable of innovations in either the institutional or the technological sense. Institutionally, despite the availability of commercial capital on a gigantic scale (witness the Yang-chou salt merchants and the Canton Hong merchants), the traditional Chinese economy failed to develop a genuine capitalistic system such as characterized the Europe of the seventeenth and eighteenth centuries. The reasons were many and varied. In the first place, by far the easiest and surest way to acquire wealth was to buy the privilege of selling a few staples with universal demand, like salt and tea, which were under government monopoly. The activities of the Hong merchants, and of other powerful merchant groups, also partook of the nature of tax-farming rather than genuine private enterprise.

Secondly, the profit and wealth accruing to these merchant princes was not reinvested in new commercial or industrial enterprises but was diverted to various noneconomic uses. Ordinary commercial and industrial investments were less profit-able than moneylending and tax-farming in the broad sense. Furthermore, the cultural and social values peculiar to the traditional Chinese society fostered this economic pattern. In a society where the primary standard of prestige was not money but scholarly attainment, official position, or literary achieve-ment, rich merchants preferred to buy official ranks and titles for themselves, encourage their sons to become degree-holders and officials, patronize artists and men of letters, cultivate the expensive hobbies of the elite, or simply consume or squander their wealth in conspicuous ways. Consequently, up to a certain point wealth not only failed to beget more wealth; it could hardly remain concentrated in the same family for more than two or three generations.

Thirdly, the lack of primogeniture and the working of the clan system proved to be great leveling factors in the Chinese economy. The virtue of sharing one's wealth with one's immediate and remote kinsmen had been so highly extolled since the rise of Neo-Confucianism in the eleventh and twelfth centuries that few wealthy men in traditional China could escape the influence of this teaching. Business management, in the last analysis, was an extension of familism and was filled with nepotism, inefficiencies, and irrationalities. These immensely rich individuals not only failed to develop a capitalistic system; they seldom if ever acquired that acquisitive and competitive spirit which is the very soul of the capitalistic system.

Fourthly, the Confucian cultural and political system rewarded only the learned and studious. Technological inventions were viewed as minor contrivances unworthy of the dignity of scholars. Despite the budding scientific spirit in Chu Hsi's philosophy, China failed to develop a system of experimental science; moral philosophy always reigned supreme. Major technological inventions are seldom accidental and are necessarily based on scientific knowledge; hence traditional China could not produce a major technological revolution, which depends as much on the application of scientific knowledge to practical industrial problems as on a coordination of various economic and institutional factors. By the last quarter of the eighteenth century there was every indication that the Chinese economy, at its prevailing technological level, could no longer gainfully sustain an ever increasing population without overstraining itself. The economy during the first half of the nineteenth century became so strained and the standard of living for the majority of the nation deteriorated so rapidly that a series of uprisings occurred, culminating in the Taiping Rebellion.

Finally, throughout the Ch'ing by far the most powerful control over the economy was exerted by the state, through the bureaucracy. Such key enterprises as the salt trade and foreign commerce were jointly undertaken by the bureaucracy and a few individuals who were resourceful enough to resume the financial responsibility demanded by the state. Even in the late Ch'ing and early Republican periods the few new industrial enterprises launched by the Chinese were almost invariably financed by bureaucratic capitalists. In the cotton textile industry, for example, out of a total of twenty-six mills established between 1890 and 1913, nine were established by active and retired high officials, ten by mixed groups of officials and individuals with official titles, and seven by the new breed of treaty-port compradores, practically all of whom had official connections. It is common knowledge that after the founding of the Nationalist government in 1927 a few top-ranking bureaucrats who enjoyed Chiang Kai-shek's confidence exerted ever more powerful control over the modern sector of the national economy through the incomparably superior apparatus of four major modern banks. Genuine capitalism based on private enterprise never had a chance of success in modern China, which could only choose between bureaucratic capitalism and bureaucratic collectivism. . . .

❧ The Amateur Ideal in Chinese Culture

TODAY THERE is a struggle between "reds" and "experts" in China: the Communist leaders hope that in the future a new class of men will emerge in China who are able to combine the attributes of both red and expert (see Volume III). In the China of an earlier day the conflict was between amateurs and professionals. As Joseph R. Levenson, Professor of History at the University of California (Berkeley), shows, during the Ming and the Ch'ing the amateur ideal predominated. Officials were painters and poets because through art they could reveal their true humanism, so important in the ancient value of *wen,* "culture." They were "amateurs in the fullest sense of the word, genteel initiates in a humane culture, without interest in progress, leanings to science, sympathy for commerce, nor prejudice in favor of utility."

In spite of obvious differences, there is a similarity between yesterday's amateur official and today's red cadre. Both believe in the primacy of human values, although their conception of what these values are or should be is radically different. The amateur official believed in human harmony; the red cadre believes in human struggle. The amateur ideal contributed greatly to the richness of the eighteenth century, even though it largely benefited the gentry. Yet painting, like the other cultural media of Chinese society, had "reached the limit of its idiom," and could create little that was new: "the feeling that creativity demanded freshness in the artist's purposes, remained unfamiliar to Chinese minds." Today museums and many private homes possess the artistic products of this rich

period, the remembrances of a China that once was, but died
because she could not adapt and develop.

JOSEPH R. LEVENSON *
The Amateur Ideal in Ming and Early Ch'ing Society

While the alien Mongols ruled in China (Yuan Dynasty, 1279–
1368), Confucian literati were at one of their relatively low
points of social importance. The Ming Dynasty raised them
high again, and as a ruling intelligentsia they naturally cherished
an ideal of social stability. As a corollary, in matters of taste
they deprecated the idea of change and the quest for originality.
By and large, the literati were classicists, like Jonathan Swift
in England, and in Swift's defense of the ancients against the
moderns, in his vast preference for the humanities over the
natural sciences, and in his patrician uneasiness with material
utility as the touchstone of value, we see the pattern of literati
culture with significant clarity.

Swift died in savage indignation and derangement. The
moderns were taking his world and he knew it. Science, progress, business, and utility, the combination he deplored, would
soon be leading themes in modern western culture. But in
Ming and early Ch'ing China, the China of the four or five
centuries before Westerners came in force, science was slighted,
progress denied, business disparaged and (with possibly increasing difficulty) confined; and with these three went the
fourth of Swift's desiderata, an anti-vocational retrospective
humanism in learning. Artistic style and a cultivated knowledge of the approved canon of ancient works, the "sweetness
and light" of a classical love of letters—these, not specialized,
"useful" technical training, were the tools of intellectual ex-

* Joseph R. Levenson, *Confucian China and Its Modern Fate, Problem of
Intellectual Continuity* (Berkeley and Los Angeles: University of California
Press, 1958), pp. 15–22, 40–41.

pression and the keys to social power. These were the qualities mainly tested in the state examinations, which qualified the winners for prestige and opportunities.

The elite, in short, were not permitted (as Balázs puts it) to "impoverish their personalities in specialization." The Ming style was the amateur style; Ming culture was the apotheosis of the amateur. . . .

Probably more in the Ming period than ever before, as the extreme aestheticism of the Ming eight-legged essay suggests, Chinese officials were amateurs in office. They were trained academically and (for the most part) tested by written examinations, but they were not trained directly for tasks to be undertaken; whatever the case among aides in official yamens, mere hirelings without the proper Confucianist's claim to leadership, the higher degree-holding members of the bureaucracy—the ruling class *par excellence*—were not identified with expertise. The prestige of office depended on that fact. The scholar's belle-lettristic cultivation, a type of learning divorced from the official tasks for which it qualified him, was essential—not to performance of official functions with technical efficiency (there it was rather inhibiting), but to the cultural celebration of those functions.

If the knowledge characteristic of officials had been a vocational, technical, "useful" knowledge, then it would have been only a professional means, with no intrinsic quality to dignify the bureaucratic end. But when office could be taken to symbolize high culture, knowledge for its own sake, the terminal values of civilization, then officeholding was clearly superior to any other social role. No other sort of success (commercial, military, technological, or the like), which might be assumed to depend on a body of professional knowledge devised as a logical means to produce it, could compete in prestige with success in winning office; for the peculiar preparation for the latter success, by its aesthetic independence, its very irrelevance, logically, to the bureaucratic end—at least in a specialized, technical sense, if not in a broadly moral one—

made of that end the end of life. A course in classical letters might train the official ideally to rule by virtuous example— to be himself, as it were, the finest product of art and thought, radiating harmony to society—but it was far from a training in special techniques for effecting social harmony, not by magical sympathy, but by logical consequence.

In China, of course, because of the nature of its institutions, this aesthetic brand of knowledge really was for the sake of something: office. But it was a symbolic, not a logical qualification. To see the genuine significance of this distinction, let us compare the Ming situation with the modern English one, for in England, too, classical training has frequently given entrée to civil office. A recent tribute to a British civil servant, after praising his classical scholarship, attempted, rather defensively, it seems, to make an ordinary logical reference of his classical training to his official role:

> He read classics at Malvern and became a humanist. . . . Then in 1932, like many a classical scholar before him, he entered the Home Civil Service. . . . He is certainly a great civil servant, and I have no doubt whatever that he owes his quality to his humanism. It is that which gentles his will and disciplines his mind to the delicacies of human relationships.

Living, as he does, in a highly specialized society, in which the amateur yields to the expert almost all along the line, a society in which "amateur" as a term, in fact, has developed rather its connotation of imperfect skill than of disinterested love, the writer here must strike us as quasi-apologetic (which no Ming classicist, in a similar case, would ever have been) in making such a "professional" plea for the classical curriculum: he writes as though he feels that his public—a practical, vocationally-minded public with a common-sense indifference to educational frills—must be doubting the genuine relevance of antique studies to modern professional tasks. He cannot simply assume a general public acceptance of an obvious affinity between classical education and a managerial office. The prestige of letters, it is true, has lent a greater prestige to the higher bureaucracy in England than it has to its western counterparts. But in England—and here it has differed from China—the bureaucracy, though thus enhanced, has not been able to reflect its glory back to the source. For while the social facts of Chinese history made bureaucracy the central point of power, the social facts of English history have relegated bureaucracy to a role of service to other powers in the English state. Socially, the rise of "business" (which Swift had seen with such distress), with its anti-traditional, anti-humanist bias, put bureaucracy in the shade, while intellectually it forced the classics from their solitary eminence. To be sure, the nineteenth-century Oxford and Cambridge ideal, like the Confucian, was the educated gentleman, prepared for the world of affairs and his place in the governing class by a course in humane letters, with nothing crudely purposive about it; but this ideal in the Victorian age has been called "almost the sole barrier against an all-encroaching materialism and professionalism." In England, instead of the splendid, symbolic Ming alignment of the highest cultural values with the highest social power, we finally find bureaucracy rather more just a useful employment, while the classics, insofar as they preserve vestigial links with power, tend to be justified as a logically useful means to an end which is only a means itself.

Culture, "the best that has been thought and known" (as Matthew Arnold paraphrased "sweetness and light"), has a bad time in a world of utilitarians. When the "yahoos" and "philistines" of Swift and Arnold dominate society, the defense of culture may tend to lean on philistine criteria. An amateur's love of the liberal arts, his belief that they justify themselves, may be complicated by society's insistence that he find a professional point in their cultivation. But in China, the men of social consequence in the Ming and early Ch'ing periods were hardly cultural philistines; the professional point in their humanistic studies was in their failing to have any specialized professional point. They were amateurs in the fullest sense of the word, genteel initiates in a humane culture, without interest in progress, leanings to science, sympathy for commerce, nor prejudice in favor of utility. Amateurs in government because their training was in art, they had an amateur bias in art itself, for their profession was government.

Long before, in the Sung Dynasty, Wang An-shih (1021–1086) had tried, among other things, to make the civil-service examinations more practical than aesthetic. Although Wang was unquestionably a dedicated Confucianist, trying to revive in Confucianism its primal concern with political science, his finest official and scholarly contemporaries, who began by largely sharing his convictions, finally turned away, and ordinary Confucianists never forgave him. Was it only impracticability they saw in his sweeping program, or disputable points in his classical exegesis, or an immediate material challenge to their perquisites; or did they also sense that a Confucian landed bureaucracy would rule as intellectual amateurs, or not at all? Had Wang struck a false note, a possible knell for the omnicompetent, socially superior sophisticates, who were no mere scribes in a feudal state, nor professional civil servants in a business one?

Su Tung-p'o (1036–1101), one of the foremost serious opponents of Wang An-shih, seems to have been the first painter to speak of *shih-ta-fu hua,* the "officials' style" in painting, a term which became in the Ming era one of the several interchangeable terms for the "amateur style."

By the end of the Ming Dynasty, one rule had been firmly established in the world of painting: officials themselves were painters, and they liked their painting best. Painters *by profession* were disparaged. The Ming Emperors had revived the court academy of painting (*Hua-yüan*), associated mainly with the names of Hui-tsung (*regn.* 1101–1126, the last real Emperor of the Northern Sung) and his Southern Sung successors. But the Ming academy differed from the Sung in that the latter had merely honored painters with official titles, while their Ming counterparts were genuinely court painters, working to specifications. Accordingly, the Ming academy, unlike Hui-tsung's, was never put on an equal footing with the *Han-lin yüan,* the highest circle of literary scholars, and Ming *Hua-yüan* painters by no means had the rank or prestige of *Han-lin* literati. There were court painters in the Imperial Guard—a surprising place for them, on the face of it, but not so surprising when one reflects that the Imperial Guard was a catch-all for non-bureaucratic types, and that it represented the emperor and his personal corps of eunuchs in their character as rivals to the civil-official interest.

Wen Cheng-ming (1470–1567), a scholar who had the *Han-lin* rank, and a famous painter as well, clearly expressed the amateur's creed. "The cultivated man," he said, "in retirement from office, frequently takes pleasure in playing with the brush and producing landscapes for his own gratification." Or for the gratification of his cultivated friends—like the gentleman-painter Shen Shih-t'ien (1427–1509), a model of leisurely, exquisite taste; he identified a stray ink-landscape in his hall as the calling-card of one of his fellow-spirits, who had splashed it playfully on a bit of silk that was lying at hand, and whom Shen recaptured and kept as his guest for a casual matter of three months. Mo Shih-lung, a very important late-Ming critic, highly approved of some earlier artists for looking at painting as a joy in itself, not as their profession. His friend, Tung Ch'i-ch'ang (1555–1636), echoed Mo in praising one of the fourteenth-century Yuan masters as the first to make the painter's pleasure as well as expression the end of his art. Tung himself, painter and calligrapher as well as the foremost critic of his time, was perfectly careless about what became of his own productions. It was said of him that if a person of station asked directly for some of his work, the petitioner might be fobbed off with anything—Tung's signature, perhaps, or a poem from his brush, on a painting by somebody else. If people wanted a Tung original, they learned to seek it from the women of his household, for whom he would frequently, idly, paint or write.

Tung had, quite simply, a contempt for professionalism. One of its connotations, he felt, was narrowness of culture.

The true *wen-jen,* the "literary man," the amateur, had a
feeling for nature and a flair for both painting and poetry.
It was a familiar thing for painters to deprecate their special
talents by offering themselves as rounded personalities; the
sixteenth-century painter Hsü Wei, for example, said of himself (though critics disagreed) that his calligraphy came first,
poetry second, prose composition next, and painting last. The
Ch'ing scholar Shen Tsung-ch'ien (*fl. ca.* 1780?) summed up
the persisting amateur's bias against narrow specialization:
"Painting and poetry are both things with which scholars divert
their minds. Generally, therefore, those who can participate
in the writing of poetry can all take part in painting."

The amateur's scorn of professionals had an aspect, too,
of patrician contempt for the grasping climbers who were not
the gentry's sort. There were overtones of anti-commercial
feeling in the scholar's insistence that the proper artist is fi-
nancially disinterested. Mi Fu (1051–1107), the famous in-
tuitive Sung artist who was a classical hero to the Ming amateur
school, had written, "In matters of calligraphy and painting,
one is not to discuss price. The gentleman is hard to capture
by money." That was the finding of the hapless nobleman who
came to Lu Chih (1496–1576) with a letter from one of Lu's
friends, secured a picture on the strength of it, and then committed the horrible gaffe of offering sums of money; there is
something almost mythic in the account of Lu's passionate act
of rejection, as though a vital nerve of a culture had been
touched. Much later, the *Mustard-seed Garden Manual* (*Chieh-
tzu yüan hua chuan*), an encyclopedic instruction book for
painters, appearing in several parts between 1679 and 1818
(though its earliest stratum was late Ming), made the same
equation between professionalism and a falling short of literati
standards of gentility. "When one has the venal manner," it
loftily proclaimed, "one's painting is very vulgar." And the
Ch'ing painter Tsou I-kuei (1686–1772) laid down the rule that
the *shih-ta-fu* painter, the amateur painter-official, "is not acquisitive in the world, nor does he distract his heart with considerations of admiration or detraction."

In short, in the amateur's culture of the Ming and early Ch'ing, officials as critics commended officials as painters to officials as connoisseurs. "Wang Yü, tzu Jih-ch'u, hao Tung-chuang Lao-jen painted landscapes and grasped in them the very marrow of the Vice-President of the Board of Revenue's art." A remark like this, ordinary enough in its own day, will joyously strike the modern reader as comically incongruous; he could hardly sense more vividly the individual quality of the culture which knew it as commonplace. . . .

Historians of the arts have sometimes led their subjects out of the world of men into a world of their own, where the principles of change seem interior to the art rather than governed by decisions of the artist. Thus, we have been assured that seventeenth-century Dutch landscape bears no resemblance to Breughel because by the seventeenth century Breughel's tradition of mannerist landscape had been exhausted. Or we are treated to tautologies, according to which art is "doomed to become moribund" when it "reaches the limit of its idiom," and in "yielding its final flowers" shows that "nothing more can be done with it"—hence the passing of the grand manner of the eighteenth century in Europe and the romantic movement of the nineteenth.

How do aesthetic values really come to be superseded? This sort of thing, purporting to be a revelation of cause, an answer to the question, leaves the question still to be asked. For Chinese painting, well before the middle of the Ch'ing period, with its enshrinement of eclectic virtuosi and connoisseurs, had, by any "internal" criteria, reached the limit of its idiom and yielded its final flowers. And yet the values of the past persisted for generations, and the fear of imitation, the feeling that creativity demanded freshness in the artist's purposes, remained unfamiliar to Chinese minds. Wang Hui was happy to write on a landscape he painted in 1692 that it was a copy of a copy of a Sung original, while his colleague, Yün Shou-p'ing, the flower-painter, was described approvingly by a Ch'ing compiler as having gone back to the "boneless" painting of Hsü Ch'ung-ssu, of the eleventh century, and made his work one with it. (Yün had often, in fact, inscribed "Hsü Ch'ung-ssu boneless flower picture" on his own productions.) And Tsou I-kuei, another flower-painter, committed to finding a traditional sanction for his art, began a treatise with the following apologia:

> When the ancients discussed painting, they treated land-scape in detail but slighted flowering plants. This does not imply a comparison of their merits. Flower painting flour-ished in the northern Sung, but Hsü [Hsi] and Huang [Ch'üan] could not express themselves theoretically, and therefore their methods were not transmitted.

The lesson taught by this Chinese experience is that an art form is "exhausted" when its practitioners think it is. And a circular explanation will not hold—they think so not when some hypothetically objective exhaustion occurs in the art it-self, but when outer circumstance, beyond the realm of purely aesthetic content, has changed their subjective criteria; other-wise, how account for the varying lengths of time it takes for different publics to leave behind their worked-out forms? There were Ch'ing experiments in Western-style perspective, but these remained exoticisms; suspicion of sterility in modern Chinese painting, embarrassment about the extent of traditional disciple-ship (instead of a happy acceptance of it) began in China only late in the nineteenth century, when Chinese society began to change under Western pressure and along Western lines, and when modern Western value judgments, accordingly—like praise of "originality"—were bound to intrude their influence. We have seen how the amateur commitments of the literati-official class in early-modern China brought Chinese painting to its late Ming, early Ch'ing condition. A reassessment of that condition never came until a change in role was thrust on the official class, and a change in its education, and a change in the general currency of its amateur ideal. . . .

🌑 The Scholar-Official: the Road to Success

THE FOLLOWING selection is taken from the famous Ch'ing Dynasty novel *Ju-lin Wai-shih* (*An Unofficial History of the Literati*), by the gifted but often cynical author Wu Ching-tzu (1701-1754). Wu, an aspiring young scholar, repeatedly failed to get his higher degree in the Chinese civil-service examination system.

In this satire of the Chinese literati-official class Wu shows the great importance of the examination system as a means of social mobility. He recounts the triumph of Fan Chin, a man of humble origins, who because of persistence and uprightness finally passes the provincial examination. He is suddenly transformed from an abused pauper into a wealthy man of vast prestige, and even his foul-mouthed father-in-law, Butcher Hu, changes his tune and grovels in respect before him.

But one must also note the hostility and scorn in which the author holds the examination system and the bureaucracy through which Fan Chin was forced to wade before his triumph. Wu mocks the hypocrisy and self-seeking generated by the system, satirizes the blind manner in which men crumple in awe before a scholar simply because he has successfully passed an examination, and is highly critical of those who seek office to attain wealth. In short, it is the shallowness and formalism of the whole Chinese bureaucratic system which is being satirized.

WU CHING-TZU *
From *The Scholars*

Now though Chou Chin engaged several secretaries, he thought, "I had bad luck myself so long; now that I'm in office I mean to read all the papers carefully. I mustn't leave everything to my secretaries, and suppress real talent." Having come to this decision, he went to Canton to take up his post. The day after his arrival he burnt incense, posted up placards, and held two examinations.

The third examination was for candidates from Nanhai and Panyu Counties. Commissioner Chou sat in the hall and watched the candidates crowding in. There were young and old, handsome and homely, smart and shabby men among them. The last candidate to enter was thin and sallow, had a grizzled beard and was wearing an old felt hat. Kwangtung has a warm climate; still, this was the twelfth month, and yet this candidate had on a linen gown only, so he was shivering with cold as he took his paper and went to his cell. Chou Chin made a mental note of this before sealing up their doors. During the first interval, from his seat at the head of the hall, he watched this candidate in the linen gown come up to hand in his paper. The man's clothes were so threadbare that a few more holes had appeared since he went into the cell. Commissioner Chou looked at his own garments—his magnificent crimson robe and gilt belt—then he referred to the register of names, and asked, "You are Fan Chin, aren't you?"

Kneeling, Fan Chin answered, "Yes, Your Excellency."

"How old are you this year?"

* Wu Ching-tzu, *The Scholars* (*An Unofficial History of the Literati*) (Peking: Foreign Language Press, 1957), pp. 65–77.

"I gave my age as thirty. Actually, I am fifty-four."

"How many times have you taken the examination?"

"I first went in for it when I was twenty, and I have taken it over twenty times since then."

"How is it you have never passed?"

"My essays are too poor," replied Fan Chin, "so none of the honorable examiners will pass me."

"That may not be the only reason," said Commissioner Chou. "Leave your paper here, and I will read it through carefully."

Fan Chin kowtowed and left.

It was still early, and no other candidates were coming to hand in their papers, so Commissioner Chou picked up Fan Chin's essay and read it through. But he was disappointed. "Whatever is the fellow driving at in this essay?" he wondered. "I see now why he never passed." He put it aside. However, when no other candidates appeared, he thought, "I might as well have another look at Fan Chin's paper. If he shows the least talent, I'll pass him to reward his perseverance." He read it through again, and this time felt there was something in it. He was just going to read it through once more, when another candidate came up to hand in his paper.

This man knelt down, and said, "Sir, I beg for an oral test."

"I have your paper here," said Commissioner Chou kindly. "What need is there for an oral test?"

"I can compose poems in all the ancient styles. I beg you to set a subject to test me."

The commissioner frowned and said, "Since the Emperor attaches importance to essays, why should you bring up the poems of the Han and Tang dynasties? A candidate like you should devote all his energy to writing compositions, instead of wasting time on heterodox studies. I have come here at the imperial command to examine essays, not to discuss miscellaneous literary forms with you. This devotion to superficial things means that your real work must be neglected. No doubt your essay is nothing but flashy talk, not worth the reading.

Attendants! Drive him out!' At the word of command, attendants ran in from both sides to seize the candidate and push him outside the gate.

But although Commissioner Chou had had this man driven out, he still read his paper. This candidate was called Wei Hao-ku, and he wrote in a tolerably clear and straightforward style. "I will pass him lowest on the list," Chou Chin decided. And, taking up his brush, he made a mark at the end of the paper as a reminder.

Then he read Fan Chin's paper again. This time he gave a gasp of amazement. "Even I failed to understand this paper the first two times I read it!" he exclaimed. "But, after reading it for the third time, I realize it is the most wonderful essay in the world—every word a pearl. This shows how often bad examiners must have suppressed real genius." Hastily taking up his brush, he carefully drew three circles on Fan Chin's paper, marking it as first. He then picked up Wei Hao-ku's paper again, and marked it as twentieth. After this he collected all the other essays and took them away with him.

Soon the results were published, and Fan Chin's name was first on the list. When he went in to see the commissioner, Chou Chin commended him warmly. And when the last successful candidate—Wei Hao-ku—went in, Commissioner Chou gave him some encouragement and advised him to work hard and stop studying miscellaneous works. Then, to the sound of drums and trumpets, the successful candidates left.

The next day, Commissioner Chou set off for the capital. Fan Chin alone escorted him for ten miles of the way, doing reverence before his chair. Then the commissioner called him to his side. "First-class honors go to the mature," he said. "Your essay showed real maturity, and you are certain to do well in the provincial examination too. After I have made my report to the authorities, I will wait for you in the capital."

Fan Chin kowtowed again in thanks, then stood to one side of the road as the examiner's chair was carried swiftly off. Only when the banners had passed out of sight behind the next hill did he turn back to his lodgings to settle his bill. His home was about fifteen miles from the city, and he had to travel all night to reach it. He bowed to his mother, who lived with him in a thatched cottage with a thatched shed outside, his mother occupying the front room and his wife the back one. His wife was the daughter of Butcher Hu of the market.

Fan Chin's mother and wife were delighted by his success. They were preparing a meal when his father-in-law arrived, bringing pork sausages and a bottle of wine. Fan Chin greeted him, and they sat down together.

"Since I had the bad luck to marry my daughter to a scarecrow like you," said Butcher Hu, "heaven knows how much you have cost me. Now I must have done some good deed to make you pass the examination. I've brought this wine to celebrate."

Fan Chin assented meekly, and called his wife to cook the sausages and warm the wine. He and his father-in-law sat in the thatched shed, while his mother and wife prepared food in the kitchen.

"Now that you have become a gentleman," went on Butcher Hu, "you must do things in proper style. Of course, men in my profession are decent, high-class people; and I am your elder too—you mustn't put on any airs before me. But these peasants round here, dung-carriers and the like, are low people. If you greet them and treat them as equals, that will be a breach of etiquette and will make me lose face too. You're such an easygoing, good-for-nothing fellow, I'm telling you this for your own good, so that you won't make a laughingstock of yourself."

"Your advice is quite right, Father," replied Fan Chin.

"Let your mother eat with us too," went on Butcher Hu. "She has only vegetables usually—it's a shame! Let my daughter join us too. She can't have tasted lard more than two or three times since she married you a dozen years ago, poor thing!"

So Fan Chin's mother and wife sat down to share the meal with them. They ate until sunset, by which time Butcher Hu was tipsy. Mother and son thanked him profusely; then, throwing his jacket over his shoulders, the butcher staggered home bloated. The next day Fan Chin had to call on relatives and friends.

Wei Hao-ku invited him to meet some other fellow candidates, and since it was the year for the provincial examination, they held a number of literary meetings. Soon it was the end of the sixth month. Fan Chin's fellow candidates asked him to go with them to the provincial capital for the examination, but he had no money for the journey. He went to ask his father-in-law to help.

Butcher Hu spat in his face, and poured out a torrent of abuse. "Don't be a fool!" he roared. "Just passing one examination has turned your head completely—you're like a toad trying to swallow a swan! And I hear that you scraped through not because of your essay, but because the examiner pitied you for being so old. Now, like a fool, you want to pass the higher examination and become an official. But do you know who those officials are? They are all stars in heaven! Look at the Chang family in the city. All those officials have pots of money, dignified faces and big ears. But your mouth sticks out and you've a chin like an ape's. You should piss on the ground and look at your face in the puddle! You look like a monkey, yet you want to become an official. Come off it! Next year I shall find a teaching job for you with one of my friends so that you can make a few taels of silver to support that old, never-dying mother of yours and your wife—and it's high time you did! Yet you ask me for traveling expenses! I kill just one pig a day, and only make ten cents per pig. If I give you all my silver to play ducks and drakes with, my family will have to live on air." The butcher went on cursing at full blast, till Fan Chin's head spun.

When he got home again, he thought to himself, "Commissioner Chou said that I showed maturity. And, from ancient times till now, who ever passed the first examination without going in for the second? I shan't rest easy till I've taken it." So he asked his fellow candidates to help him, and went to the city, without telling his father-in-law, to take the examination. When the examination was over he returned home, only to find that his family had had no food for two days. And Butcher Hu cursed him again.

The day the results came out there was nothing to eat in the house, and Fan Chin's mother told him, "Take that hen of mine to the market and sell it; then buy a few measures of rice to make gruel. I'm faint with hunger."

Fan Chin tucked the hen under his arm and hurried out.

He had only been gone an hour or so, when gongs sounded and three horsemen galloped up. They alighted, tethered their horses to the shed, and called out: "Where is the honorable Mr. Fan? We have come to congratulate him on passing the provincial examination."

Not knowing what had happened, Fan Chin's mother had hidden herself in the house for fear. But when she heard that he had passed, she plucked up courage to poke her head out and say, "Please come in and sit down. My son has gone out."

"So this is the old lady," said the heralds. And they pressed forward to demand a tip.

In the midst of this excitement two more batches of horsemen arrived. Some squeezed inside while the others packed themselves into the shed, where they had to sit on the ground. Neighbors gathered round, too, to watch; and the flustered old lady asked one of them to go to look for her son. The neighbor ran to the market place, but Fan Chin was nowhere to be seen. Only when he reached the east end of the market did he discover the scholar, clutching the hen tightly against his chest and holding a sales sign in one hand. Fan Chin was pacing slowly along, looking right and left for a customer.

"Go home quickly, Mr. Fan!" cried the neighbor. "Congratulations! You have passed the provincial examination. Your house is full of heralds."

Thinking this fellow was making fun of him, Fan Chin pretended not to hear, and walked forward with lowered head. Seeing that he paid no attention, the neighbor went up to him and tried to grab the hen.

"Why are you taking my hen?" protested Fan Chin. "You don't want to buy it."

"You have passed," insisted the neighbor. "They want you to go home to send off the heralds."

"Good neighbor," said Fan Chin, "we have no rice left at home, so I have to sell this hen. It's a matter of life and death. This is no time for jokes! Do go away, so as not to spoil my chance of a sale."

When the neighbor saw that Fan Chin did not believe him, he seized the hen, threw it to the ground, and dragged the scholar back by force to his home.

The heralds cried, "Good! The newly honored one is back." They pressed forward to congratulate him. But Fan Chin brushed past them into the house to look at the official announcement, already hung up, which read: "This is to announce that the master of your honorable mansion, Fan Chin, has passed the provincial examination in Kwangtung, coming seventh in the list. May better news follow in rapid succession!"

Fan Chin feasted his eyes on this announcement, and, after reading it through once to himself, read it once more aloud. Clapping his hands, he laughed and exclaimed, "Ha! Good! I have passed." Then, stepping back, he fell down in a dead faint. His mother hastily poured some boiled water between his lips, whereupon he recovered consciousness and struggled to his feet. Clapping his hands again, he let out a peal of laughter and shouted, "Aha! I've passed! I've passed!" Laughing wildly he ran outside, giving the heralds and the neighbors the fright of their lives. Not far from the front door he slipped and fell into a pond. When he clambered out, his hair was disheveled, his hands muddied, and his whole body dripping with slime. But nobody could stop him. Still clapping his hands and laughing, he headed straight for the market.

They all looked at each other in consternation, and said, "The new honor has sent him off his head!"

His mother wailed, "Aren't we out of luck! Why should passing an examination do this to him? Now he's mad, goodness knows when he'll get better."

"He was all right this morning when he went out," said his wife. "What could have brought on this attack? What *shall* we do?"

The neighbors consoled them. "Don't be upset," they said. "We will send a couple of men to keep an eye on Mr. Fan. And we'll all bring wine and eggs and rice for these heralds. Then we can discuss what's to be done."

The neighbors brought eggs or wine, lugged along sacks of rice or carried over chickens. Fan Chin's wife wailed as she prepared the food in the kitchen. Then she took it to the shed, neighbors brought tables and stools, and they asked the heralds to sit down to a meal while they discussed what to do.

"I have an idea," said one of the heralds. "But I don't know whether it will work or not."

"What idea?" they asked.

"There must be someone the honorable Mr. Fan usually stands in awe of," said the herald. "He's only been thrown off his balance because sudden joy made him choke on his phlegm. If you can get someone he's afraid of to slap him in the face and say, 'It's all a joke. You haven't passed any examination!'—then the fright will make him cough up his phlegm, and he'll come to his senses again."

They all clapped their hands and said, "That's a fine idea. Mr. Fan is more afraid of Butcher Hu than of anyone else. Let's hurry up and fetch him. He's probably still in the market, and hasn't yet heard the news."

"If he were selling meat in the market, he would have heard the news by now," said a neighbor. "He went out at dawn to the east market to fetch pigs, and he can't have come back yet. Someone had better go quickly to find him."

One of the neighbors hurried off in search of the butcher, and presently met him on the road, followed by an assistant who was carrying seven or eight catties of meat and four or five strings of cash. Butcher Hu was coming to offer his congratulations. Fan Chin's mother, crying bitterly, told him what had happened.

"How could he be so unlucky!" exclaimed the butcher. They were calling for him outside, so he gave the meat and the money to his daughter, and went out. The heralds put their plan before him, but Butcher Hu demurred.

"He may be my son-in-law," he said, "but he's an official

now—one of the stars in heaven. How can you hit one of
the stars in heaven? I've heard that whoever hits the stars in
heaven will be carried away by the King of Hell, given a
hundred strokes with an iron rod, and shut up in the eighteenth
hell, never to become a human being again. I daren't do a
thing like that."

"Mr. Hu!" cried a sarcastic neighbor. "You make your
living by killing pigs. Every day the blade goes in white and
comes out red. After all the blood you've shed, the King of
Hell must have marked you down for several thousand strokes
by iron rods, so what does it matter if he adds a hundred
more? Quite likely he will have used up all his iron rods
before getting round to beating you for this, anyway. Or maybe,
if you cure your son-in-law, the King of Hell may consider that
as a good deed, and promote you from the eighteenth hell to
the seventeenth."

"This is no time for joking," protested one of the heralds.
"This is the only way to handle it, Mr. Hu. There's nothing
else for it, so please don't make difficulties."

Butcher Hu had to give in. Two bowls of wine bolstered
up his courage, making him lose his scruples and start his
usual rampaging. Rolling up his greasy sleeves, he strode off
toward the market, followed by small groups of neighbors.

Fan Chin's mother ran out and called after him, "Just
frighten him a little! Mind you don't hurt him!"

"Of course," the neighbors reassured her. "That goes without saying."

When they reached the market, they found Fan Chin
standing in the doorway of a temple. His hair was tousled, his
face streaked with mud, and one of his shoes had come off. But
he was still clapping his hands and crowing, "Aha! I've passed!
I've passed!"

Butcher Hu bore down on him like an avenging fury,
roaring, "You blasted idiot! What have you passed?" and
fetched him a blow. The bystanders and neighbors could
hardly suppress their laughter. But although Butcher Hu had
screwed up his courage to strike once, he was still afraid at

heart, and his hand was trembling too much to strike a second time. The one blow, however, had been enough to knock Fan Chin out.

The neighbors pressed round to rub Fan Chin's chest and massage his back, until presently he gave a sigh and came to. His eyes were clear and his madness had passed! They helped him up and borrowed a bench from Apothecary Chen, a hunchback who lived hard by the temple, so that Fan Chin might sit down.

Butcher Hu, who was standing a little way off, felt his hand begin to ache; when he raised his palm, he found to his dismay that he could not bend it. "It's true, then, that you mustn't strike the stars in heaven," he thought. "Now Buddha is punishing me!" The more he thought about it, the worse his hand hurt, and he asked the apothecary to give him some ointment for it.

Meanwhile Fan Chin was looking round and asking, "How do I come to be sitting here? My mind has been in a whirl, as if in a dream."

The neighbors said, "Congratulations, sir, on having passed the examination! A short time ago, in your happiness, you brought up some phlegm; but just now you spat out several mouthfuls and recovered. Please go home quickly to send away the heralds."

"That's right," said Fan Chin. "And I seem to remember coming seventh in the list." As he was speaking, he fastened up his hair and asked the apothecary for a basin of water to wash his face, while one of the neighbors found his shoe and helped him put it on.

The sight of his father-in-law made Fan Chin afraid that he was in for another cursing. But Butcher Hu stepped forward and said, "Worthy son-in-law, I would never have presumed to slap you just now if not for your mother. She sent me to help you."

"That was what I call a friendly slap," said one of the neighbors. "Wait till Mr. Fan finishes washing his face. I bet he can easily wash off half a basin of lard!"

"Mr. Hu!" said another. "This hand of yours will be too good to kill pigs any more."

"No indeed," replied the butcher. "Why should I go on killing pigs? My worthy son-in-law will be able to support me in style for the rest of my life. I always said that this worthy son-in-law of mine was very learned and handsome, and that not one of those Chang and Chou family officials in the city looked so much the fine gentleman. I have always been a good judge of character, I don't mind telling you. My daughter stayed at home till she was more than thirty, although many rich families wanted to marry her to their sons; but I saw signs of good fortune in her face, and knew that she would end up by marrying an official. You see today how right I was." He gave a great guffaw, and they all started to laugh.

When Fan Chin had washed and drunk the tea brought him by the apothecary, they all started back, Fan Chin in front, Butcher Hu and the neighbors behind. The butcher, noticing that the seat of his son-in-law's gown was crumpled, kept bending forward all the way home to tug out the creases for him.

When they reached Fan Chin's house, Butcher Hu shouted: "The master is back!" The old lady came out to greet them, and was overjoyed to find her son no longer mad. The heralds, she told them, had already been sent off with the money that Butcher Hu had brought. Fan Chin bowed to his mother and thanked his father-in-law, making Butcher Hu so embarrassed that he muttered, "That bit of money was nothing."

After thanking the neighbors too, Fan Chin was just going to sit down when a smart-looking retainer hurried in, holding a big red card, and announced, "Mr. Chang has come to pay his respects to the newly successful Mr. Fan."

By this time the sedan-chair was already at the door. Butcher Hu dived into his daughter's room and dared not come out, while the neighbors scattered in all directions. Fan Chin went out to welcome the visitor, who was one of the local gentry, and Mr. Chang alighted from the chair and came in. He was wearing an official's gauze cap, sunflower-colored gown, gilt belt, and black shoes. He was a provincial graduate, and had served as a magistrate in his time. His name was Chang Chin-chai. He and Fan Chin made way for each other ceremoniously, and once inside the house bowed to each other as equals and sat down in the places of guest and host. Mr. Chang began the conversation.

"Sir," he said, "although we live in the same district, I have never been able to call on you."

"I have long respected you," replied Fan Chin, "but have never had the chance to pay you a visit."

"Just now I saw the list of successful candidates. Your patron, Mr. Tang, was a pupil of my grandfather; so I feel very close to you."

"I did not deserve to pass, I am afraid," said Fan Chin. "But I am delighted to be the pupil of one of your family."

After a glance round the room, Mr. Chang remarked, "Sir, you are certainly frugal." He took from his servant a packet of silver, and stated, "I have brought nothing to show my respect except these fifty taels of silver, which I beg you to accept. Your honorable home is not good enough for you, and it will not be very convenient when you have many callers. I have an empty house on the main street by the east gate, which has three courtyards with three rooms in each. Although it is not big, it is quite clean. Allow me to present it to you. When you move there, I can profit by your instruction more easily."

Fan Chin declined many times, but Mr. Chang pressed him. "With all we have in common, we should be like brothers," he said. "But if you refuse, you are treating me like a stranger." Then Fan Chin accepted the silver and expressed his thanks. After some more conversation they bowed and parted. Not until the visitor was in his chair did Butcher Hu dare to emerge.

Fan Chin gave the silver to his wife. When she opened it, and they saw the white ingots with their fine markings, he asked Butcher Hu to come in and gave him two ingots, saying, "Just now I troubled you for five thousand coppers. Please accept these six taels of silver."

Butcher Hu gripped the silver tight, but thrust out his

clenched fist, saying, "You keep this. I gave you that money to congratulate you, so how can I take it back?"

"I have some more silver here," said Fan Chin. "When it is spent, I will ask you for more."

Butcher Hu immediately drew back his fist, stuffed the silver into his pocket and said, "All right. Now that you are on good terms with that Mr. Chang, you needn't be afraid of going short. His family has more silver than the Emperor, and they are my best customers. Every year, even if they have no particular occasions to celebrate, they still buy four or five thousand catties of meat. Silver is nothing to him."

Then he turned to his daughter and said, "Your rascally brother didn't want me to bring that money this morning. I told him, 'Now my honorable son-in-law is not the man he was. There will be lots of people sending him presents of money. I am only afraid he may refuse my gift.' Wasn't I right? Now I shall take this silver home and curse that dirty scoundrel." After a thousand thanks he made off, his head thrust forward and a broad grin on his face.

True enough, many people came to Fan Chin after that and made him presents of land and shops; while some poor couples had to serve him in return for his protection. In two or three months he had menservants and maidservants, to say nothing of money and rice. When Mr. Chang came again to urge him, he moved into the new house; and for three days he entertained guests with feasts and operas. On the morning of the fourth day, after Fan Chin's mother had got up and had breakfast, she went to the rooms in the back courtyard. There she found Fan Chin's wife with a silver pin in her hair. Although this was the middle of the tenth month, it was still warm and she was wearing a sky-blue silk tunic and a green silk skirt. She was supervising the maids as they washed bowls, cups, plates, and chopsticks.

"You must be very careful," the old lady warned them. "These things don't belong to us, so don't break them."

"How can you say they don't belong to you, madam?" they asked. "They are all yours."

"No, no, these aren't ours," she protested with a smile.

"Oh yes, they are," the maids cried. "Not only these things, but all of us servants and this house belong to you."

When the old lady heard this, she picked up the fine porcelain and the cups and chopsticks inlaid with silver, and examined them carefully one by one. Then she went into a fit of laughter. "All mine!" she crowed. Screaming with laughter she fell backwards, choked, and lost consciousness. . . .

2. CHINA AND THE WORLD

❦ The Emperor's Decree to the Outer Barbarians

WHEN WESTERN traders first arrived in China, they found themselves in a strange new world governed by a totally alien system. The East Asian nations were barely aware of the existence of Europe, and their traditions had matured far beyond the pale of Western civilization.

Relations between states were based on the idea of a Confucian hierarchy, very similar to the Confucian idea of family in which each member occupies a proscribed place. China stood at the center of the East Asian family, and the smaller nations—Korea, Japan, Vietnam, and Burma—occupied inferior positions around her. They accepted a peripheral status which demanded that they pay tribute to China in the form of periodic missions to Peking to perform the three kneelings and nine prostrations before the Emperor. The Tribute System, as these missions came to be known, presupposed inequality among nations. Since this system endured for thousands of years, it was logical for the Ch'ien Lung Emperor (1736–1795) to approach the Western nations, when they arrived on China's doorstep, in this traditional Chinese manner. No matter how loudly Britain protested, no matter how powerful she claimed to be, no matter how unreasonable she found the Chinese system, she was to receive the same treatment as all other inferior tribute-bearing nations. In this time-honored system, no exceptions could be made, even for the "European barbarians."

The following selection from the Chinese Emperor Ch'ien Lung to King George III exemplifies China's tradition-bound attitude toward the outside world. We may find it naïve and amusing, but we must remember that the Tribute System had served the Chinese well for centuries. The logic of the British Ambassador's (Lord Macartney) demand for equal representation and free trade completely escaped the Emperor. The granting of such requests was in no way compatible with the traditional manner of handling such matters, and the British demands were summarily dismissed.

One does not have to read far into this selection to appreciate the vast gulf that separated China from the West. Britain knew little about China, but China knew less about the West and evidenced no desire to learn. Why should a superior study an inferior? The sources of future conflict are all too obvious. The Chinese Emperor's arrogance and determination to remain isolated were incompatible with the British Crown's ambitious plans for imperialist expansion. A head-on collision was inevitable.

THE CH'IEN LUNG EMPEROR *
A Decree

You, O King, live beyond the confines of many seas, nevertheless, impelled by your humble desire to partake of the benefits of our civilization, you have dispatched a mission respectfully bearing your memorial. Your Envoy has crossed the seas and paid his respects at my Court on the anniversary of my birthday. To show your devotion, you have also sent offerings of your country's produce.

I have perused your memorial: the earnest terms in which it is couched reveal a respectful humility on your part, which is highly praiseworthy. In consideration of the fact that your Ambassador and his deputy have come a long way with

* The Ch'ien Lung Emperor in Harley Farnsworth MacNair, *Modern Chinese History, Selected Readings* (Shanghai: Commercial Press Ltd., 1923), pp. 2–9.

your memorial and tribute, I have shown them high favor and have allowed them to be introduced into my presence. To manifest my indulgence, I have entertained them at a banquet and made them numerous gifts. I have also caused presents to be forwarded to the Naval Commander and six hundred of his officers and men, although they did not come to Peking, so that they too may share in my all-embracing kindness.

As to your entreaty to send one of your nationals to be accredited to my Celestial Court and to be in control of your country's trade with China, this request is contrary to all usage of my dynasty and cannot possibly be entertained. It is true that Europeans, in the service of the dynasty, have been permitted to live at Peking, but they are compelled to adopt Chinese dress, they are strictly confined to their own precincts and are never permitted to return home. You are presumably familiar with our dynastic regulations. Your proposed Envoy to my Court could not be placed in a position similar to that of European officials in Peking who are forbidden to leave China, nor could he, on the other hand, be allowed liberty of movement and the privilege of corresponding with his own country; so that you would gain nothing by his residence in our midst.

Moreover, Our Celestial dynasty possesses vast territories, and tribute missions from the dependencies are provided for by the Department for Tributary States, which ministers to their wants and exercises strict control over their movements. It would be quite impossible to leave them to their own devices. Supposing that your Envoy should come to our Court, his language and national dress differ from that of our people, and there would be no place in which to bestow him. It may be suggested that he might imitate the Europeans permanently resident in Peking and adopt the dress and customs of China, but, it has never been our dynasty's wish to force people to do things unseemly and inconvenient. Besides, supposing I sent an Ambassador to reside in your country, how could you possibly make for him the requisite arrangements? Europe consists of many other nations besides your own: if each and all demanded to be represented at our Court, how could we possibly consent? The thing is utterly impracticable. How can our dynasty alter its whole procedure and system of etiquette, established for more than a century, in order to meet your individual views? If it be said that your object is to exercise control over your country's trade, your nationals have had full liberty to trade at Canton for many a year, and have received the greatest consideration at our hands. Missions have been sent by Portugal and Italy, proferring similar requests. The Throne appreciated their sincerity and loaded them with favors, besides authorizing measures to facilitate their trade with China. You are no doubt aware that, when my Canton merchant, Wu Chao-ping, was in debt to the foreign ships, I made the Viceroy advance the monies due, out of the provincial treasury, and ordered him to punish the culprit severely. Why then should foreign nations advance this utterly unreasonable request to be represented at my Court? Peking is nearly two thousand miles from Canton, and at such a distance what possible control could any British representative exercise?

If you assert that your reverence for Our Celestial dynasty fills you with a desire to acquire our civilization, our ceremonies and code of laws differ so completely from your own that, even if your Envoy were able to acquire the rudiments of our civilization, you could not possibly transplant our manners and customs to your alien soil. Therefore, however adept the Envoy might become, nothing would be gained thereby.

Swaying the wide world, I have but one aim in view, namely, to maintain a perfect governance and to fulfill the duties of the state: strange and costly objects do not interest me. If I have commanded that the tribute offerings sent by you, O King, are to be accepted, this was solely in consideration for the spirit which prompted you to dispatch them from afar. Our dynasty's majestic virtue has penetrated unto every country under heaven, and kings of all nations have offered their costly tribute by land and sea. As your Ambassador can see for himself, we possess all things. I set no value on objects strange or ingenious, and have no use for your country's manufactures. This then is my answer to your request to appoint a representative at my Court, a request contrary to our dynastic usage, which would only result in inconvenience to yourself. I have expounded my wishes in detail and have commanded your tribute Envoys to leave in peace on their homeward journey. It behoves you, O King, to respect my sentiments and to display even greater devotion and loyalty in future, so that, by perpetual submission to our Throne, you may secure peace and prosperity for your country hereafter. Besides making gifts (of which I enclose an inventory) to each member of your Mission, I confer upon you, O King, valuable presents in excess of the number usually bestowed on such occasions, including silks and curios—a list of which is likewise enclosed. Do you reverently receive them and take note of my tender good will toward you! A special mandate.

(A further mandate to King George III dealt in detail with the British Ambassador's proposals and the Emperor's reasons for declining them.)

You, O King, from afar have yearned after the blessings of our civilization, and in your eagerness to come into touch with our converting influence have sent an Embassy across the sea bearing a memorial. I have already taken note of your respectful spirit of submission, have treated your mission with extreme favor and loaded it with gifts, besides issuing a mandate to you, O King, and honoring you with the bestowal of valuable presents. Thus has my indulgence been manifested.

Yesterday your Ambassador petitioned my Ministers to memorialize me regarding your trade with China, but his proposal is not consistent with our dynastic usage and cannot be entertained. Hitherto, all European nations, including your own country's barbarian merchants, have carried on their trade with Our Celestial Empire at Canton. Such has been the procedure for many years, although Our Celestial Empire possesses all things in prolific abundance and lacks no product within its own borders. There was therefore no need to import the manufactures of outside barbarians in exchange for our own produce. But as the tea, silk, and porcelain which the Celestial Empire produces are absolute necessities to European nations and to yourselves, we have permitted, as a signal mark of favor, that foreign *hongs* (Chinese business associations) should be established at Canton, so that your wants might be supplied and your country thus participate in our beneficence. But your Ambassador has now put forward new requests which completely fail to recognize the Throne's principle to 'treat strangers from afar with indulgence,' and to exercise a pacifying control over barbarian tribes, the world over. Moreover, our dynasty, swaying the myriad races of the globe, extends the same benevolence toward all. Your England is not the only nation trading at Canton. If other nations, following your bad example, wrongfully importune my ear with further impossible requests, how will it be possible for me to treat them with easy indulgence? Nevertheless, I do not forget the lonely remoteness of your island, cut off from the world by intervening wastes of sea, nor do I overlook your excusable ignorance of the usages of Our Celestial Empire. I have consequently commanded my Ministers to enlighten your Ambassador on the subject, and have ordered the departure of the mission. But I have doubts that, after your Envoy's return he may fail to acquaint you with my view in detail or that he may be lacking in lucidity, so that I shall now proceed to take your requests *seriatim* and to issue my mandate on each question separately. In this way you will, I trust, comprehend my meaning.

(1) Your Ambassador requests facilities for ships of your nation to call at Ningpo, Chusan, Tientsin, and other places for purposes of trade. Until now trade with European nations has always been conducted at Macao, where the foreign *hongs* are established to store and sell foreign merchandise. Your nation has obediently complied with this regulation for years past without raising any objection. In none of the other ports named have *hongs* been established, so that even if your vessels were to proceed thither, they would have no means of disposing of their cargoes. Furthermore, no interpreters are

available, so you would have no means of explaining your wants, and nothing but general inconvenience would result. For the future, as in the past, I decree that your request is refused and that the trade shall be limited to Macao.

(2) The request that your merchants may establish a repository in the capital of my Empire for the storing and sale of your produce, in accordance with the precedent granted to Russia, is even more impracticable than the last. My capital is the hub and center about which all quarters of the globe revolve. Its ordinances are most august and its laws are strict in the extreme. The subjects of our dependencies have never been allowed to open places of business in Peking. Foreign trade has hitherto been conducted at Macao, because it is conveniently near to the sea, and therefore an important gathering place for the ships of all nations sailing to and fro. If warehouses were established in Peking, the remoteness of your country lying far to the northwest of my capital would render transport extremely difficult. . . .

This request is also refused.

(3) Your request for a small island near Chusan, where your merchants may reside and goods be warehoused, arises from your desire to develop trade. As there are neither foreign *hongs* nor interpreters in or near Chusan, where none of your ships have ever called, such an island would be utterly useless for your purposes. Every inch of the territory of our Empire is marked on the map and the strictest vigilance is exercised over it all: even tiny islets and far-lying sandbanks are clearly defined as part of the provinces to which they belong. Consider, moreover, that England is not the only barbarian land which wishes to establish relations with our civilization and trade with our Empire: supposing that other nations were all to imitate your evil example and beseech me to present them each and all with a site for trading purposes, how could I possibly comply? This also is a flagrant infringement of the usage of my Empire and cannot possibly be entertained.

(4) The next request, for a small site in the vicinity of Canton city, where your barbarian merchants may lodge or,

alternatively, that there be no longer any restrictions over their movements at Macao, has arisen from the following causes. Hitherto, the barbarian merchants of Europe have had a definite locality assigned to them at Macao for residence and trade, and have been forbidden to encroach an inch beyond the limits assigned to that locality. Barbarian merchants having business with the *hongs* have never been allowed to enter the city of Canton; by these measures, disputes between Chinese and barbarians are prevented, and a firm barrier is raised between my subjects and those of other nations. The present request is quite contrary to precedent; furthermore, European nations have been trading with Canton for a number of years and, as they make large profits, the number of traders is constantly increasing. How would it be possible to grant such a site to each country? The merchants of the foreign *hongs* are responsible to the local officials for the proceedings of barbarian merchants and they carry out periodical inspections. If these restrictions were withdrawn, friction would inevitably occur between the Chinese and your barbarian subjects, and the results would militate against the benevolent regard that I feel toward you. From every point of view, therefore, it is best that the regulations now in force should continue unchanged.

(5) Regarding your request for remission or reduction of duties on merchandise discharged by your British barbarian merchants at Macao and distributed throughout the interior, there is a regular tariff in force for barbarian merchants' goods, which applies equally to all European nations. It would be as wrong to increase the duty imposed on your nation's merchandise on the ground that the bulk of foreign trade is in your hands, as to make an exception in your case in the shape of specially reduced duties. In future, duties shall be levied equitably without discrimination between your nation and any other, and, in order to manifest my regard, your barbarian merchants shall continue to be shown every consideration at Macao.

(6) As to your request that your ships shall pay the duties leviable by tariff, there are regular rules in force at the Canton custom house respecting the amounts payable, and since

I have refused your request to be allowed to trade at other ports, this duty will naturally continue to be paid at Canton as heretofore.

(7) Regarding your nation's worship of the Lord of Heaven, it is the same religion as that of other European nations. Ever since the beginning of history, sage Emperors and wise rulers have bestowed on China a moral system and inculcated a code, which from time immemorial has been religiously observed by the myriads of my subjects. There has been no hankering after heterodox doctrines. Even the European (missionary) officials in my capital are forbidden to hold intercourse with Chinese subjects; they are restricted within the limits of their appointed residences, and may not go about propagating their religion. The distinction between Chinese and barbarian is most strict, and your Ambassador's request that barbarians shall be given full liberty to disseminate their religion is utterly unreasonable.

It may be, O King, that the above proposals have been wantonly made by your Ambassador on his own responsibility, or peradventure you yourself are ignorant of our dynastic regulations and had no intention of transgressing them when you expressed these wild ideas and hopes. I have ever shown the greatest condescension to the tribute missions of all states which sincerely yearn after the blessings of civilization, so as to manifest my kindly indulgence. I have even gone out of my way to grant any requests which were in any way consistent with Chinese usage. Above all, upon you, who live in a remote and inaccessible region, far across the spaces of ocean, but who have shown your submissive loyalty by sending this tribute mission, I have heaped benefits far in excess of those accorded to other nations. But the demands presented by your Embassy are not only a contravention of dynastic tradition, but would be utterly unproductive of good result to yourself, besides being quite impracticable. I have accordingly stated the facts to you in detail, and it is your bounden duty reverently to appreciate my feelings and to obey these instructions henceforward for all time, so that you may enjoy the blessings of perpetual peace.

If, after the receipt of this explicit decree, you lightly give ear to the representations of your subordinates and allow your barbarian merchants to proceed to Chêkiang and Tientsin, with the object of landing and trading there, the ordinances of my Celestial Empire are strict in the extreme, and the local officials, both civil and military, are bound reverently to obey the law of the land. Should your vessels touch the shore, your merchants will assuredly never be permitted to land or to reside there, but will be subject to instant expulsion. In that event your barbarian merchants will have had a long journey for nothing. Do not say that you were not warned in due time! Tremblingly obey and show no negligence! A special mandate!

🏵 China as Viewed by an
Eighteenth-Century Physiocrat

EIGHTEENTH-CENTURY Europeans became increasingly aware of China, and men like Voltaire, Malebranche, Montesquieu, and Quesnay turned to China in their search for a remedy for France's ills. Some, like Montesquieu, rejected China as nothing more than ruthless despotism; others, like Voltaire and Quesnay, were fascinated by China. Disheartened by religious oppression and monarchy in their own country, they were only too eager to see China through rose-tinted lenses, as a model not of popular government but of humane enlightened despotism, where the Emperor ruled by moral persuasion and love rather than by force. But their vision of China was constructed from sketchy and frequently inaccurate information, and their idealization of the Celestial Kingdom of peace and harmony was as much a product of their own disenchantment with Europe as of an objective evaluation of China's actual circumstances. Although they partially captured the essence of the Confucian ideal of rule, in which the people bend before the righteous example of the ruler like rice seedlings before the wind, they failed to recognize that in practice the Chinese system could be as brutal and unjust as the worst European monarchy.

The following selection is from François Quesnay's *Despotism in China,* written in 1767. The admiration Quesnay held for that distant and prosperous land is clearly discernible. It is interesting to note that less than a century later China became, for Europe, an object of humor and scorn rather than adulation.

FRANÇOIS QUESNAY *
From *Despotism in China*

Whatever may have been the period when Europeans gave the name China to this empire—the name which it carries at present—no one can deny that this state is the most beautiful in the world, the most densely populated, and the most flourishing kingdom known. Such an empire as that of China is equal to what all Europe would be if the latter were united under a single sovereign.

China is divided into fifteen provinces; the smallest, according to the report of Father LeComte, is so fertile and so populous that it alone could form a considerable state. "The ruler who is master of it," says this author, "will assuredly have enough wealth and enough subjects to satisfy any reasonable ambition."

Each province is divided again into a number of cantons or *fu,* each one of which has for its capital a city of the first rank. This city contains a superior tribunal, under which several other jurisdictions, located in districts of the second rank, are set up; these districts are called *chou.* The secondary courts, in their turn, preside over lesser areas, counties, called *hsien,* with cities of the third rank—not to speak of a multitude of other towns and villages, some of which are as large as our cities.

To give a general idea of the number and grandeur of the cities of China, it will suffice to quote the description of Father LeComte.

"I have seen," he says, "seven or eight cities, all larger

---

* François Quesnay in Lewis A. Maverick, *China, A Model for Europe* (San Antonio: Paul Anderson Co., 1946), pp. 164–172, 141–142.

than Paris, without counting several others that I have not
seen, to which Chinese geography attributes the same size.
There are more than eighty cities of the first order, comparable
to Lyons, Rouen, or Bordeaux. Among two hundred of the
second order, there are more than a hundred like Orléans, and
among about twelve hundred of the third order there are to be
found five to six hundred as large as Dijon or La Rochelle, not
to speak of a prodigious number of villages that surpass in
grandeur and in the number of inhabitants the cities of
Marennes and St. Jean-de-Luz. There are no exaggerations here;
nor reports based on the word of others; I myself have traveled
over the greater part of China, and the two thousand leagues
that I have covered should make my testimony valid."

From the vast extent of China one may readily perceive
that the temperature of the air and the influence of the celestial
bodies are not the same throughout; and it may be concluded
from this that diversity of climate does not necessitate different
forms of government. The northerly provinces are very cold
in winter, whereas those of the south are always temperate; in
the summer the heat is tolerable in the former, but excessive
in the latter. . . .

If China enjoys a happy abundance, it is owing not only
to the depth and fertility of the soil, but also to the great number of rivers, lakes, and canals that water it. There is no city,
not even a small village, especially in the southern provinces,
that is not located on the edge of a river or a lake or some
canal or stream.

The great lakes and many lesser ones, added to the numerous springs and streams that descend from the mountains, have
stimulated the industry of the Chinese; they derive great benefits from the multitude of canals that serve to irrigate their lands
as well as to establish easy communication from one province
or from one city to another.

In order not to interrupt land communication, bridges have
been erected at intervals. These bridges have five or six arches,
the middle one of which is extremely high. The vaults are well
girded and the piers so slight that one would say from afar
that all the arches were suspended in the air.

All the canals in China are very well maintained, and the greatest care is taken to make the rivers navigable. Even though there are several of them that wind through mountains and rocks that are extremely rough and steep, nevertheless the hauling of the barges and boats is made easy. By dint of great toil they have succeeded in cutting the base of the rocks in an infinite number of places, making a level towpath for those who haul the barges.

However, in spite of the industry and sobriety of the Chinese people, the fertility of the soil, and the abundance that reigns, there are few countries that have so much poverty among the humbler classes. However great that empire may be, it is too crowded for the multitude that inhabit it. All Europe combined would not number so many families.

This prodigious multiplication of people, regarded as so useful and desirable in the states of Europe, sometimes produces appalling results. In Europe it is thought that a large population is the source of wealth, but this is to take the effect for the cause, for population exceeds wealth everywhere; it is wealth that multiplies both wealth and men; but the propagation of men always exceeds the wealth. People may be seen (in China) so poor that, unable to provide their infants with food, they expose them in the streets. . . .

Misery produces in China an enormous number of slaves, or persons who indenture themselves under the condition that they may sometime redeem their freedom. A man sometimes sells his son or even himself and his family for a very small price. The government, so attentive in other matters, closes its eyes to these difficulties, and this frightful spectacle is repeated every day. . . .

The authority of masters over slaves is limited to ordinary duties, and they treat them like their own children; also, the slaves' loyalty to their masters is inviolable. If any slave acquires money by his own industry, the master has no right to take the slave's wealth, and the slave may buy back his freedom if his master consents or if he has retained the right to do so in his indenture. . . .

Everyone tries to earn a decent living, and it is only by

continuous labor that one can provide this; and is there in the
world a nation more laborious, a people more sober and industrious!

A Chinese spends whole days digging or plowing by hand.
Often, even after having spent all day in the water up to his
knees, he considers himself very lucky to find at his home in
the evening rice, some vegetable, and a little tea. This peasant,
however, has his liberty and property assured; there is no
chance of his being despoiled by arbitrary impositions, nor by
exactions of tax collectors who harass the inhabitants of the
countryside, making them abandon an employment that brings
down upon them contempt much more overwhelming than the
work itself. Men are very hardworking, wherever they are
assured the benefits of their labor. However small the earning
may be, it is the more precious to them, because it is their sole
resource to provide for their needs.

The artisans run about the cities from morning until night
looking for business; most of the workers in China do their work
in the private homes. For example, does one want to have a
costume made?—the tailor comes to your house in the morning
and stays until the evening. So it is with all the other artisans.
They continually go about the streets looking for work; even
the blacksmiths carry their anvil and forge about with them for
ordinary work; the barbers, if the missionaries may be believed,
walk through the streets with a chair on their shoulders, a basin
and kettle in their hands. Everyone of good will, not crippled or
sick, finds the means to subsist; thus there is not an inch of
cultivable land unused in the empire, nor is there anyone, man
or woman, of any age, deaf or blind, who does not manage to
make a living. The mills for grinding grain are mostly operated
by hand; a great number of poor and blind people are occupied with this work.

In conclusion, all the inventions that industry can discover, all the improvements that necessity brings to attention,
all the resources that self-interest inspires, are here employed
and used profitably. . . .

         .   .   .

Only two classes may be distinguished among the Chinese people, the nobility and the people; the first include the princes of the blood, those with titles, the Mandarins, and the scholars; the second, the husbandmen, merchants, artisans, etc.

There is no hereditary nobility in China; a man's merit and capacity alone mark the rank he is to take. Children of the prime minister of the empire have their fortune to make and enjoy no special consideration. If they are inclined toward idleness, or if they lack talent, they fall to the rank of the common people, and are often obliged to adopt the vilest of occupations. However, a son inherits the property of his father; but to succeed him in his dignities and to enjoy his reputation, the son must elevate himself by the same steps; thus all of the son's hopes depend upon study, as the only avenue to honors. . . .

The term despotism has been applied to the government of China, because the sovereign of that empire takes into his own hands exclusively the supreme authority. Despot means master or lord; this title may therefore be applied both to rulers who exercise an absolute power provided by law, and to rulers who have usurped an arbitrary power, which they exercise, for good or for evil, over nations whose government is not protected by fundamental laws. Thus there are legal despots and arbitrary or illegal despots. In the first case, the title of despot does not seem to differ from that of monarch, a title that is given to all kings, that is to say both to those who have sole and absolute authority, and to those whose authority is limited or modified by the constitutions of the governments of which they are the heads. The same statement applies to emperors. Therefore, there are monarchs, emperors, and kings, who are despots, and others as well. In arbitrary despotisms the name of despot is nearly always considered a derogatory title referring to a tyrannical and arbitrary ruler.

The Emperor of China is a despot, but in what sense is that term applied? It seems to me that, generally, we in Europe have an unfavorable opinion of the government of that em-

pire; but I have concluded from the reports about China that
the Chinese constitution is founded upon wise and irrevocable
laws which the Emperor enforces and which he carefully ob-
serves himself.

🏵 The Distant and Strange Continent of Europe

WHILE THE eighteenth-century European perspective of China would hardly have satisfied contemporary standards of objectivity, the Chinese conception of Europe could only be termed a caricature. Despite the attempts of the Jesuits in the fifteenth and sixteenth centuries to teach mapmaking to the Chinese (a time in Europe when mapmaking became a skilled and scientific craft), the Chinese took little interest in geography, their own or other countries', and Chinese maps remained crude until well into the nineteenth century. The following anonymous and undated selection was probably written shortly before the Opium War, a time when China was already being pressed by Britain. The description of Europe is not only vague, it is comical. Centuries earlier Chinese had written some remarkable travel accounts of neighboring countries, notably India, and Central and North Asia. But since Ming times, Chinese interest in foreign areas waned, as evident in the disinterest shown the great voyages of the Ming explorer Cheng-ho.

Aside from the exoticism of the description, two points might be noted about the following selection. First, there is no sign of deep interest, such as Europeans had for China, or of analysis. A section, not presented here, blandly lists the three types of political system in Europe: monarchy, democracy, and mixed monarchical-democratic government. The absence of analysis, except by a few scholars, was characteristic of the scholarship of the entire Ch'ing period, with its stress on voluminous compilation. Second, though the author notes the

racial difference of Europeans, he seems mainly fascinated by
their hair rather than their skin color; even today, the Chinese
are not particularly race conscious, and never refer to themselves as "yellow men."

This selection is translated from the *Hsiao-fang hu-chai
yü-ti ts'ung-ch'ao,* a compilation of descriptions of countries
China had dealings with in the early nineteenth century. The
compiler was Wang Hsi-ch'i, a native of Kiangsu. The collection
was published in 1891. The name of the author of the section
on Europe is not given.

WANG HSI-CH'I *
Europe to a Chinese Observer

Europe (*Ou-lo-pa*) is one of the five great continents. In land
area it is the smallest, but it is compensated for this in other
ways. Europe is about 7,700 miles (= 2,570 English miles)
long, and 1,000 miles (= 333 English miles) broad, in all making 20 million square miles. To the north it borders the Arctic
Ocean. To the east it rises from the Ural Mountains. The Ural
River turns southward. There its boundaries are formed by
the Caspian Sea, the Caucasus Mountains, and the Black Sea.
To the south it is cut off by the Mediterranean. And to the
west it ends at the Atlantic. Though it is smaller than the
other four continents, its soil is fertile, its products are plentiful, it has many talented people and many famous places. For
this reason, Europe's power in the present world is pre-eminent,
and it has become a leading force in the five continents. Yet in
ancient times its people hunted for a living, ate meat, and wore
skins. Their customs were barbaric, and their spirit was wild
and free. But during our own Shang period (2000 B.C.) Greece

---

* Franz Schurmann, trans., Wang Hsi-ch'i, *Hsiao-fang hu-chai yü-ti ts'ung-
ch'ao.*

and other countries gradually came under the influence of the Orient. For the first time they began to till fields and manufacture products, build cities and dig lakes. They began to do all kinds of things. Before long, writing and civilization began to flourish. Thus they became beautiful like the countries of the East.

During the time of our own P'ing Wang of the Chou Dynasty (around 770 B.C.) Rome arose in Italy and began to extend its rule over surrounding regions. By the time of the beginning of our Western Han Dynasty (206 B.C.) Rome succeeded in acquiring rule over the entire Western world. It was known everywhere, and even in our *Book of the Han Dynasty* where it was called Ta-ch'in. The Chin and the Wei Dynasties too called Rome Ta-ch'in, but also called it Li-chien.

But then internal conflicts arose, the military became more arrogant, and life was luxurious. During the Western Chin (A.D. 265–317) the Empire split in two parts, east and west. The western part still had its capital in Rome, but it lasted for only another hundred years or so. Toward the end of our first Sung Dynasty (A.D. 420–478) it was finally destroyed by local feudatories and barbarians. But the part which founded its rule in Constantinople lasted for many hundreds of years more. Yet rebellion and murder were frequent, disorder repeatedly broke out, and it too finally declined. With the decline of Rome during the reign of our illustrious Emperor Ching (A.D. 258–263), many great lords began to fight among each other for territory and cities, and so Europe gradually fell apart into many warring countries. During the middle of the T'ang Dynasty (A.D. 618–906) Charlemagne, a wise and learned man, gifted with civil and military talents, became Emperor of the Germans and the French. His fame and virtue spread far afield, and all the barbarians submitted to him. He reorganized the army, instituted discipline, and revived the Roman Empire, thereby unifying Europe. When Charlemagne died, however, his descendants turned out to be incompetent. Hardly a hundred years elapsed, when Europe once again broke up. The great lords set up their own domains over which they made themselves king. This is how the countries of France, Germany, and Italy arose.

During the time of our Five Dynasties period (A.D. 907–960) the settlements of Northern Europe for the first time set up stable systems of rule, and laid down the various ranks, which then spread to other countries. In this way countries like Russia, Sweden, Norway, and Denmark arose. These countries all made alliances with each other. . . .

As the situation is now, Russia controls the northeast of Europe. It is shaped like a palm-leaf fan. Hanging down from it is Sweden. From its southern cliffs, suddenly springing forth like an arm, is Denmark, sometimes also called the country of Lien. South of Lien are the various countries of the Germans. To the east is Prussia; to the south is Austria; to Austria's southeast is Western Turkey. Way down in the south and shaped like a human palm and bordering on the Mediterranean is Greece. The country shaped like a human leg with a shoe stuck on is Italy. The country in Europe's northwest corner is Switzerland. Northwest of Germany and bordering the sea is Holland. To the south of Holland you have Belgium, and southwest of Belgium you have France. To the southwest there is Spain. Also on the west, bordering the Great Sea, there is Portugal. The big island located in the great-cliff sea northwest of France is England.

These are the divisions of Europe. Those interested in geography can thus get an idea of its shape.

Europe's people are all tall and white. Only those who live in the northeast where it is very cold are short, and dwarfish. They have big noses and deep eyes. But their eyes are not of the same color, with brown, green, and black being most frequent. They have heavy beards that go up to their temples, or are wound around their jaws. Some of their beards are straight like those of Chinese. Some are crooked and twisted like curly hairs. Some shave them all off. Some leave them all on. Some cut off their beards but leave their mustaches. Some cut off their mustaches and leave their beards. They do what they wish. Whether old or young, all have beards. They let their hair grow to two or three inches. But if it gets longer they cut it. The women leave on all of their hair. The women dress their hair somewhat like Chinese women, but gather it together in a net. The color of their whiskers and hair is different. They have yellow, red, mottled, or black, all kinds. The men wear flat-topped, tubelike, narrow-brimmed hats of different heights ranging from four inches to over one foot. They are made of felt or of silk. When they meet people, they lift their hats as a sign of respect. Their clothes are narrow and their sleeves are tight. The length only goes down to their bellies. Their trousers are bound tightly around their waists. But their outer garments are loose and long, and reach as far down as their knees. They wear collars in front and back. Their inner garments are of cotton, but their outer garments are of wool. They often wear boots which are made of leather.

Women's clothes are also tight and their sleeves stick to their bodies. They wear skirts which are long and brush the ground. This is how they generally dress. For their ceremonial hats, ceremonial clothes, their military helmets and garments, they have different practices.

For their eating and drinking utensils they use gold, silver, and ceramics. When they eat they use knife and fork, and they do not use chopsticks. They eat mainly bread. Potatoes are staple. They mostly roast or broil fowl and game. They usually season it with preserves or olive oil. They drink spirits and soda water, as well as coffee in which they mix sugar. Its fragrance enlivens teeth and jaws, and makes the spirit fresh and clear.

Now as to the way they build houses. On the outside they have no surrounding walls, and inside they have no courts. They do not pay much attention to the exact direction and position (geomancy), they do not have fixed standards; square or round, concave or convex—all depends on the discretion of the owner. Sometimes they have many-storied buildings that go up for five or six, or seven or eight floors. They usually also dig out another underground floor; they use it for storage or go there to escape the heat. Their foundations are deep and solid. Their walls are substantial and thick. In hot or in cold weather nothing comes through them. In the winter they are warm inside and in the summer cool. They are very convenient. The upper classes use stone. The middle classes use brick. The lower classes use earth. For covering tiles, they use lead or sometimes ceramic pieces or light stones and boards. They make them depending on how wealthy they are.

Inside the rooms are clean and swept. They try very hard to keep dirt out. Looking at them they seem like silver. You feel comfortable in them. They are also very good at decorating places. All their gold and jade, their precious objects, antiques, and objects of amusement they place in the front rooms, so that people can see them. Their palaces, temple buildings, pavilions, parks and lakes, and all their museums and scientific buildings are designed to delight the tourist. In size they are all very spacious, and ingeniously built. This indicates that the Westerners respect the arts, and try hard to become famous. Therefore they strive to be refined in everything they do, and overlook no small details.

Now for their machines. When they first invented them, they just relied on common sense. They tried this and rejected that, without ever finding out from anyone else how it ought to be done. However, they did some research and found people who investigated the fine points and propagated their usage. In this way they gradually developed all their machines such as steamships, steam trains, spinning machines, mining and canal-digging machines, and all machines for making weapons and gunpowder. Things improved day by day and helped enrich the nation and benefit the people. Day by day they became more prosperous and will keep on becoming so.

II. Decline and Humiliation:
The Nineteenth Century

Like Egypt of the pharaohs, Rome, and the Byzantine Empire, Imperial China flourished and prospered and finally sank into irreversible decline. But China, unlike the others, was the only great ancient empire to survive until modern times.

The fortunes of China had risen and fallen with the regeneration and decline of the dynasties. Invasion from the borderland steppes and disintegrating government brought dynasty after dynasty to its demise. Chaos reigned while China readjusted. And then out of the ruins, like the mythical Chinese phoenix, a new dynasty arose, built on the same traditional principles, often different only in name. China changed only within her own tradition, meeting new challenges by turning to the past for time-tested solutions, and failure was blamed not on the system but on its administration. Confucianism remained throughout as a system of thought and of government.

In the nineteenth century China found herself in an entirely new kind of decline, but for half a century she remained stubbornly unaware of its substance. When attacked, she struck out to defend herself as she had during previous thousands of years, but this time the West brought weapons, machines, and ideas which could not be fitted into the Chinese universe or be dealt with by Chinese institutions without tearing at the roots of her most basic traditions. China was obsolete by Western standards, and while this was obvious to the West, which could make the comparison, to the culture-bound and isolated Chinese the idea that any nation had found principles of civilization superior to China's was laughable fantasy.

It took over fifty years of failure, humiliation, and defeat before China could see herself clearly in the new world context. The Opium War, the Arrow War, the Taiping Rebellion, and the Boxer Rebellion rocked Imperial China but did not deliver the *coup de grâce*. The Chinese response to these attacks from without and revolts from within was various attempts at reform, none of which reached down to the roots of the problem, for the distressing truth was that the Chinese had not yet understood the nature of their affliction. China was clearly on a disaster course, but her leaders—retaining supreme trust in the ancient system—remained confident that disaster could be allayed by adjustments and housecleaning. Somehow the barbarians would again be taken care of; they might rule for a while, but sooner or later they would be absorbed into the Chinese polity. Now their clever instruments would be used against the Chinese, but ultimately they would end up in Chinese arsenals. And their ideas, distasteful as they were, might yet be accommodated into the Chinese intellectual universe, as was earlier done with Buddhism.

The problem was not that China did nothing to meet the challenge, but that what she chose to do was inappropriate and ineffective. Confucianism was never a rigid doctrine, but rather a flexible set of principles, and so, when reform was necessary, the Chinese worked out and put into practice many commendable schemes. Yet China's unshaken faith in the past as a guide to the present prevented her from understanding her new enemies and the world of science, organized power, and revolution out of which they had sprung. China believed confidently that the dikes holding back the flood were basically secure, even though cracks were everywhere visible, and she occupied herself by filling in the cracks, hoping that sooner or later the flood would subside. The flood did not subside, and the cracks were less significant than the crumbling sand on which the dikes rested. Nineteenth-century Chinese accepted the need for reform, but only as a means to return once again to a traditional stability. The West believed in change and progress as the basis of all modern human life. The Chinese could not yet conceive of it.

1. THE WEST MOVES INTO CHINA
🏵 *Opium, Free Trade, and the*
Expansion of British Power

HISTORIANS USUALLY consider the Opium War to be the first milestone in modern Chinese history. Indeed, the Nanking Treaty (1842) signed at the conclusion of the war represented China's point of no return: hereafter, the tide of foreign penetration could not be reversed. A fault appeared in China's defense system, and through it poured the heterodoxy of the West which ultimately tolled the death knell of traditional China.

No episode in Chinese history has been more disputed than the Opium War. For many Chinese the British declaration of war represented a flagrant example of imperialist aggression, and they regarded their resistance, as feeble as it was, as a patriotic attempt to stamp out the opium trade sapping China of her riches and her people of their health.

Contemporary Chinese look back with bitterness on Britain's forceful entry into China. It represents to them the beginning of almost a century of foreign privilege, domination, and gunboats on the Yangtze River. For them the Opium War marks the beginning not only of modern Chinese history but of national humiliation.

The British, of course, viewed the war and its causes from a very different vantage point. Of all the issues at stake, the problem of opium was of secondary importance. The British concern was with the inequity of their relations with the Chinese government: they were not pleased with their treatment as just another tribute-bearing nation. The Chinese authorities consented to communicate with the British only in the context of an inferior-superior relationship, but even then they refused to negotiate directly with the foreigners, insisting that one of the Hong merchants be used as a middleman. The British, inconvenienced and incensed by such abuse and nonsense, demanded to be represented in the person of an ambassador posted in Peking with explicit rights to discuss affairs of state on the basis of diplomatic equality. The Chinese naturally (natural to the Chinese) refused to consider such an outrageous demand, and with no other recourse, the British felt fully justified in going to war.

The following selection is a translation from *Modern Chinese History* by the late Nationalist Chinese Ambassador to the United Nations, Tsiang Ting-fu. It is interesting to note that the author does not try to excuse his countrymen for their handling of the Opium War, but says only, "We do not castigate them because they are not really worth our castigation."

TSIANG TING-FU *
The English and the Opium Trade

Before the eighteenth century England produced no major product marketable in China, and for the most part her ships carried silver rather than goods to China. Economists at that time, whether Chinese or foreign, appreciated the fact that a steady drain of gold and silver was detrimental to a nation's economy, and each nation sought to increase exports, thereby increasing the inflow of gold and silver. After many years in the China trade the British discovered that opium was an extremely lucrative item; thus the British East India Company encouraged the cultivation of opium in India while controlling

* Orville Schell, trans., Tsiang Ting-fu, *Chung-kuo chin tai-shih* (Hong Kong: Li-ta Publishers, 1955), pp. 12–24.

its transport to China. During the first few years of the Ch'ien-lung Emperor's reign (1736–1795) the Chinese imported only about four hundred chests annually (each chest was about a hundred *chin;* a *chin* is about a kilo). The Ch'ien-lung Emperor had forbidden Chinese merchants to sell opium, but his efforts came to nought. By the time of the Chia-ch'ing Emperor (1796–1820) the import of opium had increased to almost four thousand chests a year. Finally, the Chia-ch'ing Emperor prohibited further imports, but because of corruption among the official class, the enforcement of inspection and prohibition proved to be extremely difficult. The opium trade continued to expand.

The Tao-kuang Emperor was more concerned than all his predecessors over the opium problem. He proved the most determined to suppress its use, and upon ascending the throne, he issued ordinances strictly prohibiting opium smoking. But opium imports increased faster than ever before. During the first year of the Tao-kuang Emperor's reign (1821) the amount of opium coming into China was still quite low, only five thousand chests, but by 1850 it had jumped to over thirty thousand chests (worth about eighteen million Chinese *yuan*). The result was that Chinese silver was rapidly drained away in return for opium which was of no benefit to her whatsoever. The whole country regarded this as a calamity, but officials in Kwangtung felt that the prohibition on opium was utterly impractical in view of the fact that the opium trade was in the interest of those who gave the orders to suppress it. This group suggested instead that the tax on foreign opium be increased, and that local production in China be stepped up simultaneously to compete with the foreign opium trade, thus rendering it no longer profitable for foreign merchants to bring opium from India and thereby halting importation.

By the fourteenth year of the Tao-kuang Emperor's reign (1824) the advocates of this policy were in ascendancy, but no one except Hsü Nai-chi dared publicly speak in its favor. In the eighteenth year of the Tao-kuang Emperor's reign (1838) Huang Chüeh-tzu memorialized the Emperor, clamoring angrily for prohibition and advocating summarily stamping out all opium smoking. He claimed that if no one smoked opium, no one would buy opium, and he suggested that those who smoked opium might be cured by capital punishment.

After Huang Chüeh-tzu's memorial had reached the Emperor, the Emperor asked that each provincial governor present his views on the subject. Although no one came forward and directly opposed Huang Chüeh-tzu, they felt that his policy was obviously too extreme, maintaining that opium smokers harmed only themselves while the merchants who dealt in opium harmed many. Were not the merchants' crimes much graver than the addicts'? They concluded that since Canton was the main port of entry and sale of opium, outlawing its use should begin there.

Lin Tse-hsü, Viceroy for Hunan and Hupei, agreed with Huang Chüeh-tzu's proposal and advised that all measures be taken to enforce them. The Tao-kuang Emperor decided that the prohibition of the sale and use of opium ought to be enforced with greater severity; thus he sent Lin Tse-hsü to Canton as his High Commissioner to look into the problem. Lin, a Fukienese and one of the most renowned and capable officials in political circles of his time, and greatly respected by the scholar-official class, was a tremendously self-confident and arrogant man. He had no real experience handling "barbarians," but he recklessly announced that, "I am intimately acquainted with the wily ways of the barbarian from my sojourn in Fukien."

Actually, people at that time were rather hypocritical about the whole opium problem. They admitted in private correspondence to the difficulties of suppressing opium, but in their official memorials they toed the line with ceremonious ostentation. This sort of lack of candor was a great problem among the scholar-official class.

In reality, opium suppression was an extremely complicated and difficult problem, and it would have been no easier without foreign interference. But how much more difficult it was during the Tao-kuang reign, when the English were totally unwilling to allow us to carry out the policy of suppression.

Opium was not only commercially very profitable then, it also constituted the greater part of the revenues earned by the Indian government, and in view of this, the English were uneasy about our policy of trying to close the country to free trade. They were eager to settle matters once and for all, and had we given them the slightest pretext over the opium problem, they would not have hesitated to deal with us by force of arms.

We call the war that followed the Opium War; the English call it the Trade War. Both sides had their own reasons. In regard to the opium problem—we tried to get rid of the curse altogether, while the English hoped to maintain the situation as it was; we were the ones who wished to alter the status quo. In regard to the trade problem—the English sought new opportunities and freedom, and it was we who strongly favored keeping the situation as it was; they were the ones who wished to alter the status quo. Under these circumstances, war was unavoidable.

CLASH BETWEEN EAST AND WEST

On March 10 of the nineteenth year of the Tao-kuang Emperor's reign (1839), Lin Tse-hsü arrived at Canton. He spent a week pondering the situation and settling himself before he made his first move. He then issued a proclamation to all foreigners, saying that it was not right to harm others for the sake of one's own profit: "How dare you bring your country's vile opium into China, cheating and harming our people?"

Lin made two demands of the foreigners: first, he asked that they take all the unsold opium and "hand it all over to Chinese officials"; second, he asked that the foreigners pledge not to import any more opium into China. If they continued, said Lin, "the opium will be confiscated and those involved will be decapitated." Unfortunately, the foreigners did not understand that Lin meant business, thinking that he was just another ordinary official who, as a matter of course, had issued a pious proclamation as a formality at the beginning of his term of office. But after all, they thought, would not Lin be willing to sell out like all the other officials after they got around to settling the price of the squeeze and, would not trade then be able to continue as usual? They did not realize that Lin was not this sort of man. Lin said, "If the opium trade does not cease, I, the Imperial High Commissioner, will not leave my post. I will persevere in this matter until the end."

By the end of March the foreigners were still unwilling to hand over their opium stocks. Lin Tse-hsü then issued an order forbidding any movement to and from Canton, and sent troops to encircle the thirteen foreign factories (foreign trading establishments). He ordered all Chinese to leave the factories and he later forbade anyone at all from entering or leaving. In short, Lin turned the thirteen factories into foreign prisons and prohibited the sale of foodstuffs to the inmates.

At that time there were roughly three hundred and fifty foreigners inside the thirteen factories, among whom was the English Superintendent of Trade, Captain Charles Elliot. Naturally, those inside did suffer a certain amount of privation— they had to do chores, like boil their own water, wash their own dishes, and do their own housework—but there was enough food, since the foreigners had previously stored up a large quantity and were also being clandestinely supplied.

Captain Elliot had originally hoped to compromise, but Lin stood firmly to his two demands. At that time the English, unfortunately, happened to have only two small gunboats in Chinese waters, and the troops on board had no chance of landing at Canton. Captain Elliot had no means by which to protest, and to yield was his only alternative. But the way in which he chose to yield is worth our attention: instead of simply ordering the English merchants to hand over their opium to Lin, he ordered them to hand the opium over to him; in his capacity as Superintendent of Trade, he gave each merchant a receipt, and by one quick maneuver all British opium became the property of the British Crown.

Captain Elliot then handed over 20,280 chests of opium to the Chinese. This was a great victory for Lin, who, with one toss of the net, had trapped a million *chin* of opium. The Tao-kuang Emperor was indeed pleased, and he commended Lin, saying, "Your great loyalty to the throne and your unbounded love of your country are unequaled and unmatched by any within or without the Empire."

But still the foreigners did not quite believe that Lin was genuinely determined to suppress the opium trade, and they thought that he must be in some way profiting. They soon learned otherwise.

At Hu-men, on the Pearl River Delta, Lin ordered two huge pools to be dug in the sandy banks. He later wrote:

> First I had a series of trenches dug and then I dug ditches to connect them. After this was completed, I had water diverted into the trenches through the ditches. Then I had salt sprinkled on the pools. Finally, I had the unprocessed opium thrown into the pools and added lime to boil the opium. The opium was thereby turned into ashes and completely destroyed. The nauseating odor was more than we could bear. When the tide finally receded we opened the trenches and let the residue flow away. We then used brushes to clean the bottom of the pools so that nothing remained. The process took twenty-three days. Every bit of opium was completely destroyed. Each day civilian and military officials were there to supervise. Even the foreigners came to watch and to record the events in detail. They lavishly praised the Commissioner's integrity.

Meanwhile Captain Elliot had made a thorough report to London and was quietly awaiting further orders. After his apparent success, Lin was greatly relieved. The Emperor was so pleased that he offered Lin a new position—Viceroy to Kwangtung and Kwangsi—but Lin humbly turned down the offer, claiming that "although all the opium in the factories had been completely destroyed, there is still the possibility that more may be smuggled in." Lin wanted to do the job thoroughly, and thus subsequently demanded that all foreign merchants sign a bond committing themselves thenceforth to observe the Chinese regulations prohibiting opium trade. Captain Elliot refused to sign, thereby stirring up the simmering conflict once again. But by this time Lin was swelled with new confidence, and claimed that the English power was nowhere near as menacing as in fact it was. In addition, he believed that the English were utterly dependent on the Chinese since they needed Chinese *tea* and *rhubarb!* He thought that if he simply cut off their supply of tea and rhubarb he could bring about their ruination.

The forts at Hu-men were repaired and overhauled. Lin also took a huge iron chain and stretched it across the entrance of Hu-men harbor as a blockade.

That winter Chinese junks clashed on numerous occasions with British ships in the waters around Canton. Each time Lin memorialized the Emperor claiming smashing victories, putting the whole country in a very optimistic mood.

When the British government finally received Elliot's letter, they dispatched Admiral George Elliot as plenipotentiary in charge of an expeditionary force to China. Britain's Foreign Minister, the well-known moralist-imperialist Lord Palmerston, not only demanded that China pay an indemnity to cover the confiscated opium and expenses for the British expeditionary force, but that China renounce her traditional policy of limiting trade and refusing to grant Western nations equality in diplomatic relations.

Admiral Elliot arrived off the coast of Canton in the summer of 1840. If Admiral Elliot had really understood what was happening in China, he would probably have gone directly to Canton and fought it out immediately with Lin who was, after all, the hard-line faction's major advocate. But the British had made different plans. Admiral Elliot did not attack Canton; he merely announced British intentions to blockade the port and moved on. The Chinese explanation was that the English were actually afraid of Lin.

After laying the blockade, Admiral Elliot proceeded north to Tinghai, where there were no defenses whatsoever, and as the Chinese had feared, the British were able to take the city without firing a shot. Captain Elliot and Admiral Elliot then turned the main body of their fleet north again and sailed for Taku Bar off Tientsin.

When the news of the fall of Tinghai finally reached Peking, the Emperor was extremely disturbed, and ordered troops from Shensi, Yunnan, Kweichou, and Hunan to proceed immediately to the two coastal provinces. The whole country was plunged into a state of tremendous agitation. Having ordered so many troops into action, the Tao-kuang Emperor was confronted with a supply problem for which he was very reluctant to allocate funds. His confidence in Lin was greatly shaken, and on July 22 he issued an edict criticizing Lin, saying, "You have accomplished nothing and have caused a great deal of disturbance. In pondering the situation, I cannot control my rage. I await to see in what manner you choose to reply." Meanwhile, at Tientsin, Ch'i-shan, the Viceroy of Chihli, had been placed in charge of negotiations with the British, and he had adopted a policy of trying to learn about both sides of the conflict. He sent his men on board English ships under the pretense of negotiation, while in actuality they were checking on the state of English preparedness. Ch'i-shan realized that the firepower of the English warships far outclassed that of the Chinese; about English steam vessels he wrote: "Without any wind, or even a favorable tide, they glide along against the current and are capable of fantastic speed." About British naval guns he said: "Their carriages are mounted on swivels, enabling the guns to be turned and aimed in any direction."

Any comparison to the state of Chinese military preparedness was simply laughable. The guns at Shanhaikuan "were remnants of the early Ming which had to be overhauled for use." The Yangtze River, the so-called "natural barrier" of defense, had already been occupied by the British. Ch'i-shan commented: "Those who are in charge of military affairs are all literary officials. Although their literary accomplishments are distinguished, they have no knowledge of armaments," and he concluded that there was no alternative but to adopt a policy of appeasement toward the barbarians.

The note sent to China by the British Foreign Minister

seemed to give Ch'i-shan every reason to believe that his policy of appeasing the barbarians had been effective. The first half of the note strenuously criticized Lin's former policy, asking what was to be gained by such arbitrariness and vindictiveness; the second half of the note outlined British demands. Ch'i-shan interpreted the letter in a typically Chinese way, concluding that the English were just filing a routine protest. Lin had treated the English too harshly as inferiors and so they were demanding that the Emperor redress their grievances. With an eye to the future Ch'i-shan told the British:

> Last year Commissioner Lin and those who participated in the inspection and prohibition of opium did not truly embody the temperate and just intentions of the Emperor. They were cheated and deceived by others. Therefore, their handling of the situation was improper. This matter will be investigated in detail and the culprits will be severely punished. Since this affair occurred at Canton and since we do not have the necessary information here (at Tientsin) to handle the matter, it is imperative that you set sail for the South and wait until the Commissioner arrives in Canton. We can then investigate and handle the matter fairly. I am sure the Commissioner can clear up any false accusations made against you.

As for indemnities, China even agreed to give a modest sum so that the British representative could return home without a loss of face. As for the old trade system, Ch'i-shan told the British that after the treaty was settled they could carry on as they always had without any revisions. Since Admiral Elliot and Captain Elliot had never wanted to get embroiled in a war in North China in the first place, they consented to return to Canton for further negotiations, even expressing their willingness to withdraw their troops from Tinghai. The Tao-kuang Emperor was exceedingly pleased, and believed that Ch'i-shan had convinced the British to withdraw their army and navy by his cleverness. Ch'i-shan's diplomacy seemed infinitely superior to Lin's policy of belligerence and rudeness.

The Emperor thereupon ordered all troops from the inland provinces to return to their original defense positions. He called the whole troop movement "a period of wasted extravagance," degraded Lin, and appointed Ch'i-shan to replace him.

After Ch'i-shan arrived in Canton he discovered how much more complex the situation was than he had originally anticipated. The British were insistent that they be paid an indemnity and that they be given Hong Kong or that other ports be opened for trade. Ch'i-shan was of the opinion that granting territory to the British would be much more damaging than allowing new ports to be opened, but he was afraid the Emperor would disagree. He thought it just as well to procrastinate a while and do some bargaining, but British patience soon gave out, and in the beginning of December they opened fire (outside of Canton).

It was not until after Ta-chiao and Sha-chiao were lost that Ch'i-shan agreed to sign a treaty with Captain Elliot in which he agreed to pay an indemnity of six million *yuan,* to cede Hong Kong to Britain, and, at a later date, to establish direct official intercourse between the two countries on an equal footing. But the Emperor refused to agree to the terms and cursed Ch'i-shan for "having obstinately pursued a misbegotten policy." He degraded him, divested him, and confiscated all his official property. At the same time, he ordered troops to proceed to Canton to repel the invaders.

The English, however, were not content with the way Captain Elliot had handled the affair either, and they dispatched a new representative and more troops to China. From this point on, Britain and China both were of the same mind; both advocated war and refused further negotiation. Britain's attitude was very simple: If China did not concede to their demands, they would not cease hostilities. The Emperor was equally as obstinate: as soon as one soldier fell, he was determined to call another to fill his place.

In the Chinese ranks there were soldiers who had never before been in combat and who fled as soon as they could.

There were others who suffered death or defeat rather than surrender or flee. There were those commanders who had bragged recklessly before the war began, but once in battle made a hasty retreat. There were also those noble commanders who died bravely, worn out from the struggle. One does not hesitate to say that the equipment was unworthy of the men; but neither was army discipline and morale worthy of the men. One cannot avoid mentioning that our people had a tendency to become traitors—because of hunger and cold they frequently gave up and joined the ranks of the British as coolies.

By the summer of 1842, when the British had decided to attack Nanking, the Emperor realized at last the hopelessness of the situation and the futility of further resistance, and agreed to accept British demands and to sign the Treaty of Nanking.

THE CHINESE NATION STANDS STILL FOR TWENTY YEARS

The fundamental reason for the defeat of China in the Opium War was our backwardness. Our troops and armaments were anachronisms, our government was medieval, and our people, including the official class, had a medieval mentality. Although we risked our lives resisting, we were finally defeated. There was no mystery in our defeat; it was inevitable.

Looking at the Opium War's place in our national history, we see that the military defeat we suffered during the war did not presage the total collapse of our old notion of "nationality." Even after the defeat we still failed to comprehend the reason for it, and we failed to initiate any reforms which would have truly dealt a fatal blow to our concept of "nationality." If the reforms of the T'ung-chih restoration (see pp. 205–235) could have been carried out during the reign of the Tao-kuang Emperor or the Hsien-feng Emperor, our modernization would have come about twenty years earlier than Japan's, thus completely changing Far Eastern modern history. But during the Tao-kuang Emperor's reign men were unfortunately unable to grasp the meaning of their military defeat. After the war they continued on as though everything were just the same, numb and insensitive, opinionated and arrogant. The situation remained unchanged until the end of the Hsien-feng Emperor's reign, when the Anglo-French expeditionary forces attacked Peking (1860).

In the wake of this disaster only a small minority finally woke up to the necessity of studying the West, and so we call this period the "twenty precious years when China stood still."

Why did the Chinese under the Tao-kuang Emperor not begin to initiate reforms after the Opium War? The reasons are complicated, but worth our attention. First, Chinese have traditionally tended to be conservative, too conservative. Our culture had endured for several thousands of years, its roots deep, its branches long. It was not easy for our people to recognize the necessity for reform. The second reason was that our culture was the lifeblood of the scholar-official class, and any tremors which jostled our culture threatened to smash the rice bowls of the scholar-officials. As soon as we attempted to implement any new political ideas, all those venerable souls who had won their positions through the old examination system ran the risk of losing their jobs; one can hardly blame them for opposing reform. The third reason was that the Chinese scholar-official class lacked a spirit of independence and individualism. There was always a small group of men who saw matters with greater foresightedness and perception than the others, but afraid of public criticism, they remained silent. Lin Tse-hsü is a perfect example. Actually, there were two Lin Tse-hsüs: the Lin whom the scholars and officials knew, and the real Lin. The first Lin was Lin the ever victorious Commissioner, who advocated the hard line and who had always used traditional Chinese methods of diplomacy. Unfortunately these officials thought the traitorous Commissioner Ch'i-shan had been bribed by the English to collaborate with them and that before the English had gotten rid of Lin, they dared not attack Canton. But once Lin was gone, the war began. These officials concluded that they were defeated, not because of any fallacy in their traditional way of handling such affairs, but because they had been betrayed by Ch'i-shan. That officialdom should have understood things in this way at this time was natural; Lin's memorials to the Emperor had been filled with self-confidence.

It is a pity that after Tinghai fell, Lin did not have a chance to confront Britain and pit his might directly against hers. It is no wonder that the Chinese, laboring under a sense of false omnipotence and power, did not readily acknowledge their defeat. It is true that Lin did gradually become aware of what was really happening around him. After he arrived at Canton, he realized that the Chinese military equipment was no match for that of the British, and he did his best to buy foreign cannon and boats. At the same time, he appointed men to translate foreign publications, and he later passed all the material that he had collected to Wei Mo-shen (Wei Yüan) who subsequently used it to compile his *An Illustrated Gazetteer of the Maritime Countries* (*Hai-kuo T'u-chih*), which revived the idea of using the barbarians to control the barbarians (*I-i Chih-i*), but what was more important, it presented the idea of using barbarian armaments to control the barbarians. The Japanese scholars later translated this book into Japanese to help push their own reform movement forward. Although Lin was quite aware of the realities of the situation, he was still afraid of public criticism, and thus did not dare publicly suggest reform.

In the end, Lin was exiled by the Emperor to Ili in Sinkiang. En route, he wrote a letter to a close friend in which he sadly admitted that the English rapid-fire guns were vastly superior to any the Chinese possessed. He said that he recognized the superiority of English technical knowledge, and recounted all the Chinese military's painfully obvious shortcomings. He concluded with: "But alas, what was to be done, what was to be done?"

This letter was written in confidence in 1842, and Lin asked his friend not to make it public. In other words, the "real" Lin did not want others to know his private thoughts. It is no wonder that even later on, when Lin had been reinstated as Viceroy of Shensi and Kansu, and of Yunnan and Kweichou, he was not willing to raise openly the subject of reform, allowing instead the scholar-officials to sleep undisturbed in the depths of their dreams. He allowed his country to slide gradually to destruction, because he was unwilling to sacrifice his own reputation and struggle against his contemporaries. Lin was without doubt one of the finest products of old Chinese culture, but he felt his own reputation to be more sacred than affairs of state. The scholar-officials did not yield and, of course, never advocated reform. Ch'i-shan and Ch'i-ying, who advocated appeasement of the barbarians, were both aware of the glaring differences between the strong West and weak China, and openly propagandized for their cause. But the scholar-official class had no faith in them. They had no confidence in themselves or in the people. Preferring to let things take their own course, they made no attempts to shake up the system or to bring about reform.

We do not castigate them because they are not worth our castigation.

🌀 The Detestable, Strong,
but Beatable Foreign Barbarians

WHEN THE Opium War broke out, the Chinese were confident that they would beat the "insignificant and detestable race." After all, the Ch'ing Dynasty was the world's mightiest empire. When they lost, they attributed it to the superior firepower of the English.

Just before the outbreak of the Opium War a censor submitted a memorial to the Emperor, maintaining that the English would not be able to sustain a war against China: "Without, therefore, despising the enemy, we have no cause to fear them"; and he forecast easy victory if war should break out.

There is an ancient Chinese saying from Hsün-tzu: "Know yourself, know your opponent; in a hundred battles win a hundred victories." Evidently, the Chinese knew neither themselves nor their opponents.

*A CENSOR ***
Memorial to the Emperor

The English barbarians are an insignificant and detestable race, trusting entirely to their strong ships and large guns; but the immense distance they have traversed will render the arrival of seasonable supplies impossible, and their soldiers, after a

* A Censor in MacNair, *Modern Chinese History, op. cit.,* p. 136.

single defeat, being deprived of provisions, will become dispirited and lost. Though it is very true that their guns are destructive, still in the attack of our harbors they will be too elevated, and their aim moreover rendered unsteady by the waves; while we in our forts, with larger pieces, can more steadily return the fire. Notwithstanding the riches of their government, the people are poor, and unable to contribute to the expenses of an army at such a distance. Granted that their vessels are their homes, and that in them they defy wind and weather, still they require a great draft of water; and, since our coasts are beset with shoals, they will certainly, without the aid of native pilots, run ashore, without approaching very closely. Though waterproof, their ships are not fireproof, and we may therefore easily burn them. The crews will not be able to withstand the ravages of our climate, and surely waste away by degrees; and to fight on shore, their soldiers possess not sufficient activity.* Without, therefore, despising the enemy, we have no cause to fear them. While guarding the approaches to the interior, and removing to the coast the largest guns, to give their ships a terrific reception, we should at the same time keep vessels filled with brushwood, oil, saltpeter, and sulphur, in readiness to let them drive, under the direction of our marine, with wind and tide against their shipping. When once on fire, we may open our batteries upon them, display the celestial terror, and exterminate them without the loss of a single life.

* The Emperor was assured that the English soldiers were buttoned up so tight, that, if once down, they could never get up again.

🕸 A Nineteenth-Century Western China-Expert

THE FOLLOWING passage is from a small volume written in 1847 by a British Consulate interpreter, Thomas Meadows, author of the well-known volume *The Chinese and their Rebellions*. The passage speaks for itself. After reading it, one begins to get some idea of the chasm which lay between East and West.

THOMAS MEADOWS *
From *Desultory Notes on the Government and People of China*

There seems to be an idea, now somewhat prevalent in England, that the Chinese generally have, in consequence of the late war, attained a much more correct knowledge of foreigners and the power and state of their countries than formerly. This is, however, very far from being the case. Those who saw and felt us, though sufficient in number to populate a first-rate European kingdom, form but a very small portion of the Chinese people; and the great body of the nation, inhabiting districts and provinces that we have never yet reached, can only look on the late war as a rebellious irruption of a tribe of barbarians, who, secure in their strong ships, attacked and took some places

* Thomas Meadows in *ibid.*, pp. 193–197.

along the coast, and even managed to get into their possession an important point of the grand canal, whereby they forced the Emperor to make them certain concessions. Nearly all they know of the fighting and of the character of the invading forces they must have learned from the Mandarins' reports to the Emperor, and his answers to them, published in the *Peking Gazette,* and from copies of local proclamations which may have reached them. We may easily imagine, from the tone of these papers, that the Chinese, who from want of experience would be unable to form sound judgments on such matters from *correct* data, must entertain opinions on the subject as erroneous as the accounts in these documents are distorted.

It will be difficult for the Englishman, who is in the habit of obtaining speedy and correct information through the newspapers of all unusual occurrences, not only in his own, but in nearly every country in the world, to comprehend this fully; but he must remember that the Chinese have (with the single exception of the *Peking Gazette,* containing nothing but official documents full of misrepresentations) no newspapers, and that the great body of the nation have no means of learning what passes at a distance from their own township. This is a circumstance which must always be kept in view when reflecting on and drawing conclusions with regard to China and the Chinese, as it accounts for much that will otherwise appear extraordinary.

So much for the nation generally; as to those who have come, and continue to come into contact with us, let the reader remember how very few foreigners speak Chinese; that only the Canton and Macao Chinese speak a little English, and that so badly as to be barely intelligible even when speaking of matters relating to their own occupations of tradesmen, mechanics, or menials;—let the reader recall this to his mind, and he will perceive that even if the Chinese were eager inquirers into foreign matters, and knew how to put their questions, they must, from the want of opportunity alone, be woefully ignorant of us. But the apathy with respect to foreign things generally, even of the higher and, in the Chinese sense of the word, educated classes, and that when they meet a foreigner who understands their own language, is to an European quite astonishing. They very seldom ask questions, still more seldom is the information they seek after of a kind that tends to enlighten their minds on the state of foreign nations. An intelligent European, accustomed to reflect on the state of a number of countries enjoying a variety of different advantages, and laboring each under peculiar disadvantages, could, by a few well-directed questions, and from very little data, form a tolerably correct notion of the state of a people hitherto unknown to him; but it would be a great error to suppose that this is the case with the Chinese. Their exclusion of foreigners and confinement to their own country has, by depriving them of all opportunities of making comparisons, sadly circumscribed their ideas; they are thus totally unable to free themselves from the dominion of association, and judge everything by rules of purely Chinese convention.

If we except one or two of the Chinese officers who have constantly been engaged in the late negotiation with foreigners, and, it may be, a few of those who have had business to transact with the consulates at the five ports, those Chinese who speak the Canton English, know all that is known of us in China. These people being, as above stated, tradesmen, mechanics, and domestics, are of course nearly all ignorant, in a Chinese point of view; and the following speech of a master carpenter, a man who has probably worked exclusively for foreigners from his youth up, uttered in an unaffected and earnest manner, in the course of a conversation about the building of the British consulate, gives what is by no means an unfair sample of the extent of their information respecting foreign countries. When arguing, not on the state of nations, but on the very businesslike subject of work to be done, and the amount of dollars to be given for it, he in support of some argument, said, "Cuttee outo Yingkelese king my tingke allo la-che Yingkelese man savay my;" *i.e.,* "With the exception of the Queen" (so he meant it) "of England, I think all Englishmen of consequence know me." He had been in the habit of doing work for the company's factory, and the idea of the class is that China, being a large and fertile country, abounding in all good things, while all other places are small and barren, all our most important possessions must, therefore, lie in China; hence they conceive that our headmen, who come here, and principal merchants, are in fact the chiefs of what we call our country.

"It is in the great size and wealth and the numerous population of our country; still more in its excellent institutions, which may contain some imperfections, but which after all are immeasurably superior to the odd confused rules by which these barbarians are governed; but, above all, in its glorious literature which contains every noble, elegant, and in particular, every profound idea; everything, in short, from which true civilization can spring, that we found our claim to national superiority." So thinks even the educated Chinese; and so the whole nation will continue to think until we have proved to them—no easy nor short task—our mental as well as our physical superiority. When some good works shall have been compiled in Chinese on natural law, on the principles of political economy, and on European national and international policy, then (after such works shall have obtained a wide circulation) when they perceive how much more deeply metaphysics have been explored by us than by them, and how studiously the best established principles of the sciences included under that term have been brought into practical operation by us, then, but not till then, will the Chinese bow before the *moral* power of the civilized West.

At present they take the tone of superiors quite unaffectedly, simply because they really believe themselves to be superior. I do not remember meeting among educated Chinese with a single instance of any want of candor in regard to this subject; whenever their minds once acknowledge anything foreign as superior to the Chinese article of the like sort, they at once admit it to be so. For instance, when a Mandarin who has never spoken to a barbarian, and never seen one of their books, who, perhaps, has hitherto always doubted that they had anything deserving of the name, is first shown one, he admires the decided superiority of the paper at once; but when he finds that instead of commencing at the left hand, as it (according to his belief) *of course* ought, its beginning is at the (Chinese) end; when he sees that all the lines, instead of running perpendicularly down the page, in the (to a Chinese) natural way, go sidling across it; when he further asks the meaning of the words in a sentence, and finds, as may easily happen, that the first comes last, and the last first, "Ah!" says he, without however the slightest intention of giving offence, "it's all confused, I see; you put the words anywhere, just as it suits your fancy. But how do you manage to read it?" When you, however, explain to him at length, that there is no *natural* way for the lines to run, and no absolutely proper place for books to begin; that there can scarcely be said to be any natural order for the succession of words in sentences, but that it is fixed by custom, and differs in every language, and that the uneducated Englishman would consider the Chinese method as quite absurd; when you explain this to him, and he begins to comprehend your reasoning, there is no obstinate *affectation* of contempt. He cannot, of course, have much respect for the shallow productions of barbarian minds, but he handles the book gravely, no longer regarding it as an absurdity.

All Chinese who have seen them are perfectly ready to allow that our ships, our guns, watches, cloths, etc., are much superior to their own articles of the like sort; and most of them would frankly admit us to be superior to them in all respects, if they thought so. But as above said, they do not. They are quite unable to draw conclusions as to the state of foreign countries, from an inspection of the articles produced or manufactured in them. They cannot see that a country where such an enormous, yet beautiful fabric as a large English ship is constructed—an operation requiring at once the united efforts of numbers and a high degree of skill—*must* be inhabited by a people not only energetic but rich and free to enjoy the fruits of its own labor; that such a country *must,* in short, have a powerful government, good laws, and be altogether in a high state of civilization. All this the Chinaman, having never compared the various states of different nations, is not only quite unable to perceive of himself, but often not even when it is pointed out to him at great length. We have, it is true, the power to do some great and extraordinary things, but so have the elephants and other wild animals, he occasionally sees and hears of; in his eyes, therefore, we are all barbarians, possessing perhaps some good qualities, congregated perhaps together in some sort of societies, but without regular government, untutored, coarse, and wild. . . .

🏵 War: An Instrument of Western Truth and Justice

A PREVIOUS selection was an account of the Opium War and the first Chinese defeat as seen through the eyes of a Chinese. The next selection is from the account of a British officer, Lt. Col. G. J. Wolseley, who took part in the second major Western expedition.

The immediate objective of the Anglo-French expedition against China in 1860 was to force ratification of a new treaty, for while the Chinese had pledged themselves to renegotiate the Treaty of Nanking twelve years after its signing (1842), they had succeeded in consistently evading the issue. By 1856 neither Britain nor France was willing to countenance further Chinese procrastination. They were determined to press for immediate resolution.

The nominal *casus belli* was a Chinese refusal to apologize for a dubiously legitimate claim that the British flag had been insulted. But the real issues were more profound and reminiscent of the Opium War: on whose terms would relations between China and the West be based? Which side should prevail? It was a conflict of wills. Should the Chinese accept British demands and establish diplomatic and trade relations with the West based on equality and free intercourse between sovereigns and capitals? Or should the British accede to Chinese demands, accept their status as an inferior, and be content to limit their trade to the treaty ports? There was much at stake: the British stood to lose four hundred million potential customers and their imperial honor; the Chinese stood to lose two thousand years of tradition and a way of life.

Wolseley shows little awareness of the problem as it must . have appeared to the Chinese, and does not perceive that the Chinese were attempting to protect more than a few ridiculously quaint rules and customs by their isolation. He talks blithely of "doing justice" and raising the Chinese "to our standard of knowledge," never realizing how relative these concepts are, and showing little awareness that the West was dealing not with a pack of uneducated savages but with a highly sophisticated and developed culture. His writing is interesting in that it shows clearly the moralism and self-righteousness with which the West set out to open China.

LT. COL. G. J. WOLSELEY *
From *War With China*

Thus ended the China War of 1860, the shortest, most brilliant, and most successful of all that we have waged with that country. Let us hope that it may be the last, by procuring for our merchants a perpetual immunity from those acts of violence and oppression, which have led to all our disputes with the Peking government. May its prophylactical effects enable us to trade on freely at every port along the great seaboard of the empire, and so open out new channels for our commercial enterprise.

It has cost us a large sum of money, but unlike many of our expensive European wars, we may with justice look forward to a liberal return for what we have expended.

To have refrained from a war with China in 1860, and at the same time have maintained our position at the several ports where we traded, would have been impossible. If we had pocketed our defeat of 1859, and contented ourselves with

---

* Lt. Col. G. J. Wolseley, *War With China in 1860* (London: Longmans, Green, 1862), pp. 323–328.

written demands for apology or reparation, we might, perhaps, have struggled on for some little time without any very violent rupture with the Chinese authorities; but the day must soon have arrived when we should have been forced to decide whether we should fight or withdraw finally from the country.

The one great object which we have ever had in view there has been freedom of action for our merchants, and unrestricted permission to trade with all parts of the empire. To prevent this last mentioned object has ever been the aim of all Chinese politicians. They sought to confine foreign trade to a few ports, where they wished our mercantile community to exist merely upon sufferance, and exposed to insult and exactions, in order to demonstrate publicly its dependent position. By Sir Henry Pottinger's treaty, access for British subjects at all times into Canton was stipulated for, but, most improperly, never enforced. By the Tientsin treaty of 1858, it was agreed that we should have liberty to travel through all parts of the country, and that the treaty itself should be ratified in presence of our Minister at Peking. When endeavoring to push his way there for that purpose, Mr. Bruce was opposed by force of arms, and prevented from accomplishing his object. Not only was the clause in the treaty which declared the unrestricted liberty of traveling through China thus proved to be null, but even our Minister's right of way to the capital was at once denied. That right of visiting Peking at pleasure, and carrying on direct and personal communications with the government there, was the principal advantage which Lord Elgin's mission in 1858 had obtained for us; but upon our first attempt to avail ourselves of the engagement it was forcibly denied. To have quietly allowed them to recede from their contracts, would have been indeed a bad precedent to have established. The best guarantee we have for the fulfillment of the treaty now ratified, is the very act of ratification itself, which was a public recognition of our equality with China as a nation, and a renunciation, on their part, of those conceited notions regarding universal superiority, which has ever been one of the great difficulties in all our dealings with them.

Surely no one can accuse our government of having un-
necessarily plunged into this war, although many may with
justice find fault with its having been postponed so long. The
British nation is always slow to engage in war. John Bull has
certain received notions as to right and wrong, justice and injustice, etc., etc., which, although essentially applicable in all
his relations with the civilized nations of the West, are as un-
suited for Eastern politics as red brick would be for ancient
Grecian architecture. His repugnance to spill blood has sometimes the very opposite effect of causing it to flow in quantities,
which a slight effusion earlier in the affair would have prevented.
He prefers, in all matters likely to entail war, to concede to the
utmost limits of concession. In disputes with Asiatics such is
not the line of action to pursue. To renounce any demand previously made, or to fail in enforcing any stipulated agreement,
is simply to incur a reputation of weakness or cowardice with
them. Notwithstanding our century's experience in India, the
English people really know little of the Asiatic mind. The advice
and instruction frequently put forward in print upon the subject
by our Indian administrators is rejected by the people at home.
They insist upon considering that all our public servants in
India are imbued with bigoted notions from long residence in
the East, and that what is applicable to England and its people
must be equally so to the enslaved Negroes of America and the
ancient governments of Asia. But to these, on the contrary,
new ideas regarding international policy never penetrate, and
the same motives influence the ruler and the subject now which
actuated those classes when our ancestors went naked and
painted their bodies sky blue. If any European monarch of
the twelfth century had pursued the system of international
policy at present general in the Western world, he must have
entailed upon himself the hatred of his own people and the
scorn of all others. Such a revolution in the minds of men cannot be effected in a day. We might as well expect to Christianize
the Eastern nations at once, by giving them the Bible, as expect
to overthrow their secular faith in political economy by simply
enunciating that system which our superior wisdom teaches us.

To engraft the enlightened institutions of the nineteenth upon the ignorance of the twelfth century, and expect the tree to bear fruit immediately, is folly. Before the Asiatic world can be led to believe in the justice of our polity, or before it will be applicable to Eastern nations, it will be necessary first to raise them up to our standard of knowledge, and enable them to reason in the same logical manner with ourselves. Time, bringing with it increased learning, alone can eradicate traditional errors. If it took many centuries to overcome in us the fear of witchcraft, and to enable us to discover how wrong it was to burn our fellow creatures for differing with us upon religious matters, surely many generations must pass away before our essentially British code of proceeding in the East is appreciated there in its true light. Year after year the local authorities of Canton oppressed our merchants, and offered insults to our officials, but rather than plunge into hostilities we left those injuries unredressed. Every individual slight that we submitted to was the sure precursor of another, until at last an impression was established that we would sooner bear with any indignity than draw the sword. If we had insisted from the first upon the right of entry within Canton, and had been sharp in avenging at once all serious attempts at violence upon the part of the local authorities there, we should have saved the millions which we have since had to expend in war. Nothing, however, but the presence of an armed force effecting a chronic intimidation could have enabled us to accomplish that end; and the British nation, taking but little interest in the matter, as long as trade somehow or other went on, preferred ignoring the difficulties encountered by our officials to incurring the yearly expense which the maintenance of such a force would have entailed. So strong was our disinclination to embroil ourselves that Sir John Davis was disgraced for having insisted upon the right of entry into Canton, and severe strictures were made by many upon those who were responsible for the active measures taken in the Arrow affair. Before entering upon the war of 1860, an ultimatum was despatched to Peking by orders of the Home government, offering the most liberal terms for reconciliation. These terms were so favorable to the Imperial government that all who were ignorant of the train of reasoning common to Asiatic minds were certain of their acceptance, and believed our war-like preparations uncalled for in consequence. The liberality of the proffered terms, however, only made war the more inevitable after all. They were supposed to be dictated by fear arising from our recent defeat. By placing ourselves gratuitously in the position of suppliants we gave His Celestial Majesty cause for imagining that he was really our superior in strength, and consequently entitled to dictate terms to us. His impertinently evasive answer was the result.

By the residence of our Minister at Peking, we can now apply directly to the authorities there for redress in all matters of local grievance, and the authorities at the various ports will henceforth hesitate before they embroil themselves with foreigners who have a minister at the Chinese seat of government in direct personal communication with their immediate superiors there.

By this war we have practically opened out the trade of the Yangtze River, whence a vastly increased commerce is to be expected. We have inflicted such a severe blow upon the inflated pride of the Hsien-feng Emperor that the whole face of Chinese politics, and our relations with that country, must change, before he will again dare to insult our flag or obstruct our commerce.

It is to be hoped, also, that intercourse with such men as Mr. Bruce, and those now acting under him, may serve in a measure to open the eyes of Chinese politicians to a just appreciation of their own shortcomings and real interests.

❦ The Legal Foundations of Western Superiority in China

THE "unequal treaties" forced upon the Chinese after the Opium War and the Arrow War "brought to China a rich fare of good and evil." In major ports up and down the Chinese coast foreign concessions sprang up, immune to Chinese jurisdiction. Western traders, missionaries, and diplomatic officials lived in their Western-style houses, drank good Scotch, and went piously to church. Over the years they succeeded in creating a world almost as remote from China as London or Paris —a world clean, wealthy, and well ordered in comparison to the seething Chinese quarter outside. If a foreigner was accused of murdering a Chinese, he rested assured that he would not be tried in a Chinese court. If trouble was afoot, he was comforted by the Western gunboats in the harbor. In short, if he wished, it was possible to shut the whole Chinese world out of his life. One recalls the infamous sign which allegedly hung above the gate of a Shanghai park: NO DOGS OR CHINAMEN.

Needless to say, many Chinese found galling and humiliating this impairment of their country's sovereignty. China accepted the unequal treaties because she had no choice, but the old feelings of cultural superiority and pride were slow to die. The treaty ports and the foreign quarters were constant reminders of Chinese weakness, and the source of profound resentment against the West.

The treaty ports were, of course, not all evil. Providing vital points of contact between China and the West, they were, in a sense, the gateway from old China into the modern world, and as such they served as an incubator for a new generation of

Westernized Chinese. Equally important, they gave birth to a new and powerful economic class, a Chinese urban bourgeoisie heretofore so conspicuously absent from traditional Chinese society.

As Fairbank points out in the following selection, the treaty system was not without its redeeming graces. If not for the treaty ports and Western presence, China might not have modernized as soon as she did. But like bitter medicine, the treaty system was often difficult for a proud Chinese to swallow.

JOHN K. FAIRBANK *
The Western Impact

The legal structure established by the unequal treaties in the period 1842–1860 resulted directly from the two wars fought by the British against the Ch'ing government (see pp. 131, 154). The first war in 1840–1842, which has been called, particularly in China, the Opium War, resulted directly from the doughty Commissioner Lin Tse-hsü's vain effort to suppress the drug trade at Canton. But the British expeditionary force was sent to Canton and thence up the coast to secure privileges of general commercial and diplomatic intercourse on a Western basis of equality, and not especially to aid the expansion of the opium trade. The latter was expanding rapidly of its own accord, and was only one point of friction in the general antagonism between the Chinese and British schemes of international relations.

The principles embodied in the Treaty of Nanking in 1842 were not fully accepted on the Chinese side and the treaty privileges seemed inadequately extensive from the British side. Consequently the treaty system was not really established until the British and French had fought a second war and secured treaties at Tientsin in 1858. Even then the new order was not

* Fairbank, *The United States and China, op. cit.,* pp. 120–123.

acknowledged by the reluctant dynasty until an Anglo-French expedition had occupied Peking itself in 1860. The transition from tribute relations to treaty relations occupied a generation of friction at Canton before 1840, and twenty years of trade, negotiation, and coercion thereafter.

Although the new treaties were signed as between equal sovereign powers, they were actually quite unequal in that China was placed against her will in a helpless position, wide open to the inroads of Western commerce and its attendant culture. By the twentieth century, after three generations of energetic Western consuls had developed its fine points, the treaty structure was a finely articulated and comprehensive mechanism. It was based first of all on treaty ports, at first five in number, and eventually more than eighty.

The major treaty ports had a striking physical and institutional resemblance to one another. Each had a crowded, noisy bund and godowns (warehouses) swarming with coolies, who substituted for machinery, under the supervision of Chinese compradores (business managers), who managed affairs beneath the overlordship of the foreign taipan (firm managers), teatasters, and other personnel. Each treaty port centered in a foreign section newly built on the edge of a teeming Chinese city and dominated by the tall white flagstaff of Her Majesty's Consulate. Its institutions included the club, the race course, and the church. It was ruled by a proper British consul and his colleagues of other nations and protected by squat gunboats moored off the bund. At Canton, Amoy, Swatow, and Foochow this foreign community got further protection by being established on an island adjacent to the shipping. At Ningpo, Shanghai, and other places the foreign area was separated from the Chinese city by a river, canal, creek, or other waterway.

Extraterritoriality. This legal system, under which foreigners and their activities in China remained amenable to foreign and not Chinese law, was not a foreign nor a modern invention. In a manner rather like that of the Turks at Constantinople, the Chinese government in medieval times had expected foreign communities in the seaports to govern themselves under their own headmen and by their own laws. This had been true of the early Arab traders in China. The British and Americans at Canton before the Opium War demanded extraterritoriality because they had suffered from Chinese attempts to apply Chinese criminal law to Westerners, without regard for Western rules of evidence or the Western abhorrence of torture. But most of all the foreign traders needed the help of their own law of contract.

As applied in the treaty ports, extraterritoriality became a powerful tool for the opening of China because it made foreign merchants and missionaries, their goods and property, and to some extent their Chinese employees, converts, and hangers-on all immune to Chinese authority. France in particular undertook the protection of Roman Catholic missions and communicants. All this was, to say the least, an impairment of Chinese sovereignty and a great handicap to China's self-defense against Western exploitation. The Japanese, who were saddled with the same system also, after 1858, made tremendous efforts to get out from under it and did so by the end of the century.

A further essential of the treaties was the treaty tariff which by its low rates prevented the Chinese from protecting their native industries. Since, for various reasons, the administration of the low treaty tariff was not effective in Chinese hands, a foreign staff was taken into the Chinese custom house. Under Sir Robert Hart as Inspector General, the Westerners who served as commissioners of Chinese Maritime Customs became leading figures in every port, guardians both of the foreign trade and of the modest Chinese revenue of about 5 per cent derived from it.

Under the new dispensation of the treaties Western civilization brought to China a rich fare of good and evil. The opium trade which supplied 10 or 15 per cent of the revenue of British India went hand in hand with the Protestant missionary movement which was nourished by the shillings and dimes of devout congregations in the Christian West. Beginning about 1830 British and American Protestant missionaries found that modern medicine carried more weight in China than the scriptures.

Missionary hospitals were soon attempting to repair the ravages of disease, including the effects of opium. In Chinese eyes this was no more anomalous than the general gap between Christian precept and imperialist practice.

By the most-favored-nation clause (the neatest diplomatic device of the century) all foreign powers shared what any one of them could squeeze out of China. The treaty system kept on growing as the fortunes of the Manchu Dynasty deteriorated. The dynasty became increasingly dependent upon British administrative and diplomatic support. During the century of the treaties the Chinese people were consequently subjected to a most far-reaching, cumulative, and violent process of change. The opium trade that had begun as a joint Sino-foreign traffic was taken into the country. After the 1880s China's native opium production began to supplant the Indian product, importation of which ceased in 1913. From the treaty ports along the coast and up the Yangtze, Western ways as well as goods spread into the interior, aided in the remote centers by zealous evangelists like those of the China Inland Mission. Christianity opened the way for the acceptance of Western values which upset the old order entirely.

2. INTERNAL REBELLION
🕉 Rebellion: A Recurrent Tradition

SINCE TIME immemorial China has been plagued by internal revolts and rebellions. More often than not these rebellions gained momentum through affiliation with one or another of the myriad religious societies which abounded in China. Thus the ruling dynasties—justifiably afraid that during troubled times and with the proper leadership such organizations could be their undoing—tended to look with great suspicion on all heterodox religious organizations.

In the following selection C. K. Yang, Professor of Sociology at the University of Hawaii, examines the role of religious movements in political rebellion during the Ch'ing Dynasty. He discusses the social setting of religious rebellion and finally studies the failure of the Confucian orthodoxy to fulfill China's spiritual need during times of disorder and upheaval. He concludes that the proliferation of religio-political rebellions in China was in large measure the result of an inability of the Confucian orthodoxy to provide the common man with a promise of deliverance and salvation.

Both the Taiping Rebellion, (see pp. 178–192), which succeeded in occupying a large part of central China, and later the Boxer Rebellion (see pp. 193–204), which resulted in the siege of Peking by the Western powers, were rebellions embracing the lethal combination of religion and politics. Both proved disastrous for China.

C. K. YANG *
Religion and Political Rebellion

In the present science-oriented age, religion is often regarded as a conservative or even reactionary agency bent upon protecting the social and political status quo. In China, facts show that religion was indeed a strong undergirding force for the established institution of government. But, on the other hand, the rejection and persecution of heresy indicated a clear threat to the ruling political power by religion in its heterodox forms. Max Weber has already pointed out the revolutionary role of religion, and other scholars in the sociology of religion have also noticed that religion could uphold as well as tear down a political structure. The purpose of the present chapter is to consider the role of religion in political revolts and some of the ways by which religion contributed to the development of rebellious political movements in modern China.

RELIGIOUS SOCIETIES IN POLITICAL REBELLION

History shows ample evidence of the persistent role of religion in political struggles against ruling dynasties. The Taoist Yellow Turban Rebellion in the Han period; the scattered uprisings of Buddhist groups in the period of disunion; the sporadic nationalistic resistance led by the Taoist sect Ch'üan-chen Chiao (Complete Truth religion) against the Chin and Yüan rulers; the White Lotus Rebellion that helped topple the Mongol rule and gave the succeeding dynasty its name, Ming, through its mes-

* C. K. Yang, *Religion in Chinese Society* (Berkeley and Los Angeles: University of California Press, 1961), pp. 218–229.

sianic figures of Big and Little Ming Wang (Brilliant Kings), who were thought to have been sent by Buddha Maitreya to the world to restore peace and order: these are only prominent instances in an endless chain of religious rebellions that spread across the pages of Chinese history for two thousand years.

In the Ch'ing period, religious rebellions crowded the records of every decade after the middle of the eighteenth century. Military operations of that dynasty were marked by two major types of campaigns, one the expeditions to the borderlands against non-Chinese peoples in the earlier part of the dynasty, and the other the suppression of religious revolts during the latter half of the dynasty. Except for several uprisings, such as that of the twice-renegade Wu San-kuei, when the dynasty was still struggling to establish itself, very few political rebellions of any appreciable proportion were totally unconnected with some religious element or organization. This broad historical outline is significant, for it indicates the intimate relation between religious forces and political movements, arising from the domestic population, which seriously weakened the dynastic rule and finally helped to bring about its collapse.

The vast complexity of the religious rebellions in the Ch'ing period defies summary here, and it must suffice to consider a few prominent examples. The reign of Emperor Ch'ien Lung, the climax of the dynasty's power and glory, was marred by repeated religious rebellions, such as the uprisings of the White Lotus (also known as the Incense Smelling and the White Yang) sect in 1774, the Eight Diagrams and the Nine Mansions sects in 1786–1788, the Heaven and Earth society in 1786–1789, and the re-emergence of the White Lotus forces in 1794, which spread over nine provinces and took eight years to suppress, seriously sapping the government's strength and marking the beginning of the dynasty's decline.

The nineteenth century was marked by three major domestic events, all dealing heavy blows at the dynastic power. The century started with the great rebellion of the Eight Diagrams or T'ien Li (Celestial Principle) sect in 1813, which followed closely upon the heels of the temporary pacification of the White Lotus revolt. The middle of the century saw the dynasty shaken to its foundations by the great explosion of the Taiping Rebellion, the first major religious uprising to derive its inspiration from a European religion. The century ended with the development of the Boxers' association, which began as a domestic opposition movement but was diverted by the Empress Dowager against foreign powers in the Boxer Rebellion of 1900. In between these three leading events were a continuous series of local revolts by religious societies in every part of the empire.

The political nature of these religious revolts, large or small, can hardly be denied. An Imperial decree gave what seemed to be an accurate analysis of the Eight Diagrams Rebellion of 1813: "In normal times, the [Eight Diagrams or Celestial Principle] Society was engaged in daily worship of the sun and reciting scripture, claiming thereby to make its members invulnerable to weapons, fire, or drowning; and, in times of famine and disorder, they might plot for the 'great enterprise.' " This appears to characterize the course of development of many religious societies in China. In times of peace and order, the organizations would gather a following through their salvational activities, and in times of widespread suffering and disorder, they would emerge to try their hand at the "great enterprise." The "great enterprise" (*ta shih*) referred to the founding of a new dynasty. The Eight Diagrams insurrectionists broke into the Forbidden City in Peking, aiming at nothing less than capturing the throne. Further back, in the early seventeenth century, the White Lotus sect leader, Hsü Hung-ju, assumed for himself the title of Chung-hsing Fu-lieh Ti, or the Renaissance Great-Blessedness Emperor, at the height of his bid for power, which ended in his execution.

Other religious rebellions were more modest in their attempts, but were nonetheless involved in unmistakable political action. In 1834, the persecution of the T'ien-chu Chiao (Celestial Bamboo) religion in Honan province was based mainly on the discovery of weapons, gunpowder, and some rebellious-sounding documents in the house of the leader of the sect. In

1835, the persecution against the Hsien T'ien (Prebirth) sect was prompted by the discovery of an alleged plot of rebellion, and one branch of the sect in Shansi province did briefly occupy the county city of Chao-ch'eng, burn the government office buildings, liberate all the prisoners from the county jail, attack a post station near the city, and take the postal horses. In 1837, in the eastern part of Shantung province, a religious leader, Ma Kang, and a large number of his fellow sectarians met death at the hands of the law partly because they had attacked the county city of Wei Hsien, killed the magistrate, and liberated prisoners from the county jail.

From here, as the tide of rebellion rolled on toward the great Taiping explosion, local religious uprisings became more numerous. These local revolts repeated a classic pattern: killing the local magistrate, burning government buildings, and freeing prisoners from the county jail as a symbol of rectifying the injustices of misgovernment. At times even some Chinese local police and Manchu soldiers would cast their lot with the rebels. Religious sects were rife in the 1840s in the mountainous territory bordering upon the southern provinces of Hunan, Kweichow, Kwangsi, and Kwangtung, a territory long troubled by armed local bands that defied the authorities, and an area destined to become the home base of the powerful Taiping rebels. By 1850, leaders of religious sects counted among them such colorful titles as the "Great King of Red Heaven" in Honan, the "Great King of Red Earth" in Szechwan, and the "Great King of Red Mankind" in Kwangtung. The Taiping revolt, therefore, was but the climax of a half century of widespread political action by religious societies that blanketed every part of the Ch'ing empire at a time when dynastic strength was on the decline.

After the Taiping revolt there was a respite of two or three decades when religious uprisings tapered off in frequency. But toward the end of the nineteenth century, politically rebellious religious sects were again on the march. The Boxer movement raged in the north, while in the south smoldering elements of the Triad society and the Heaven and Earth society, once among the basic forces of the Taipings, were rekindling political resistance and contributing their underground systems to the revolutionay movement that brought the end of the Ch'ing Dynasty.

Under the Republic, the chaotic 1920s saw the rise of the Red Spear and the Big Sword societies in North China, offering their members magical invulnerability to firearms and resisting the provincial authorities. In Shantung province, Ma Shih-wei led the I-hsin T'ien-tao Lung-hua Sheng-chiao Hui (the Single-Hearted Celestial Principle Dragon-Flower Sacred Religion Society), and set himself up as Emperor until the local warlord, Han Fu-ch'ü, finally crushed his organization in 1930 and drove him off to the then Japanese-occupied city of Dairen in Liaoning province. In the long Japanese occupation of China during World War II, one of the many White Lotus ramifications, the I-kuan Tao (Unity sect), re-emerged, becoming a nationwide movement that has had varied political implications. The Communist regime started its rule with a series of persecutions against religious societies, the I-kuan Tao being one of the main objects for elimination. As late as 1956, the Communist government was still pursuing an active campaign against a host of religious sects operating around the central theme of *pien t'ien* or "changing Heaven," that is, changing the ruling power.

The persistent association of religious movements with political rebellions in the Ch'ing period resulted in a popular attitude which regarded all heterodox religious organizations as politically dangerous. This traditional attitude partly accounts for the Communist government's crusade against all sectarian societies. As pointed out, many sectarian groups were nonpolitical in nature, and the government's persecution of them was based not on finding rebellious intention or action but on the age-old fear that, given a politically ambitious leadership in troubled times, such groups could easily become instrumental in rebellion. Whatever the motivation, constant government suppression reinforced the popular attitude concerning the political nature of sectarian organizations.

The opposition between institutional religion and the government grew out of an inherent conflict between the two parties in an authoritarian political tradition. As indicated in the last chapter, the government considered that the established social and political order was threatened by heterodox movements with dissenting social and political orientations. The Buddhist organization before the tenth century clearly presented such a threat, though it never resorted to large-scale armed resistance. Through the expansion of its monastic orders and its creed of universal salvation, it hoped eventually to replace the existing world order. Buddhist undermining of the Confucian social and economic order reached appreciable proportions during its periods of successful organized development, such as between the third and the tenth centuries and during the Liao rule in north China. Confucian statesmen, for whom the study of historical lessons always constituted an important part of their intellectual orientation, were wary of a repetition of the same situation if they countenanced a similar organized growth of other heterodox movements.

Under the traditional authoritarian control and repeated persecutions, heterodox religious movements which did not win a legally recognized position like that of Buddhism and Taoism were forced to seek cover, and frequently were ready to offer armed resistance to the ever present threat of suppression in order to develop their own forms of religious life. Secrecy and readiness to resist suppression were particularly necessary for religious sects that aimed at universal salvation, as their doctrine usually claimed superior power for their deities over the world order—a dogma that was obviously offensive to the authoritarian temporal power, which would tolerate no superior doctrine other than the accepted orthodoxy.

The assumption of spiritual superiority over the temporal power is clearly illustrated in the reason given by the modern I-kuan Tao (Unity sect) in its refusal to register with the government as required by Republican law in the 1930s and 1940s. An instruction to its membership stated:

> . . . we all are [Unbegotten] Mother's children, and the officials in the government are also her children. How

can there be any reason for the Mother to register with
her children? Ch'u Min-i [an important Nationalist figure]
is already converted, and all the other prominent officials
are also fated to be converted sooner or later. . . .

Under the Ch'ing Dynasty, such a document would undoubtedly
have been regarded as an expression of rebellious intentions,
thus bringing persecution and possible armed resistance. The
claim of the superior power of certain deities to control the
world order was made by most of the leading sects in the
Ch'ing period, as will be considered in the following discussion
on salvation and prophecy.

But not all religious rebellions were the result of political
oppression and the necessity to defend a chosen way of religious
life. Political cause or ambition was clearly an integral part of
many sectarian movements, as is shown by the repeated efforts
of the White Lotus sect to overthrow the Ch'ing Dynasty and
to restore the Ming house. Other sects began as purely religious movements but turned into open rebellion when troubled
times presented favorable opportunities for political struggle.
The Taiping Rebellion seems to fall into this category. Still
other sects exhibited a dominant political character at the very
beginning, as shown by the many sects in which the leaders assumed the titles of emperors and kings, distributed official ranks
among their followers, used official government seals, and included military tactical books in their religious literature.

Whatever the basic cause of rebellion, the important fact
remains that at least during the Ch'ing period most of the leading political opposition movements were linked with religious
societies.

SOCIAL SETTING OF RELIGIOUS REBELLION

In what social settings were religious rebellions most likely to
rise? One obvious setting was persecution by the authoritarian
government. Persecution could provoke many a purely religious

organization into armed resistance. And, under an authoritarian government, many otherwise purely political movements were forced to operate in disguise as religious enterprises, ending in the form of religious rebellion. The Eight Diagrams Rebellion at the beginning of the nineteenth century represented the former, and rebellions led by the Great Kings of Red Heaven, Red Earth, and Red Mankind in the 1840s were illustrations of the latter. During the Republican period, heterodox religious movements thrived in many parts of the country, but the removal of the anti-heretic law and the relaxation of government control of religion resulted in a far smaller number of religious rebellions than during a similar length of time in the latter part of the Ch'ing rule.

In addition to the authoritarian setting, there was the important factor of social crisis arising from the inadequacy of the existing institutions to meet the needs of the people. A religious rebellion was basically a collective effort by a group to introduce or to force a change in the existing social or political order. In this respect, religious rebellions might resemble other movements of social reform or revolution; when the established social and political order failed to provide a solution for a critical situation, and when the people were at a loss as to what to do, religious movements rose to improvise an answer which would cause a situation of conflict with the government.

In other cases, a public crisis which the government had failed to cope with would provide a politically dormant religious organization with the opportune moment to develop its political ambitions through open rebellion. The official Ch'ing comment on the Eight Diagrams Rebellion (cited previously) made an accurate observation when it remarked that the sect was engaged in religious activities in normal times, but plotted for great political enterprise in times of famine and disorder.

Economic hardship and disaster constituted a frequent type of crisis that bred religious movements and rebellions. Famine due to crop failure was a recurrent crisis typical of an agricultural society, leading to many forms of mass action. We may say that no major politico-religious upheaval in Chinese history was without some form of extensive agricultural crisis as a backdrop.

Instances of this kind were too frequent to enumerate, but we may name a few examples. The area adjoining the three northern provinces of Honan, Shantung, and Hopei was traditionally a hotbed of sectarian movements in modern times, and it was also an area of recurrent famines because of its geographical location, which subjected it to frequent rain failure and flood damage. Famine was never out of sight in the areas affected by the series of rebellions of the White Lotus and the T'ien Li sects in the closing years of the eighteenth and the early years of the nineteenth century. The rebellion of the Hsien T'ien (Prebirth) sect in the northern part of Hopei came in 1835, a year described in an official document as one when "not a drop of rain had fallen there, and all the people were in a state of agitation, anguish, and dismay, thus prepared at any moment to be stirred up by evil-brewers." The Taiping uprising arose in a mountainous southern region where tillable land was limited and the struggle for a livelihood always hard, and came at a time when famines due to drought had struck frequently.

In the hilly districts of Hunan province, where a host of rebellious groups arose in 1851 to join the sweeping Taiping uprising, the sectarian organizations bore such descriptive names as the Straw Plaiters' sect, the Grass Cutters' sect, and the Firewood Gatherers' sect. These were among the poorest occupations, and the rise of religious sects among them indicated critical economic difficulty for the lowest stratum of the population in that troubled province. Similar situations occurred even in recent decades. In the 1920s, for instance, the Red Spear society in Honan and Shantung provinces emerged from the background of a series of famines.

In addition to economic crises, there were political crises of disorder, excessive oppression, and extortion by corrupt officials, making a normal life extremely difficult. In the face of destruction by war and banditry at times when the weakened and corrupt government could no longer maintain peace and order, religious societies often turned into armed groups to help make a semblance of normal life possible. Such political crises were frequently the derivative effect of serious economic difficulties, which then led to the rise of banditry and religious sects, and these in turn offered an opportunity for the corrupt government to extort money and labor from the people, thus deepening the crisis.

This was the background of the White Lotus Rebellion in the early years of the nineteenth century, as was pointed out in the well-known Memorial on the Suppression of Heretic Sects (*Cheng Hsieh-chiao Su*) by Hung Liang-chi. "After the bandits left, the officials came. After the burning and pillaging by the bandits, there was oppression from the officials." Even a decree from Emperor Tao Kuang admitted "it was extortion by local officials that goaded the people into rebellion." Using the arrest of sectarian members as a threat, local officials and police extorted money from the people. "Whether or not an arrest was to be made depended only on the willingness or refusal to pay, and not on actual participation in sectarian worship." In different localities of Hupeh and Szechwan provinces, where the White Lotus Rebellion originated, "thousands of innocent people were implicated."

A similar picture lay behind the Taiping Rebellion half a century later.

> . . . The government grew increasingly degenerate, and corrupt officials infested the land. . . . The provinces of Kwangtung, Kwangsi, Yünnan and Kweichow [home territory of the rebellion] were struck frequently by famine due to drought, and the people lacked food and clothing. Yet the officials kept oppressing and extorting them. Adventurous elements were thus forced to turn to banditry. Innocent people suffered from corrupt officials above them and from the bandits around them; they could not maintain their livelihood and became homeless drifting migrants . . . Thus rose the Pao-liang Kung-fei Hui [Society for

Protecting the Innocent and Attacking the Bandits, the forerunner of the Taiping movement] to answer the need of the time.

ORTHODOXY, "DEVIATING ORIENTATION," AND THE SALVATION MOVEMENTS

From widespread suffering in overwhelming crises arose the eagerness for salvation in this and in the next life. Two courses appeared to be open: following the beaten path of the orthodox sociopolitical order, or contriving a divergent plan. In which direction lay salvation for the tortured populace? The government, fearing the rise of heterodox movements as a result of the crises, firmly admonished the people that their salvation lay not in incredible magic and visionary talk but in observing the established law and order and continuing their faith in orthodoxy.

The imperial decree of 1724 set the tone for many edicts during the Ch'ing period. In suppressing the Eight Diagrams Rebellion in 1813, Emperor Chia-ch'ing pontificated: beyond the Confucian social and moral principles, "no so-called religion exists, and outside the principles of nature and the laws of the ruler, happiness may not be sought after; happiness proceeds from complying with orthodoxy, and misfortune from following heresy." Again in 1835, an imperial edict forbidding the forming of pilgrim organizations ordered the officials to explain to the people that it was ignorance to assume that the worshiping of [heretic] gods would bring blessing and protection but that, through contentment with one's own occupation, blessing would be obtained.

Amid economic and political crises that condemned millions of people to starvation and misery, such admonitions were hollow, impractical, unrealistic. What people in a crisis were facing was the exact opposite of the enjoyment of "trouble-free days of universal peace." The practice of filial piety to parents and fidelity to the ruler, and the exertion of the utmost effort—all these, which brought blessing in normal times, were of no avail to a people gripped by an overpowering crisis. And even as the people knew well that blessing might be obtained by following one's own occupation with diligence and content-ment, the chaos and destruction in a crisis made it impossible for a large number of people to pursue this course.

The sociopolitical order based on the Confucian orthodoxy had proven its efficacy in periods of established peace and tran-quility, but during an economic and political crisis the call of heresy gained an immediate audience. When the orthodox path led nowhere, it was logical and natural that the people would look in a different direction for deliverance. Herein lay the magical appeal of heresy. In Chinese, heresy or heterodoxy was expressed by two characters, *i-tuan*, meaning *deviating orienta-tion.* Hence, "deviating orientation" as a salvational path may be regarded as a normal product of an extensive social crisis. With the traditional antagonism to heterodoxy, this deviating path led to collision with the authorities and often to armed rebellion.

The rise of heterodox religious movements was often at-tributed to the "earthly character" of the Confucian orthodoxy, which left a spiritual void. While there is truth in this inter-pretation, there are also decided limitations in its application to the rise of religious movements, particularly of the politically rebellious type. It is important to note that times of extensive crises saw the greatest development of religion in Chinese his-tory. Aside from the modern period mentioned above, there was the classic example of the four centuries of continuous economic and political chaos, from the third to the sixth cen-turies, which saw the greatest organized development of new religions in China. In both modern and ancient periods of great crisis, the Confucian orthodoxy failed to meet not only the spiritual need but also the basic material need of security and sustenance.

✦ China's First Inland Revolution

NO SINGLE event in the nineteenth century so shook China as the Taiping Rebellion (1850–1864). A movement which as late as 1849 the Ch'ing had regarded as a local nuisance by 1853 had occupied Nanking, much of Central and South China, and threatened the Manchu court in Peking. Far from being another of China's perennial peasant revolts, the Taiping movement had ideology and organization, preaching the overthrow of the existing order, the transformation of society, equality of all men, sharing of all property. From a small band of Hakka followers the Taiping leader Hung Hsiu-ch'üan created one of the most disciplined and effective military forces China had ever known. In the rebellion's early years the Taipings won battle after battle against their demoralized Imperial opponents. In 1853 they proclaimed the "Heavenly Kingdom of Great Peace," with its capital in Nanking, where the Ming Dynasty first established its rule.

Though commonly called "rebellion" in the West, the Taiping movement was a revolution, as Wolfgang Franke, Professor of History at the University of Malaya in Kuala Lumpur, notes. Had it been directed only against the Manchus, like earlier Ming restoration movements or like Sun Yat-sen's Revolutionary Party, the gentry might have rallied to it and it might have succeeded. But then it would only have been another of China's many dynastic changes. The Taipings were determined instead to eradicate the most basic elements of traditional Chinese society: the gentry—officials, scholars, landlords—and the Confucian ethos on which their authority rested.

The Taiping Rebellion shattered the image of eternal China. Karl Marx wrote, on January 31, 1850: "It is to be rejoiced at that the most ancient and stable empire in the world . . . is on the eve of a social upheaval which, in any case, must have extremely important results for civilization." Europe had just gone through the trauma of the 1848 revolutions, and like the Russian Revolution, which burst out seventy years later, the revolution in China came at a time when Europeans felt that the fires of revolt were dying out. The Western powers were ambivalent about the new movement, for while the Taipings' Christian ideology aroused sympathy, their revolutionary extremism made Westerners fearful that a new China might emerge to threaten their privileges. By the late 1850s Britain and France had cast their lot with the Manchu Dynasty.

The Taipings' utopian and socialist ideological doctrines were not unique; one could find similar doctrines in the eighteenth-century Buddhist revolts and even earlier. What was surprising is that these doctrines were tied to Christianity, an alien religion of only short history in southern China. Using foreign theory and traditional revolutionary practice, the Taipings achieved a degree of success unmatched by any of their predecessors in China. In the following selection Wolfgang Franke, a well-known German Sinologist who has resided in China for many years, notes the surprising similarities between the Taipings and the twentieth-century Communists.

With the Taipings the inland revolution of peasants against the gentry became one of the main social processes in the transformation of traditional Chinese society. Though unsuccessful, the causes of the upheaval remained latent until the Communists rediscovered them in the late 1920s.

WOLFGANG FRANKE *
The Taiping Rebellion

Hung Hsiu-ch'üan, leader of the Taiping Rebellion, was born into a poor peasant Hakka family in the South Chinese province of Kwangtung on January 1, 1814. In the fourth century A.D. the Hakkas (*i.e.,* "guest settlers") started to migrate from North China to Kwangtung and Kwangsi, where they formed an ethnic group whose number, including those who later emigrated to Southeast Asia, is estimated today to be about twenty million. The Hakkas, who spoke a special dialect and whose customs and habits differentiated them from the original inhabitants against whom they carried out a difficult struggle for survival, were considered brave and tough, with a strongly nationalistic spirit directed against Manchu domination.

Thus it is hardly surprising that Hung Hsiu-ch'üan and other Taiping leaders were Hakkas. Because he was a very gifted child, Hung's family, through great economic sacrifice, enabled him to go to school, but only through his fourteenth year. He studied as best he could on his own, and until 1843 he was a village teacher. Several times he took the state examinations—the passing of which was a pre-condition for entrance into a bureaucratic career and the only possibility of social mobility—but he failed.

In 1837, in Canton, a Christian-Protestant Mission Chinese-language pamphlet accidentally came into his hands; he looked through it without giving it much thought. In 1838, exceedingly disappointed and embittered by again failing to pass the state examinations, Hung suffered a psychotic episode, said to have lasted forty days, in which he lost consciousness

* Franz Schurmann, trans., Wolfgang Franke, *Das Jahrhundert Der Chinesischen Revolution 1851–1949* (München: R. Oldenbourg, 1958), pp. 47–64.

and had visions in which an old man appeared to him as his father and the old man's son appeared as his elder brother. Upon his recovery he reread the Mission pamphlet more carefully, after which he believed that his visions had been of God and Jesus Christ; Hung now saw himself as the son of God and the younger brother of Jesus Christ, chosen at God's command for a special mission: to destroy the demons on earth and establish the Kingdom of God. This constituted a practical pretext for overthrowing the Manchu Dynasty and the existing political system and for creating a new social order; thus, the Kingdom of God was brought down to earth.

From the propaganda pamphlet Hung could obviously have had only a superficial idea of Christianity, and even the two-month Christian education he got from an American missionary in Canton in 1847 could hardly have given him a deeper understanding. Thus, to him, Christianity was mostly the worship of a single God and the rejection of other gods, including the traditional Chinese ancestor worship. He knew the Ten Commandments, and though he believed that Christ forgave sins and crimes and could help one become a good person and enter Heaven after death, Hung's concepts derived mainly from the Old Testament; he knew neither the New Testament's deeper ideas nor the true Christian ethic. The real impact of his religion was on the idols of other religions, including the Confucian ancestor tablets: Hung and his disciples wrote "God" on a piece of paper and knelt in front of it, burned incense, lighted candles, and used sacramental wine and foods.

Whether or not Hung actually had visions is of only secondary importance to the development of the Chinese Revolution, but as non-Chinese Christian thoughts propagated by Western missionaries in China, they were quite important to the revolutionary movement from its beginning. It is possible that the visions were created for political purposes, but independent sources, some rather early, write of them, thus indicating that they actually did happen, and they do fit well with Hung's known psychopathic character.

We can describe only briefly the course of the revolution.

In 1847 Hung and his collaborators, calling themselves God-Worshipers, gathered thousands of disciples around them, mostly poor, miserable peasants from the Hakka as well as from the non-Chinese Miao and Yao tribes. The movement's center was the "Thistle Mountains" (Tzu-chin Shan) north of Kuei-p'ing in the eastern part of Kwangsi. Other bands, among them the members of anti-Manchu secret societies—Triad, Heaven and Earth, and so on—had formed in the same region, and after losing battles to Hung's followers, joined them. Thus, the combining of religious elements (Hung Hsiu-ch'üan's pseudo-Christian ideals) with nationalist elements (the anti-Manchu movement) and social elements (uprisings of land-less and destitute peasants) constituted the Taiping Rebellion's point of departure.

The real revolution, open rebellion, began in the summer of 1850. All God-Worshipers were called upon to undertake armed resistance against government troops, and in order to bind the movement's followers tightly to the leadership, their homes were burned and movable goods were made common property. This primitive communism gained for the movement considerable support from the Hakka, who lived in grinding poverty, and in a short time the movement's numbers had swelled to about ten thousand. By the following autumn the movement had grown rapidly, and Hung Hsiu-ch'üan, regarded as the leader chosen by God, was unanimously proclaimed "Heavenly King" (*T'ien-wang*) in the "Heavenly Kingdom of Great Peace" (*T'ai-p'ing t'ien-kuo*)—hence the name Taiping Rebellion.

The first year of the new dynasty supposed to replace the Manchu Dynasty was 1851. All followers of the movement adopted the pre-Manchu clothing and hair styles, and cut off the queue, which the Manchus had introduced obligatorily into China; since they let their hair grow on their foreheads, which Manchu rules had required to be shaven, the Imperial government's documents call them the Long-Hair Rebels. Also in that year, five other leaders received the title of King (*Wang*), though remaining subordinate to Hung Hsiu-ch'üan, the Heavenly King: Yang Hsiu-ch'ing, a charcoal-burner; Feng Yün-shan, like Hung a village teacher and a faith-healer; Hsiao Ch'ao-kuei, a poor peasant; Wei Ch'ang-hui, a businessman; Shih Ta-k'ai, a rich peasant. Wei and Shih came from relatively good families, and all except the charcoal-burner had some education; but none actually belonged to the gentry class. Their first disciples were several thousand poor Hakka peasants, several hundred charcoal-burners, thousands of mine workers, and a considerable number of former pirates who had been chased from the sea by foreign warships. There were even a few businessmen, rich peasants, and learned people in the movement, as well as deserters from the government and coolies from Canton who had lost their jobs as a result of the Opium War.

The Taipings' power grew rapidly. In the summer of 1852 they abandoned their base at Kwangsi and moved northward toward Hunan, where they were joined by a large number of impoverished peasants and followers of other revolts. From Hunan the main force moved toward Hupei down the Yangtze, and after an eleven-day siege in the spring of 1853 captured Nanking, southern capital of the Ming Dynasty, where the Heavenly King established his residence. When the Taipings moved an army northward with the aim of capturing Peking, there was great panic, and the government made preparations to move the capital to the Manchu rulers' summer residence in Jehol. It seemed as if the Taipings would soon occupy all of China, but because of their insufficient preparations the revolutionary army was able to reach only the area south of Tientsin. Their communications lines to the rear did not function; they had no cavalry; soldiers from the South were unused to the rough North Chinese food and cold winters. Thus the northward push failed. Another army moved westward in order to secure Taiping domination in Kiangsi, Anhwei, Hupei, and Hunan, where Tseng Kuo-fan arose as an opponent who blocked the revolution's further expansion and was ultimately to play a major role in its suppression.

The revolution could not sustain a fever pitch of power and

action, inwardly or outwardly. In 1856 a severe internal crisis developed in Nanking, and as a consequence of its bloody results some of the movement's most important leaders, their followers, and twenty or thirty thousand other people died. With this the rebellion's offensive ended; in the following years it could be only defensive. Despite increasing corruption and disintegration in the Heavenly King's Nanking court, until 1864 some powerful military leaders were able to achieve some successes and resist the enemy, who was moving ever closer to Nanking.

When the city fell in the summer of 1864, the rebellion's fate was sealed. The fame for its suppression went mostly to Tseng Kuo-fan and his army. Tseng, a stern Confucian, had trained his troops in Hunan in the best traditional Confucian spirit; hence there had developed a struggle between two ideologies—the traditional Chinese Confucian against the foreign pseudo-Christian. Tseng was a Chinese scholar, originally a civil official, and an honest person; thus it was possible for him, despite all the corruption of the Manchu Dynasty and the government of Peking, to instill in his troops a superb fighting spirit. Despite severe setbacks, his counter-revolution was to be victorious. His attempts to re-establish the traditional order— known as the T'ung-chih Restoration, named after the Emperor T'ung-chih who came to power in 1862—were models for the future, particularly for Chiang Kai-shek. There have been recent criticisms of Tseng for using his power for the salvation of an alien, reactionary, and corrupt dynasty instead of for having espoused the cause of the Chinese against foreign and domestic oppressors. Tseng certainly represented the interests of the landholding Hunan gentry, which strongly resisted the Taipings' revolutionary program—indeed, he had been able to set up and maintain his army only because of the material and spiritual support of the Hunan gentry—but his critics do not see his problem from his perspective. His struggle against the Taipings was in defense of traditional Chinese culture and a struggle of Confucianism against the foreign Christianity imported from the West. Other counter-revolutionary leaders than Tseng played an important role in the rebellion's suppression, particularly Li Hung-chang and Tso Tsung-t'ang, both of whom were Chinese rather than Manchu.

The so-called Ever Victorious Army, which consisted of Chinese, European, and especially American mercenaries under foreign leadership, primarily the well-known Englishman Charles George Gordon, was an important factor. England and France, initially friendly toward the Taipings, later favored the Manchu Dynasty and began to give it major support, particularly through the Ever Victorious Army, whose official commander was Li Hung-chang. It has often been said that the foreign powers had become disillusioned about the revolution's Christian aims; actually their reasons were less idealistic than imperialistic. England and France feared that if the Taipings were victorious, the concessions and advantages gained from the Manchu Dynasty through the Treaty of Tientsin (1858) would be lost, especially the significant military reparations and the important profits from the opium trade. In addition, the Taipings followed a much more nationalistic policy than the weak Manchus and behaved more resolutely toward the foreigners. The foreign powers' favored position in China was also very closely tied in with the fate of the Manchu Dynasty.

THE TAIPINGS' REVOLUTIONARY ACTIONS

Many of the Taiping Rebellion's principles and actions constituted a direct break with China's traditions, and provided stimuli and models for Sun Yat-sen and the Kuomintang, as well as for the May Fourth Movement and for the Communists. From Christianity the Taipings took the idea of equality of all people, thus explaining to some extent some of their social program's particularly revolutionary points. But traditional Chinese thought also played an important role. The administrative organization, for example, including the officials' names, was taken from the *Ritual of Chou,* a third- or fourth-century B.C. work describing the state organization of the Chou Dynasty (*ca.* 1050–255 B.C.). With regard to the Taipings' primitive communism, it is hard to decide whether Christian ideas or descriptions of the primeval condition of humanity in early Chinese and particularly Taoist writings had greater influence.

The most important points of the Taipings' revolutionary program may be listed as follows:

Common property. There was no private property; instead there were a common bank and granary from which appropriations were made for weddings, births, and funerals of individual members of the community.

Land reform program. All land was divided into nine categories of quality; in amounts varying with the quality, land was distributed equally to the population according to the number of people involved, for their use but not as freely disposable property. Men and women were treated as equals, children under age sixteen got half the amount. Everyone could take from the harvest only what he needed for his subsistence, and everything else went into the common granary; other agricultural as well as handicraft products were divided in the same way. There are no reliable accounts to indicate that the system was ever actually implemented practically in a particular area, for in so short a time such a thorough revamping of the whole agricultural system could have been realized only in a very restricted area, if at all. But the theory goes far beyond even the Communist government's agrarian reforms. It is known that the existing agrarian and tax system was retained in such areas as Chekiang and Kiangsu, but the taxes collected by the Taipings were lower than those taken by the Imperial government, thus considerably lightening the peasants' burdens. But as long as there were taxes, the agrarian reform movement could not really be carried out, because taxes would then no longer have been necessary. As a counter-measure, during the battles in the Yangtze Valley, the Imperial government tried to keep taxes down in order to win over the population.

The position of women. Aside from possible matriarchal relationships in the earliest period, women in traditional Chinese society were subordinate in every respect to men. The equality of men and women, carried out by the Taipings, was an unprecedented revolutionary act of great importance. Women, like men, now could take the state examinations and could hold civil or military offices; there were special female contingents in the Taiping army. Foot binding, so common among the higher classes since the twelfth century, was strictly forbidden, as was prostitution; white slavery and rape were punished by death. Monogamy was obligatory; women and girls who did not have the protection of male family members were particularly taken care of. Women were required to marry, and marriage was to rest not on a financial arrangement between families, as in the past, but on love between the two partners; even so, it sometimes happened that couples were married against their will, by officials; a Western church-marriage ceremony was introduced.

Abstinence. Opium, tobacco, and alcohol were strictly prohibited, but the prohibition, according to available reports, was not always strictly observed, particularly in later periods. But in the area controlled by the Taipings the prohibition against opium was carried through in the early years, not only in theory but in practice.

Iconoclasm. The Taipings' pseudo-Christianity was strictly monotheistic and intolerant toward other religions, though it borrowed many elements of Confucianism, Taoism, and Buddhism. The revolutionaries destroyed pictures, statues, and temples of Buddhism and Taoism, and did not shrink even before Confucian ancestor tablets. Their iconoclasm provided a valuable weapon to their enemies.

Treatment of foreigners. Because of Christian influence the Taipings regarded all people as equal and did not regard the Chinese as a chosen people. They were hostile to Catholics, and although friendly to a degree to Protestants, they did not allow Protestant missionaries to travel in the country and preach, since they regarded themselves as possessing the true doctrine and were convinced that they were best able to propagate it. The Taipings demanded that the foreigners in their area of domination subject themselves to Chinese jurisdiction, whereas they had received extraterritoriality from the Imperial government. The Taipings, with their marked nationalist attitude, were for international equality, and did not want to surrender any national Chinese rights, as did the Imperial government, albeit under force.

Calendar reform. The traditional Chinese calendar, which is in use even today and on most calendars still appears next to the official Western calendar, was a lunar calendar. The Taipings introduced an entirely new calendar—similar to the Julian calendar officially introduced in the twentieth century—with a seven-day week and a Sunday, and which constitutes a combination of solar and lunar calendar.

Literary reform. By loosening the highly traditional literary style and making it closer to the spoken and colloquial language, the Taipings were the pioneers for the later great literary reform.

REASONS FOR THE TAIPING REBELLION'S SUCCESS AND DOWNFALL

To understand the Taipings better within the framework of the entire Chinese Revolution, let us list briefly the reasons for their initial success and later downfall. These are the most important reasons for their success:

As we have indicated, the Taipings had a clear, unified, religious-political-social idea, in which they were indoctrinated and for which they fought. Buddhism, Taoism, Confucianism, opium smoking, gambling, whoring, and so on; or more personally, a rotten dynasty, with its corrupt officials and ruthless landlords—these the Taipings regarded as the Devil's representatives on earth who had to be extirpated. They saw as their divine task the creation of a heaven on earth for the blessing of all; this held them together and for this they risked their lives. On the other side, the government troops who opposed the rebellion in the early years were a ragtag mercenary band with no common ideal.

The rebels were militarily superbly organized. Like the troops, the leaders of the individual troop contingents regarded themselves as servants for the common idea and cooperated excellently. Women and children did not remain at home but followed the army separately, which helped assure the soldiers' loyalty. The government troops, on the contrary, were badly organized, and their leaders were suspicious and envious of each other, without any desire to cooperate.

The revolutionary army had superb discipline; they had a series of rigidly enforced commandments for officers and men, for example: participation in religious ceremonies, strict obedience, cooperation, absolute loyalty (treason and desertion were punished by death), bravery, moral character (*e.g.*, propertylessness), abstinence (from opium, alcohol, tobacco, gambling). The government troops were undisciplined and degenerate; they burned, plundered, raped, and killed ruthlessly, whether foe or friend.

The Taiping leaders were able strategists whose military technique was particularly admired by the Chinese Communists, who emulated them. Its particular character consisted in hitting the opponent at his weak points, but avoiding strong, well-fortified positions, and as much as possible misleading him. Even the "fifth column" played an important role. Favorable for the rebels, furthermore, was the general situation already described. The poorly armed and badly equipped revolutionaries were thus able, through better morale, discipline, and organization, to defeat the better armed and equipped government troops. The same phenomena could be observed in the case of most Chinese revolutionary movements in their early successful stages, most recently in the fight between Communists and Nationalists (*i.e.*, the government troops).

These traits characterized mainly the Taiping movement's early period. Gradually, step by step, changes occurred which led finally to the rebellion's failure and downfall. Let us list the main reasons for this:

As in the case of almost all Chinese dynasties or in the case of only partially successful revolts against the existing order, the moral decay of the Taipings' elite stratum constituted the main reason for their final downfall. Shortly after the capture of Nanking the Heavenly King and other leaders, against all commandments of the revolutionary movement, began a life of excesses—high living, luxury, many concubines. Decay at the top naturally was contagious to those in the lower echelons.

The Taiping movement initially had a clear-cut revolutionary and anti-traditional character. Gradually, however, it became infected with many traditional vices. Several different groups and cliques of local origins appeared, fighting one another for power—an old Chinese evil from way back, something that even today has not entirely disappeared. The main roles were played by a Kwangtung and a Kwangsi clique. For those from other provinces it was very difficult to get into the higher and more influential positions; nepotism began to spread. Eventually, close cooperation between the different leaders, such as had been characteristic of the Taipings' early period, no longer existed. Following the example of the Heavenly King, the other Taiping leaders also wished to lead a luxurious life, for which they needed considerable private property. Thus they violated the prescriptions concerning common property and appropriated for themselves the living habits of the very gentry they had fought.

As the Taipings increasingly lost their revolutionary élan, important reforms were carried out on the other side. We have already mentioned that Tseng Kuo-fan and others understood how to build up the local militias, set up by the gentry for self-protection, into a new, well-trained, well-organized army, which gradually gained dominance over the increasingly demoralized rebels. Whereas earlier many commanders were directly subject to the Imperial government and had hardly any contact with each other, let alone cooperated, now Tseng Kuofan became the leader of a great army; his subcommanders were personally loyal to him, and had direct connection with neither the government nor the court in Peking. This change meant a voluntary renunciation of power by the Manchu Dynasty, agreed to only under the threatening attack of the Taipings. Tseng Kuo-fan was the ancestor of the later "war lords"; from this time on, troops were subject not to the Emperor and the central government but to individual marshals, like Tseng Kuo-fan, Li Hung-chang, Tso Tsung-t'ang, and later Yüan Shih-k'ai. After the fall of the Manchu Dynasty, all political power passed to the "war lords."

Many of the earlier Taiping leaders had died in the coup of 1856. With the extension of the rebellion's domain, an increasingly greater number of able individuals were needed for leadership positions, yet everywhere they were lacking; moreover, the Heavenly King showed himself to be increasingly limited and stubborn, unwilling to take advice from anyone. Many able individuals thus went over to the government side. Most of the Taipings' officers and men were illiterate, and they did little to educate, teach, or train capable forces.

Though many supporters of the anti-Manchu revolt movement initially joined the Taipings, the latter did not know how to get along with these other, different revolt movements. Neither the revolutionary Triad society (which occupied Shanghai between 1853 and 1855) nor the peasant rebellions (known as the Nien-fei Rebellion) in the border areas of Shantung, Kiangsu, Anhwei, Honan, and North Hupei provinces had any direct connection with the Taipings. Thus, the different revolt movements remained independent of each other, enabling the other side to destroy them one by one.

As already mentioned, the Western powers' final advocacy of the Manchu Dynasty, which came about at the end of the 1850s and supplanted their initial ambivalence, made the revolutionaries' situation particularly difficult through arms shipments to the Manchus and through the support given them by the Ever Victorious Army.

The learned stratum of China was still strictly Confucianist and bitterly opposed to revolutionary ideas. Since the Taipings' ideas were very much ahead of their time, an inept leadership did not help to popularize them among the Chinese people.

The reasons for the rise and fall of the Taipings have been listed here individually because to some extent they help explain much in the later Communist movement and give us some perspective on it. The Communist leaders studied the Taiping Revolution [*sic*] in great detail, and have tried to learn its strong points while avoiding its mistakes and weaknesses. Though the Taiping Revolution can be seen as a precursor to twentieth-century revolutionary movements, it is still of considerable importance to the years immediately following it. Because of the destruction caused in Central China by struggles with the Taipings, because of the transfer of military power to various military figures, because of the concessions which had to be made to the Western powers as a result of internal pressure, the Manchu Dynasty lost much power and prestige, so that faced by a new revolutionary movement a half century later, it fell apart like a rotten building.

✿ An Imperial Despot and a Rebellious People in League Against the Foreigners and Their Chinese Sympathizers

THE SECOND great rebellion which rocked China during this period was the Boxer Rebellion (1900). Though it is regarded in the West as a simple expression of anti-foreignism, it is important to remember that its roots lay in Chinese society itself.

After the Taiping Rebellion the Manchu court allowed village self-defense forces to arise throughout China—something it had previously feared as a potential source of trouble. Since the gentry had come out in full support of the dynasty and since many of these self-defense forces were gentry-led, Peking assumed that they would be kept under control. But some of these forces began to follow other traditions, notably of rebellion. In Shantung, where economic conditions were poor, young men banded together and began to study the ancient arts of self-defense—"Chinese boxing"—and some writers have suggested there was a link with the rebellious eighteenth-century White Lotus Buddhist sects. Whatever the case, these village groups began to propagate the Robin Hood ideals: protection of the poor and hostility to venal officials. In their earliest period the Boxers were anti-dynastic: only one year before the siege of Peking they marched under the slogan "Overthrow the Ch'ing and expel the barbarians."

It is still not clear why this typical anti-dynastic, village-based rebellious movement turned suddenly to anti-foreignism. During the last years of the nineteenth century foreign missionaries in large numbers went deep into Shantung villages, where they converted people, tore down traditional temples, and built churches. In view of the great enmity the Boxers demonstrated against Chinese Christians and those Chinese officials who aided the foreigners, one can suspect that their initial hatred was directed less against the foreigners than those Chinese who had sold out to them. Fifty years later the cry *"Han-chien"* ("Traitor") was raised against thousands of Chinese who had collaborated with the Japanese. (Collaborators were often executed, while the Japanese occupiers themselves were simply imprisoned.) As we have seen time and time again in recent years, the most bloody wars are civil wars, as brother turns against brother. When the Boxers called for the overthrow of the Ch'ing and the expulsion of the barbarians, they saw the Manchu government and its officials as directly linked to the foreign barbarians who were destroying their temples. Defense of the traditional was synonymous with opposition to the government and to the barbarians with whom it was in league.

If the Boxers' initial hostility was primarily against the foreigners' Chinese supporters, internal Ch'ing politics helped shift it in the direction of outright anti-foreignism. In the wake of the Hundred Days of Reform (1898) the position of the obscurantist Empress Dowager was very tenuous. She seems to have realized that if any mass movement were launched against the dynasty, as had happened earlier with the Taipings, the chances of survival would be slim. She is reported to have said: "China is weak; the only thing we can depend on is the hearts of the people. If we lose them now, can we maintain our country?" Why not deflect this movement's growing violence away from the dynasty and toward the foreigners, particularly those reformist officials who, obviously influenced by the barbarians, were trying to subvert Manchu rule?

In the early months of 1900 the Boxers swept across the countryside of North China, burning and looting missionary settlements and slaughtering thousands of Chinese Christians. Boxer ranks were swelled with mobs of destitute vagrants who had been driven off their land by famine, flood, and drought.

In their desperation they found the Boxer sorcery, mysticism, and promise of supernatural powers (which would make them immune to bullets) most seductive.

On July 13, 1900, the Boxers stormed into Peking and lay siege to the eleven foreign legations, while the Chinese government ignored the foreigners' desperate pleas for protection. Finally, in mid-August, allied troops broke through from Tientsin to relieve the haggard, frightened prisoners of the besieged legations, and Boxer resistance quickly disintegrated, leaving the troops of the international force to take revenge on the Chinese by looting and raping.

Meanwhile the Empress Dowager had fled with her retinue deep into central China, leaving the aging Li Hung-chang in Peking to negotiate a settlement. In September of 1901 Li signed the Boxer Protocol, in which China agreed, among other things, to pay the staggering indemnity of $333 million.

Despite several wars waged by the Chinese against the foreigners, never before had the Chinese people risen in such wrathful frenzy against them. The Westerners had gotten used to Chinese evasion, trickery, and resistance, but they were supremely confident that the Chinese were basically a deeply humanistic people. The foreigners felt safe in China, particularly with extraterritoriality to protect them. What was the source of this terrible hatred? Sir Robert Hart, Inspector General of the Chinese Imperial Customs, a veteran of the Peking siege, and a man deeply sympathetic to China, tries to answer this question asked by many experienced foreigners in China.

In the preceeding selections we have distinguished two currents of nineteenth-century history: humiliation by the West and decline from within, the former expressed in the powerful West's encroachment and the latter expressed in popular internal rebellion. These two currents met in the Boxer Rebellion.

SIR ROBERT HART *
The Boxers: 1900

Every eye has latterly been turned to China, and every language has had its vocabulary enriched by a new term—but was this Boxer movement simply the growth of a starving mob, or had it a deeper significance? If it had an official origin, and pursued its course with official guidance and support, the seriousness of the episode cannot be exaggerated, and if such was not the case, the fact that the government either could not or would not interfere to oppose it calls for more than ordinary consideration and examination. Whichever explanation we accept, there is still some anterior cause to be looked for: it is never the proximate cause that gives a full answer to real inquiry, and it is to origins we must go if we would understand the causes of causes and thenceforward master them, defy them, or learn the lesson of submission. Much has been everywhere written about recent occurrences in China, but the study of disjointed phases and unconnected details will interest rather than enlighten, and may perhaps hide rather than show the more important issues. What we desire to discover is really something that will make future intercourse safe, peaceful, and profitable, and the first step to be taken in order to do that is to ascertain what it is that has made past intercourse in any form or degree the reverse. Sixty years of treaty relations have culminated in this Boxer movement: how account for such a finale?

The Chinese are a proud—some say a conceited—people, but they have very good reasons for their pride, and their conceit has its excuses. Far away from the rest of the world, they have been living their own life and developing their own civiliza-

---

* Sir Robert Hart, *These from the Land of Sinim* (London: Chapman and Hall Ltd., 1901), pp. 150–170.

tion; while others have been displaying what humanity may attain to with a revealed religion for its highest law and a Christ for its pattern, they have been exhibiting what a life a race may rise to, and live, without either. The central idea of their cult is filial piety; reverence for seniority, intensifying with every generation that transmitted it, settles all the details of family, social, and national life—instead of "Commit no nuisance," the placard on the wall says, "Respect thyself!" They are a preeminently reasonable people, and, when disputes occur, it is the appeal to right that solves them; for thirty centuries or more this recognized or inherited worship of right has gone on strengthening, and so strong is the feeling that to hint to them right must be supported by might excites something more than amazement. The relations of sovereign to subject and of man to man have so long been authoritatively defined and acknowledged that the life of the people has been poured into and shaped by a mold of duty, while the natural division of the empire into provinces has been so harmoniously supplemented by provincial and interprovincial arrangements under the metropolitan administration that law reigns everywhere and disorder is the exception. The arts of peace have ever held the first place in the estimation of all, and just as might should quail before right, so does intellectual prowess win honor everywhere, and the leaders of the people are those whom the grand national competitive examinations have proved to be more gifted than their fellows. In no other country is education so prized, so honored, so utilized, and so rewarded: along its lofty ladder, broad at the base and narrow at the top, the son of the poorest peasant may win his way to the highest post among the ministers of state around the Throne, and such is the veneration for that simple vehicle of thought, the written character, that to tread on paper with either writing or printing on it is all but desecration. Although not a warlike people by either nature or training, the force of circumstances and the prestige of a superior civilization reduced surrounding states to the position of tributaries, and thus the Middle Kingdom, soaring above all its neighbors, carried down the ages with it, for itself as a state and for its people as the people of that state, a visible, tangible, and actual supremacy; near and far, all bowed to the will of the Emperor, so judiciously manifested as to flatter rather than irritate, and so judiciously held back that tributaries could live their own lives in detail, merely recognizing Chinese suzerainty on the surface, while all responded more or less to the influence of its civilization and deferred to the teachings of its ethics—ethics which had for their central and informing doctrine that while men know nothing about the Gods, they ought to live as if in their presence, and among their fellows do nothing to others they do not want others to do to themselves. Filial piety developed mutual responsibility, and that, in its turn, made a rule of right without might more possible, and the negative precept of not doing what we do not wish others to do made it a virtue to avoid interference and fostered broad views and wide tolerance. The natural result of all this was that the Chinese government grew to consider itself the one great and civilized government beneath the skies, and expected all others to recognize it as such and admit their own inferiority, and the Chinese people—whose sons, deep-read in its many-sided literature and imbued to the core with all the teaching of its history and philosophy, were the officials and representatives of that government through the length and breadth of the land—were not less proud: supremacy in every respect had for ages been taken for granted, and a proud consciousness of it has shaped the will and attitude of both government and people.

In due time the men from the West began to appear, and when the government that had so long considered itself supreme, and the people who had so long regarded all others as barbarians, at the end of a war commenced by an attempt to put a stop to trade in a prohibited and deleterious drug, found themselves defeated in arms and forced to accept treaty relations with powers who not only challenged that supremacy, but demonstrated their ability to dictate and enforce their will, the shock their national pride received at once took root in their nature as an enduring feeling of not only *amour-propre* hurt, but right outraged; and ever since treaty relations began, this wounded feeling has been kept alive by the stipulations of the treaties and the recurrence of misunderstandings, and has increased and not decreased with the lapse of time. . . .

Foreign intercourse was simply tolerated, and was never regarded as a blessing; it was not necessary for the eighteen provinces to buy from or sell to foreigners—their own immense interprovincial trade quite sufficed to dispose of superfluous products and supply the demand of consumers; their Confucian ethics provided for the proper regulation of all the relations of men in this world—for barbarians, who so little understood the import of right here, to send missionaries to teach about preparation for the hereafter was simply ludicrous, and was becoming more than a nuisance by the quarrels that everywhere followed such teaching; as for treaties and the pleasures of foreign intercourse—China was happier and better without them. In a word, China had been living apart to the end of the eighteenth century, and was supreme in her own far Eastern world, and now we have the nineteenth ending with such an attempt to expel foreigners that the experience of a century's intercourse may be pronounced to have been neither profitable nor pleasing: if profitable, was it so displeasing that unpleasantness outweighed benefit—if pleasing, was it so little profitable that loss canceled enjoyment? Volumes would be required to detail the occurrences of this century of intercourse, to trace the interconnection of cause and effect, and to explain how each has been in turn the falling drop that wore the hole and left a rift in friendship; how can the limited space of a magazine article suffice to exhibit all lights, answer all objections, or exhaust explanations of the past and suggestions for the future? It is, in fact, surpassing strange that there should today be room for such criticism, seeing that, at all events on the surface, trade and intercourse have on the whole had such quiet times at every port, and it is all but incredible that we have so long been living on the flanks of a volcano; and yet it is apparently beyond dispute that, however friendly individuals may have appeared or been, general intercourse has all along been simply tolerated and never welcome, and now an uprising against foreign teaching and foreign intrusion, always possible, has to be faced and dealt with. Such being the case, there must be a cause for it, and surely there must be a remedy too—why is foreign intercourse seemingly under a ban, semi-governmental, semi-popular, and what can be done to make it both welcome and profitable in the future?

Foreigners in China, although increasing in numbers, are not very numerous, and may be roughly divided into three classes—mercantile, missionary, and ministerial. The mercantile class carry on their business in an orderly, legal, and unobjectionable manner, in accordance with treaty stipulations and rules framed to give effect to the same: there has been nothing in their behavior as a class or as individuals to warrant the hostility of the Chinese around them; but all the same, Chinese do complain that foreign competition in China's coasting trade has ruined junk owners and thrown out of employ the large crews they used to support—thus antagonizing the trading classes; and that the right to convey merchandise to and fro under the transit clauses has disorganized provincial finances —thus estranging all inland officials. The missionaries, it is granted, exert themselves to do good in various ways, and their medical benevolence is acknowledged with grateful appreciation; but the very fact of their presuming to teach at all is itself irritating, and for neighbors to accept their teaching is still worse, while certain abuses that have crept in—such as *soi-disant* converts joining their congregations to get protection against the consequences of misconduct, or to make use of Church connection to influence local litigation, as well as missionaries themselves intervening or interfering in local official business, a sort of poaching on official preserves which Mandarins wax wroth over—have from time to time caused local excitement and displeased both people and officials. As for the ministerial class—the foreign representatives at the capital and the consular authorities at the ports—it is absurd to suppose that their attitude and conduct have been other than propriety requires; and yet, at the same time, as the official representatives of governments that not only ignored China's claim to supremacy but exacted concessions or shared in the concessions exacted by others, they have always been viewed with suspicion, and, however popular personally, with dislike as a class, while the language and action of isolated individuals, if passing the bounds of comity, are noted rather as the characteristics of the class than the idiosyncrasies of the individual. The advent of the foreigner was unwelcome—the incidents that mark his presence create dissatisfaction—and the undercurrent of feeling is in the direction of a desire to induce him to hasten his departure rather than to prolong his stay. These blemishes disfigure the features of foreign intercourse, and neither "powder" nor "rouge" will efface them; if they, as effects, must disappear, the causes from which they spring must either be removed or neutralized.

On the Chinese side there is pride, innate pride—pride of race, pride of intellect, pride of civilization, pride of supremacy; and this inherited pride, in its massive and magnificent setting of blissful ignorance, has been so hurt by the manner of foreign impact that the other good points of Chinese character have, as it were, been stunned and cannot respond; it is not simply the claim for equality, or the demonstration of physical superiority, or the expansion of intercourse under compulsion, or the dictation of treaties, that have hurt that pride—were it only these, time would have healed the wound long ago, but it is a something in those treaties which keeps open the raw and prevents healing. Just as one can paralyze the body or corrupt the soul of a human being, so too is it possible to outrage the spirit and antagonize the nature of a people; and it is something like this which the West has done in the case of China, of course unintentionally yet not the less effectually. The most important, and from the foreign standpoint the most essential, stipulation in the treaties is that which extraterritorializes the foreigner in China; it is the principle on which the treaties are built up, and the spirit of it runs through every article: by it the foreigner is not amenable to any Chinese tribunal, and can only be dealt

with by the officials of his own country, and there is a certain
caoutchouc quality in its nature which extends its area, so that
while it is claimed not only for the individual but for his property, it leads to the supposition that he is not only to be judged
by his own laws alone, but is absolved from any obligation to
observe the laws of China—laws which, it must be remarked,
are of two kinds, the one being the written laws of the empire,
and the other the unwritten laws, the practices, prejudices, and
superstitions, of a locality, in their turn just as binding on all
people there and more likely to produce local ill-feeling if
violated. A foreign official is invoked, for instance, and his
intervention obliges Chinese officials to enforce the sale of a
certain plot of ground to missionaries against the wishes of the
neighbors, and then the missionary proceeds to put up a lofty
building on it, thereby, in the estimation and to the consternation of the whole population, irretrievably ruining the luck of
the neighborhood and the fortunes of its inhabitants. To the
foreigner the native objection is not only a something to be
laughed at, but is a superstition to be fought against and swept
away, and this is just the style of action which carries with it
the sure seed of a future riot and demands for gunboat protection; were he not withdrawn from the jurisdiction of the lords
of the soil, the Chinese government, the foreigner might possibly acquire that special plot, but he would be unable to put up
that style of building on it—would not another structure or another site do just as well, and would it not be better to have the
friendship than the hostility of the neighbors? As to the strength
of these superstitions, there is nothing stronger; and as to their
warrant, accident will always supply that. Take, for instance,
the belief that a solar eclipse on New Year's Day means bad
luck for the Emperor, and that an intercalary eighth moon
portends calamity for the country at large: well, in 1898 the
first day of the Chinese year was marked by an eclipse of the
sun, and before that year ended the Empress Dowager had
brushed aside the Emperor and strangled reform; while in 1900
the intercalary eighth moon came round, and behold, the Boxer
movement shook the whole world! What the West has said has

sounded to Chinese ears like this: "You are pagans, but we are
Christians, your laws are not our laws, your judges are corrupt,
injustice prevails, torture is practiced, punishments are bar-
barous, jails are hells, and we therefore withdraw our people
from your jurisdiction, and send missionaries to make you think
as we do; but there is money to be made in your trade, and
therefore you must share that trade with us, even though it be
along your coasts and on your inland waters, and you must
accord us—for are we not strangers and guests?—the commercial privileges which go hand in hand with the principle on
which we have made treaties, and you had better not violate
these treaties or you'll have to pay for it!" China, the proudest
of the proud, is wounded to the core, and taken the right way
the most reasonable of the reasonable, is made more obstruc-
tive than obstructionists. This is the explanation of the fact that
intercourse under treaties has not been a success, and, no matter
what safeguards be devised, as long as these treaties regulate
intercourse, so long will the irritation last, and so long will the
foreigner be unwelcome. Merchant, missionary, and minister
may one and all be animated by the best motives—they may be
sympathetic, considerate, patient, tactful, and just; and yet,
building on this foundation, the structure they run up will be as
much out of the perpendicular as the leaning tower of Pisa, and
sooner or later it must snap and collapse. . . .

Unfortunately, explanations do not always remove—they
sometimes only increase—difficulties, and to most readers it
may seem incredible that popular feeling in China has been influenced directly or indirectly by either treaties or treaty stipulations. As a matter of fact, few know anything about such international instruments, but various sections have felt their effect,
and among certain classes and their acquaintances rumors constantly spread, reflecting what has been heard by the underlings
who hang about in such numbers when Mandarins receive and
discuss business with foreign officials, or themselves talk over
foreign questions with their friends and colleagues: a Mandarin,
as is well known, has only to express annoyance at something
foreign to give the cue and set the fashion for a whole neighbor-

hood. Whatever hostility may exist, latent or expressed, it is nevertheless a fact that every foreigner has at hand numbers of Chinese friends, and that many Chinese live by, are interested in, and do not object to, foreign intercourse; China, however, is not an easy country to understand, and those who are best acquainted with it are puzzled to trace its sequence of thought or interpret its public opinion. The present outbreak may have its uses and clear the atmosphere, and years of tranquility may follow, and if this attempt to explain matters can in any way help to a better understanding, or prepare the way for such a manner of dealing with the Chinese question as to make relations more friendly and intercourse more profitable, it will not have been penned in vain. Although the Peking government had seemingly sanctioned the utterly inexcusable doings of the Boxers and others last summer, and officials in two or three provinces countenanced and took part in the infliction of the most cruel sufferings on missionaries and their families, it should not be forgotten that in the other fifteen or sixteen provinces the Viceroys and Governors maintained order, and no anti-foreign risings occurred: this fact ought not to be lost sight of when discussing the extent to which circumstances practically justify the powers in treating China as beyond the pale of civilization and Chinese claims as no longer entitled to a hearing. While conceding with Chinese thinkers that great is the might of right, one must qualify that with the thought that great also is the right of might. Where the most powerful states are also the most civilized, they not only have the right, but it is their duty sometimes to impose their will on others—only, in proportion as they are mighty and civilized, so should their action be considerate, discriminating, and just.

3. PEACE AND ATTEMPTS AT REFORM
🌀 Confucian Adaptability and
the Western Challenge

BY 1860 the Manchu Dynasty and the traditional Chinese order were teetering on the brink of collapse. Having suffered two major foreign invasions and the devastation of the Taiping Rebellion, Chinese self-confidence was at a nadir. The Emperor had fled to the Mongolian border, the summer palace had been burned to the ground, and Peking, symbolic seat of Imperial authority, had been taken by Western barbarians. Imperial China seemed at an ond.

And yet, as so often before, a last burst of energy almost succeeded in restoring to the dynasty a position of pre-eminence. As Mary Wright, Professor of Chinese history at Yale University and the author of the following selection, writes, "What was required was not merely a restoration at the eleventh hour of effective government along traditional lines but the creation of new policies that could ward off modern domestic and foreign threats and yet preserve the Confucian society and its ideology."

By 1865 observers were surprised to find that a miracle had very nearly been accomplished. By 1864 the government had retaken Nanking, the Taiping capital; the Moslem rebellions showed hopeful signs of abating; the tax system had been reformed and government coffers refilled; the examination system had been reinstituted in areas formerly under rebel control, bringing a new group of able vigorous men into the civil service. New lands were opened; Chinese trade increased. Relations with the foreign powers improved as China's statesmen adopted Western institutions and ideas; movements were launched to read Western literature. Old inflexible isolationist attitudes were reappraised and revised. In short, it seemed as though the Chinese were wiping the slate clean and were ready to embark on a new reformist tack.

But to the undiscerning eye these reforms were deceptive. Behind them ran a strong and tenacious conservative current; the object of every one of the reforms had been to insure the continued existence of the old order in the face of the encroaching West. Was there not a contradiction here? Was it possible for the new to exist alongside the old and not exert strong pressure for further change?

One is ultimately forced to concur with Professor Wright: "The T'ung-chih Restoration failed because the requirements of a modern state proved to run directly counter to the requirements of the Confucian order."

MARY C. WRIGHT *
The Modernization of China's System of Foreign Relations

The most immediate danger confronting the Chinese government during the crisis years of 1859–61 was foreign aggression. To ward off this danger, the statesmen responsible for the management of barbarian affairs faced the problem of grafting onto the traditional idea of the state and the traditional machinery of administration a series of radically new concepts and institutions. There is no more dramatic indication of the vitality that the traditional state still possessed at this late date than the speed with which the Restoration government mastered the Western system of diplomacy and used it to serve Chinese ends.

* Mary C. Wright, *The Last Stand of Chinese Conservatism* (New York: Atheneum [Stanford University Press], 1957), pp. 222–250, 190–195.

THE TRADITIONAL CHINESE VIEW
OF FOREIGN POLICY

Chinese skill in the peaceful ordering of international relations
was no new development. The tributary system, which included
all the world known to China, had proved through centuries to
be an enduring and effective system of international organization, a hierarchy in which the place of each people was determined by the degree to which it was permeated and transformed
by the Confucian doctrine. The magnetic center of this Confucian world order was China, from which civilizing influences
radiated to all nations. In the ideology that held the system together, little account was taken of the manner in which Chinese
civilization had throughout its history been influenced by contact with non-Chinese peoples. The dogma as formulated in
the Chinese Classics was: "I have heard of men using the doctrines of our great land to change barbarians, but I have never
yet heard of any being changed by barbarians."

The term barbarian (*i*) meant simply "not yet Sinicized";
the barbarians had an accepted place in the world scheme, below that of the partially Sinicized peoples. The Chinese Emperor recognized the status of the sovereigns of tributary states
and of their peoples, and bestowed upon them the immense
moral and material benefits of Chinese civilization. The tributary
states in return sent tribute missions that gave substance to the
universal pretensions of the Chinese Emperor.

The Confucian orthodoxy assumed that there was nothing
inherently evil in human nature, including the barbarian nature.
If the barbarian could be reformed by education, then tolerance
and kindness were the basis of a sound foreign policy. Prince
Kung enjoined his fellow countrymen to hate the evil that a
barbarian might do but not the barbarian himself; to be "kind
to men from afar" in accordance with the Classics, to the end
that the myriad nations might be tranquilized, that China might

flourish, and that government by virtue might prevail throughout the world.

Although leaders of the Restoration were quick to learn that the tributary system, which had been seriously disrupted during the years of rebellion, could never be rebuilt into an effective means of controlling the Western powers, the system still had considerable value in the conduct of China's relations with other Asian countries. Therefore, while a new system was constructed for dealing with the West, the old system was revived for dealing with Asia; where both the West and Asia were involved, as in the French invasion of Korea in 1866, China used the old and new systems in combination.

One of the marks of the Restoration was the resumption of tributary missions along routes that had long been closed by fighting and were now reopened. Foreign observers were amazed at these demonstrations of Chinese skill in ruling by prestige the far-flung peoples "who continue to worship the shadow after the substance has departed." The *North China Herald* of November 19, 1864, commented: "It is singular that notwithstanding its material weakness, the Chinese Government contrives to maintain unimpaired the suzerainty over neighboring states which it acquired in former days, under more energetic emperors."

Not only the Restoration conservatives but the Taiping revolutionaries as well continued to apply the concepts of the tributary system to some types of international relations. When a British warship visited Ningpo after its recapture by the Ch'ing, officers found an apparently authentic copy of a Taiping edict on world affairs. According to this document, the Taiping leaders envisioned a universal state under the Taiping Emperor. Hereditary foreign consuls would be recognized by China, would be awarded seals, and would be supervised by a Chinese foreign director:

> The affairs of foreign states will be directed by the Director under our orders. The various affairs of the foreign states will be settled by the consuls. The consuls will all

obey the order of the foreign Linguist Director, who will direct them.

Thus at the beginning of the Restoration, Chinese conservatives and revolutionaries held a common concept of a Sinocentric universal state. In the light of this basic concept, the efforts of the Western powers to advance their interests were bound to be regarded as insubordination, or, if force was used, rebellion. The traditional Chinese foreign policy had regularly been parallel to domestic policy: soothe the obedient, chastise the rebellious.

In 1859 Bruce had recognized these "maxims of China in regard to intercourse with foreign nations" as "the key":

> The subjects of foreign nations residing in China are represented as belonging to barbarous tribes, and living by trade (of all occupations the one in least repute among the Chinese), as devoid of civilization, and ignorant of the rules of reason, and by all means to be confined to the outskirts of the country.

> According to the maxims of the Government they are entitled to no rights beyond those accorded by the favour of the emperor; and though circumstances and the weakness of the Government have led it to acquiesce in the concession of considerable privileges to foreigners in distant sea-ports, it is remarkable in proving how tenaciously it holds to its traditions that it always classifies as acts of rebellion the measures of coercion adopted by foreign governments to obtain redress for wrongs done to their subjects.

This traditional system of international relations had for twenty years ceased to work to the satisfaction of either Chinese or Westerners. From the foreign point of view, constant recourse to the use of force locally was a costly and ineffective means of protecting foreign interests. From the Chinese point of view, no policy could be implemented because the foreigners were insensible to reasoning based on Chinese political thinking.

Applied to the European barbarians, the principles of the tributary system proved unworkable. In this dilemma the Chinese did not, as has often been charged, sit apathetically repeating Confucian platitudes to a contemptuous West. Instead, they learned the Western system of international relations and adapted it to Chinese needs.

During the crisis of 1860 the Chinese decided to abandon the futile effort to control a physically stronger enemy by the routine assertion of Confucian moral authority, and to appeal instead to the enemy's own moral standards. They were sufficiently acute observers to see that the foreigners granted the validity of moral arguments based on international law, Western public law, written agreements, and common-sense justice. The Chinese attempt to use these European counterparts of the Confucian ethic to control foreign activity in China was the essence of Restoration foreign policy. From the negotiations following the flight of the Hsien-feng Emperor, Prince Kung had concluded that the barbarians kept their pledged word, and that for the time being at least peaceful coexistence was possible.

THE TSUNGLI-YAMEN

The establishment early in 1861 of a modern foreign office, the Tsungli-yamen, was the most striking institutional innovation of the Restoration period. The structure of the Chinese bureaucracy had been fixed for centuries by statute and precedent, and a tremendous inertia made change difficult. Yet the system was not so moribund as to rule out executive reorganization in an emergency. At the outset, the yamen was no more than a weak and informal association of individually prominent statesmen, but its function was quickly expanded and its status consolidated. The Tsungli-yamen of 1865 was a very different institution from the Tsungli-yamen of 1861. Its intimate association with the Grand Council is no argument against its importance in its own right, but rather reflects a typical Restoration effort to modernize the functioning of the Confucian state without perceptible effect on its basic structure. The device worked well for the duration of the Restoration. Later, when the traditional state disintegrated and powerful provincial officials like Li Hung-chang assumed all the powers of government, the Tsungli-yamen, like the central government of which it was an organ, lost its effectiveness.

Before 1861 there had existed no office concerned solely with the conduct of China's foreign relations. The Board of Rites had responsibilities far beyond the handling of relations with the tributary states. The Li-fan yüan (Mongolian Super-intendency) and various other agencies considered their han-dling of relations with Russia as a minor duty. The shock of the defeat of 1860 and the burning of the Yüan-ming yüan forced a reconsideration of policy.

An edict ordered Prince Kung to take charge of the peace negotiations and appointed Kuei-liang and Wen-hsiang as his chief assistants. Prince Kung himself co-opted Ch'ung-hou and Ch'ung-lun. Heng-ch'i and Lan Wei-wen made the approaches to the allied representatives, and a number of other officials also worked under the direction of the Imperial appointees. Memori-als on foreign affairs poured in from the provinces, and copies were sent to the new office for consideration. Its responsibilities increased rapidly after the Treaties of Tientsin were finally ratified and foreign envoys took up residence in the capital.

Early in 1861 Prince Kung, Wen-hsiang, and Kuei-liang memorialized on the need for a new foreign policy to meet a new type of barbarian problem. On January 20, 1861, Prince Kung secured approval for the establishment of a formal and permanent office for the handling of foreign affairs; he com-municated his new status to the foreign envoys and received their congratulations. For the first time a single organ of gov-ernment had charge of all relations with Western powers. The superintendents of trade for the three northern ports and the five southern ports respectively were placed under the jurisdic-tion of the Tsungli-yamen. Although, like the metropolitan boards and high provincial officials, the superintendents could consult each other on problems involving foreigners and me-

morialize directly, copies of their correspondence were forwarded to the Tsungli-yamen, as were copies of relevant central
government documents.

At the beginning Prince Kung was assisted only by Wen-
hsiang and Kuei-liang, but the addition of other members was
envisioned from the outset. There was no fixed number; first
there were three, later six, and by 1869 ten members. Their
titles varied at first but were gradually standardized. The earlier
appointees were princes, ministers, and heads of boards who
held concurrent appointments to the Tsungli-yamen. As time
went on, new members tended to be specialists in foreign affairs
holding a single appointment.

For the first three years the internal organization of the
yamen fluctuated, but its structure was formalized by the reorganization of 1864. The system enacted at that time lasted
until 1901. Some overlapping jurisdictions and historic anachronisms persisted, but the system was a relatively modern and
functional one, resembling the Republic's foreign ministries
more closely than anything in the pre-1860 Ch'ing system. The
yamen suffered less than the other organs of government from
the antiquated Ch'ing system of public finance because many
of its expenditures were chargeable to other agencies. For example, since the chief members of the yamen held concurrent
appointments, their salaries and expenses were paid not by the
yamen but by the various traditional offices to which they were
concurrently assigned. Many other expenses were paid directly
from Maritime Customs revenues.

The Chinese government made a great effort to increase
and confirm the prestige and authority of the Tsungli-yamen.
The important role it was expected to play was made clear in
the first year of its existence, when the Prussian representative
asked it to request permission for foreigners to enter the walled
cities of Canton and Chaochow, near Swatow. The edict in
reply expressed concern lest foreigners think that the Tsungli-
yamen was lacking in authority to take action, and instructed
the yamen to correct this impression by taking appropriate
measures on its own authority. Hsüeh Huan in Shanghai com-

plained that he was now ignored by foreign officials, who would deal only with Peking in spite of the fact that he was the superintendent for ten ports in six provinces.

Once established, the Tsungli-yamen came to have a vested interest in the further development of international relations. To a certain extent its interests became opposed both to those of the conservative, antiforeign local officials and local gentry, and to those of the more conservative organs of the central government. The foreign envoys had almost become its protégés. There thus developed a community of interest between the Tsungli-yamen and the diplomatic corps against aggressive foreign merchants and missionaries on the one hand and Chinese obscurantists on the other. The Sinicization of foreign diplomats was paralleled by the Westernization of the Tsungli-yamen.

In consequence, the local use of force by subordinate British officials embarrassed Alcock *because* it embarrassed Prince Kung in his relations with the rest of Chinese officialdom. During the Formosan incident of 1868, when a British consul had resorted to "gunboat diplomacy," the action was reported directly to the Throne by the Governor-General of Chekiang and Fukien. Alcock, who certainly got his information from the Tsungli-yamen, reported to the Foreign Office:

> the course followed by the Vice-roy of Fukien in addressing his memorial direct to the throne, has no doubt placed, as it was intended, the Prince and his Foreign Board, of which he is president, in a very unpleasant position, as being answerable for the foreign relations maintained, and in some degree therefore held responsible for the humiliation thus inflicted by 2 subaltern officers of a foreign power. . . . [In cases of this kind, the Tsungli-yamen] were themselves on their trial before the Court and the other Boards. . . . It was necessary that the Prince should at once be able to show that, if any wrong had really been committed by the subordinate officers of a foreign power, in violation of treaty or international law and usage among civilized states, Her Majesty's Representative here would be pre-

pared, after due investigation, to give satisfaction, and, as far as possible, to afford redress for any injury inflicted.

The community of interest between foreign officials and the Tsungli-yamen against the extremists on either side was urged by Prince Kung in a shrewd memorandum to Alcock in 1868:

> The purpose of the Chinese trader is to concede as little as possible to the foreigner, and to seek his interests alone; while the foreign trader aims at his own advantage, without regard to the condition of the native merchant. Each, in short, is careful of his own interest, without thought of the other's welfare. . . . Such being the disposition of the trading class, it rests with officials to act in accordance with the principles of justice, considering both sides of a question, and inclining to neither, by which means a speedy arrangement may be concluded.

It has been responsibly charged that the organization of the yamen was faulty; that it did not permit specialization; that its members spent too much time drinking tea with foreign envoys and too little in the serious study of international affairs, of which they remained absurdly ignorant; that essentially they were conservatives reflecting the traditional outlook of the Grand Council and the boards on which they served. These statements are true in a sense, but they do not make up a balanced appraisal of the Tsungli-yamen. The organization was faulty, but it marked a considerable advance over previous machinery for handling foreign affairs; more specialization was permitted than had been permitted before, and at that time the specialist was not regarded as the ideal statesman in either Europe or China. The members of the yamen were doubtless leisurely, but their success depended on developing intimate, cordial relations with the foreign envoys, most of whom were also accustomed to leisurely social intercourse. They were certainly conservatives, but their conservatism was not the same as the conservatism of the officials in the capital who pilloried the yamen, or of the angry literati in the provinces who mobbed Kuo Sung-tao, the first minister to England.

RESTORATION SPECIALISTS IN INTERNATIONAL AFFAIRS

During the 1860s men of established position like Prince Kung and Wen-hsiang rapidly developed a competence in foreign affairs, and new appointments to the Tsungli-yamen were increasingly based on experience and ability. In the course of ten years changes in the personnel of the yamen were even more striking than changes in its structure and function. Its members quickly came to represent all the varied kinds of knowledge, prestige, and power useful in making and carrying out foreign policy: the Imperial family, the major branches of the central government, the middle bureaucracy, traditional scholarship, knowledge of the Western world, military experience, and experience in the secretariat of the yamen.

There is little foundation for the contention that the ranking members of the Tsungli-yamen were in effect honorary appointees who devoted little attention to foreign affairs. Prince Kung's responsibilities in other spheres of government were extensive, but his own writings and those of foreigners who knew him show that he was a "man of mental vigor and bold resolve," following coherent principles of foreign policy and capable of negotiating skillfully. His personal and official rank greatly strengthened the position of the new yamen within the Chinese bureaucracy and added to its prestige in foreign eyes. Wen-hsiang, "probably the ablest man who ever held a seat in the Tsung-li Yamên," was nominally second to Prince Kung within the yamen and in fact often its acting head, and his work in the Tsungli-yamen was his major responsibility. When his health failed in 1870, he attempted to resign from all his offices except the Tsungli-yamen. He was gradually relieved of his command of a Manchu Banner and of the Metropolitan Field Force, of his presidency of the Board of Works, and of several lesser offices; but until his death he remained in the Tsungli-yamen.

In its first year the Tsungli-yamen was admittedly a Manchu organization, following the pattern of Manchu metropolitan dominance of the pre-Restoration period rather than the Restoration pattern of Manchu-Chinese coalescence. The salt controller Ch'ung-lun, the skilled negotiator Heng-ch'i, and the scholarly Grand Secretary Pao-yün were excellent representatives of Manchu civilian officialdom, but of little else.

The picture changed quickly as Chinese of varying backgrounds were added. The first Chinese appointee, Tung Hsün, became a member simultaneously with the last of the high-ranking Manchu appointees, Pao-yün. At the time of his appointment Tung Hsün was a junior vice-president of the Board of Revenue. As associate general editor of the *Shih-lu* for the Hsien-feng period, he was widely read in the documents on all phases of recent Chinese history. A friend and neighbor, W. A. P. Martin, admired his vigor and flexibility of mind and personality. On his sixtieth birthday, in 1866, Tung Hsün received unusually high official honors as a reward (according to an informed younger contemporary, Weng T'ung-ho) for his outstanding achievements in the field of China's foreign relations.

The appointment of the distinguished geographer Hsü Chi-yü to the Tsungli-yamen in 1865 was striking evidence of the rapid change that had taken place in the Chinese handling of foreign affairs. The appointment was startling because Hsü and his well-known work on foreign countries, the *Ying-huan chih-lüeh,* symbolized that nascent Chinese interest in the Western world which had proved so signally inconsequential twenty years earlier. Although the geography Hsü published in the forties was "an immense stride in advance" in knowledge of the West, he had been first demoted and then in 1851 removed from office in disgrace. His official recognition in 1865 and the reissue of his book with a preface by Tung Hsün were signs of a new age.

The significance of Hsü's appointment was not fully understood by Westerners, but its importance was not overlooked.

S. Wells Williams commented at length in his dispatches. Seward, then Secretary of State, replied: "The importance which you ascribe to the appointment of Seu Ki-yu to a post in the Foreign Office seems to be well founded."

One cannot attach great importance to Tung Hsün's rendering Longfellow into Chinese verse, or to Hsü Chi-yü's writing a eulogy of Washington, for which he received a portrait of his subject as a gift from the American government. Yet details of this kind indicate a considerable change in the character of Chinese official contact with the West.

During the later years of the Restoration, three Chinese officials who had had typical successful careers were appointed to the Tsungli-yamen. T'an T'ing-hsiang had been governor-general of Chihli and junior vice-president of the Board of Revenue. Mao Ch'ang-hsi had been president of the Board of Civil Office, vice-president of the Censorate, and commander of the campaign against the Honan rebels. Shen Kuei-fen, who had also held a succession of provincial and metropolitan offices, was one of the pivotal figures of the Restoration. These appointments served both to neutralize much of the opposition to the yamen and to educate the established hierarchy in some of the new problems of foreign policy.

As the Tsungli-yamen expanded, the importance of its secretariat increased. In 1864 all the agencies of government had been invited to recommend candidates; from the resulting list thirty Chinese and thirty Manchus had been selected as yamen secretaries. These secretaryships quickly became apprenticeships for policy posts. In 1869 a secretary, Ch'eng-lin, became a minister of the yamen; and in 1872 he was joined by a second secretary, Hsia Chia-hao. Subsequently Ch'eng-fu, Li Chao-t'ang, Chou Chia-mei, and other secretaries rose to positions of responsibility because of their training in the yamen.

Experience in foreign relations became equally important in the careers of a number of Chinese officials outside the Tsungli-yamen. Ting Jih-ch'ang's extraordinary career resulted from his supposed skill in foreign affairs as well as from Li

Hung-chang's patronage. Li Feng-pao was promoted from the Foochow Shipyard to be minister to several European countries.

S. Wells Williams found China's new foreign affairs specialists "men of acute minds" who were making an intelligent effort to preserve the Confucian state by limited modernization. In his view, when they failed, they failed because they "were placed between the two great pressures of a warped and bigoted multitude of literati wedded to the old regime and the ministers of the outside powers . . . representing armies and navies which had been found invincible."

Kuo Sung-tao, himself a product of the Confucian system, went further than his colleagues in his effort to bridge the gap between Chinese tradition and the West. He argued that foreign contacts had been of benefit to China, and that the foreigners' intentions were good. In a classic review of the principles of Restoration foreign policy, written about 1875, he emphasized the many common interests between China and the West, the many instances of honorable compromise in recent years.

In examining the qualities of these men as foreign affairs specialists, it is important to remember that for each of them—even for Hsü Chi-yü, even for Kuo Sung-tao—China's domestic affairs remained the primary concern. Foreign affairs did not outweigh domestic in Chinese political thinking until much later. Communist historians have been very wrong to dismiss these men as a "foreign affairs clique," "a new production of the Tientsin Treaties," through whose agency the foreign invaders transformed old-style militarists into new-style militarists.

CHINA'S ACCEPTANCE OF THE TREATY SYSTEM

Before 1860 no Ch'ing statesman had regarded treaties as desirable. Even if specific terms had been favorable (and they were not), they would still have been limitations on the vaguely defined Imperial prerogatives of the tributary system. When tributary illusions were shattered by Western attack, a few officials, notably Ch'i-ying, had developed the beginnings of a new strategy by which China might use the treaties to control the foreigners, provided China herself observed them scrupulously. However, efforts of this type had always been short-lived and without lasting results.

The ratification of the Treaties of Tientsin in 1860 marked more than a return to the Ch'i-ying policy. In the following decade the Ch'ing government accepted and mastered the principles and practices of Western diplomacy and succeeded in using them as the main bulwark of Chinese sovereignty.

Nearly every document concerned with foreign affairs in the 1860s included a careful statement of the bearing of the treaties on the case under discussion. Where there was a treaty stipulation on the matter, the decision was automatic according to law; where a case was not clearly covered by treaty, however, the issue was debatable according to politics. The principle was clearly stated on many occasions treaties had the force of positive law. If foreign demands were based on treaties, they were to be granted regardless of where China's immediate interests might lie, because her long-term interests depended on the sanctity of treaties.

There is no recorded instance in which the officials responsible for foreign affairs advocated the violation of a treaty during the T'ung-chih Restoration. On the contrary, the Chinese documents, which were never intended for publication, record innumerable instances of the Tsungli-yamen's insistence on strict observance of the law. The yamen refused to protest against a survey of the north China coast by a British ship in 1866; British navigation rights were guaranteed by treaty. When Wen-hsiang was in charge of the purely domestic task of suppressing bandits in southern Manchuria, he devoted particular attention to maintaining order in the Yingkow area, remarking later: "It is a place where foreigners trade; it had to be protected." On the delicate question of the new Sino-Russian frontier following the cession of the Maritime Province,

Heilung-kiang officials were ordered to change their system
of border inspections so as to avoid the chance of trespassing
on what had become Russian territory. On the minor but irritating problem of renting commercial premises in the ports,
local officials were instructed not to interfere because the right
to rent was guaranteed by treaty.

This new policy of accepting and upholding treaties did
more than deprive the Western powers of legitimate grievances
that might be used as occasions for punitive action. It enabled
the Chinese government to reverse the function of the treaties
and to use them to limit the activities of foreigners to treaty
specifications. Before 1860 the treaties had represented the
minimum privileges that foreigners could expect—a line from
which they could press forward in the further opening of China.
During the 1860s the minimum became the maximum—a line
behind which the Chinese government could find security.
Japan at this early date posed a problem for Chinese diplomacy
precisely because Japan was not a treaty power, and thus not
subject to the usual sort of representations in regard to Japanese activities in Korea.

The use of treaties to "halter" the barbarian was not entirely new in the history of Chinese diplomacy. In 1845 Ch'i-
ying was instructed to try to prevent British ships from proceeding to Korea by arguing, and correctly, that no treaty had
provided for the opening of Korea. Even in 1859–60 a minority
faction had urged acceptance of the Treaties of Tientsin. But
it was only after 1860 that it became standard Chinese policy
to uphold the treaties and to insist that foreigners do likewise.

This new Chinese diplomatic strategy was most effective
against the Western powers with whom China's relations were
entirely modern in character. By appeal to the treaties, smug-
gling and illegal maritime trade could be checked and the
coolie trade to some extent controlled. Foreign efforts to legalize
the import of salt were frustrated, and the establishment of a
French salt dealer in Shanghai was closed down.

The success of this policy was indicated by widespread
indignation among foreigners in the ports. Treaties, they wrote,

had once been minimum rights to be extended by negotiation. They had become precise legal documents, and the Western powers had accepted the Chinese view that any privilege or right not specifically conceded by China could be firmly withheld by China. . . .

THE ADVANCEMENT OF WESTERN LEARNING

At the beginning of the T'ung-chih period, Chinese officials had known little of the Western world or even of some parts of China that were important in foreign relations. It was said that they were ignorant of the very names of foreign countries and confused Macao (*Ao-men*) with Australia (*Ao-chou*). In the 1862 negotiations with Russia, the members of the Tsungli-yamen found that they did not know where Lake Baikal was. By their own report, they knew too little of finance to offer an opinion on the regulations for the Maritime Customs, and very little of the geography of the Yangtze Valley or of the conditions prevailing in the ports. This initial lack of information was, however, a shortcoming that could be overcome within the Confucian tradition. Study of the problems of government had been the core of traditional education; all that was needed was to expand the concept of government to include international relations.

The effort to understand the West was not, of course, entirely new. Works such as the *Hai-lu,* the *Hai-kuo t'u-chih,* and the *Ying-huan chih-lüeh* had been in circulation for many years. There had long been a Russian-language school in Peking, and numerous Chinese in the treaty ports had had business contacts with foreigners. However, the information available from these sources was limited. Moreover, unless a knowledge of foreign affairs could be introduced into the heart of the official system, there was the great danger that such knowledge might become a monopoly of the compradores, for whom the traditional official had the greatest contempt. Feng Kuei-fen was particularly apprehensive on this score.

The introduction of Western studies in Japan provided another reason for introducing them in China. In 1863 the Censorate presented to the Throne the proposal of a district magistrate-designate that all officials whose work concerned foreign affairs be required to pass an examination on the geography, topography, customs, government, and produce of foreign countries. The petitioner reported his alarm at hearing that the Japanese had sent a mission to study shipbuilding and armament in Russia and America for ten years. To counter this increase in Japanese strength, he suggested that China set up suitable training centers in Hong Kong, Amoy, Foochow, and Shanghai on the model of the provincial academies. The Tsungli-yamen approved the plan for training future officials, but was unwilling to require the new knowledge of officials already in office.

During the Restoration the effort was made to develop new knowledge in China without sending Chinese abroad to acquire it. It was not until 1871 that Yung Wing succeeded in persuading Tseng Kuo-fan and Li Hung-chang to send the first group of students abroad under his direction, and the project was later discontinued. Foreign works were translated at an increasing rate. Tseng Kuo-fan attached a translation bureau to the Kiangnan Arsenal, and a number of other government offices were fitted out with similar branches. The Tsungli-yamen pointed out that new maps and new statistics were especially needed in the handling of foreign affairs.

In the course of twenty-five years, China's attitude toward foreign books had changed. When Russia had presented books to China in 1845, they had merely been stored in the archives. When the United States sent a gift of books in 1869, the Tsungli-yamen was interested; it also recalled the Russian books and requisitioned them for study. Foreigners in China noted these and other "symptoms of a tendency to inquire into the reasons of things which were before deemed unworthy of notice."

By the end of the T'ung-chih period, the Tsungli-yamen, which had originally limited its interest in the West to immediate considerations of technology and international law, had begun to urge a broader understanding of Western society. In commenting on the stationing of Chinese envoys abroad in 1875, it emphasized

> not simply the transaction of business in which Chinese and foreigners may be jointly concerned. . . . Men's minds, in fact, must have free access to each other before angry collisions between them can be prevented. If there are to be no collisions between them, they must thoroughly acquaint themselves each with the other.

The reading of foreign newspapers and public documents to keep abreast of current world affairs was a striking innovation. For the study of foreign books for basic learning there were Chinese precedents; but in China there had never existed any source of information comparable to the nineteenth-century Western press. Yet as early as 1862 the former chief supervisor of instruction memorialized on the importance of reading foreign newspapers in order to discover the foreigners' intentions. Hsüeh Huan regularly relayed to Peking press accounts of foreign activities in central China, although he claimed to doubt the reliability of the clippings.

Chinese officials put their new knowledge to effective use in solving problems of widely varying types. During the French invasion of Korea in 1866, the Tsungli-yamen studied Western criticisms of the French action and used them with notable success. Chinese officials on all levels were quick to locate foreign news reports and other documents that might weaken the foreign position in China. For example, in 1859 W. A. P. Martin wrote a letter casting doubt on the good faith of the allies. Years later Tung Hsün was found to have a Chinese translation, presumably made from the Blue Book text. A missionary in central China wrote:

> Our Viceroy is a very intelligent man, and anti-foreign to the backbone. He knows just as well as I do all that has been said in the House of Lords, and all that has ap-

peared in the *Times* on missionaries and the missionary enterprise. He sees that we are despised and distrusted and knows that we are at his mercy.

Alcock commented on the increasing tendency of the yamen to observe world affairs. He thought the yamen had probably found in the British press one of its favorite arguments against the extension of missionary activity: that alien Buddhist proselyters would probably meet with considerable popular hostility in England.

This new Chinese habit of newspaper reading forced British officials for the first time to take account of the effect of the foreign press on Chinese policy. The negotiations for the revision of the British Treaty of Tientsin were jeopardized by the extravagant views expressed in the press by merchant groups. According to Alcock: "The Foreign Board, here, gets translations made of such documents as these, when made public, and habitually have laid before them the comments of the local press and their more salient articles." On this occasion the Tsungli-yamen, outraged at what it read, inclined toward intransigence. To limit the damage, Alcock ordered all British consuls to publish repudiations of the merchants' view.

Restoration officials learned to use the press not only as a source of information about foreigners but as an instrument to give foreigners the desired impression of China. Hence, they became sensitive to foreign press accounts of themselves. It was generally believed at the time that Li Hung-chang had been very much aware of foreign criticism of his execution of the Taiping leaders who had surrendered at Soochow, and that he released an impounded foreign ship, the *Tsatlee,* in order to improve his press relations. Chinese officials frequently took exception to news stories printed about China; on one occasion the Tsungli-yamen ordered the local taotai to warn the *North China Herald* against making libelous remarks about Chinese officials.

THE T'UNG-WEN KUAN AND THE MODERNIZATION
OF CHINESE EDUCATION

Adapting China's highly developed traditional system of education to new needs was a basic problem of the Restoration. In modernizing education, as in modernizing foreign policy, the important thing was learning new skills. It was a cardinal principle of the Confucian state that officials should be selected on a competitive basis from among the young men who had shown the greatest proficiency in the study of government. Foreign relations would be dangerous to this traditional political system only if they could not be absorbed into it. If they were to be absorbed, they would have to be handled by competent officials with a regular status in the hierarchy without reliance on the merchants of the ports.

The compilers of the dynastic history, the *Ch'ing-shih kao,* dated the beginnings of China's new school system from the beginning of the T'ung-chih Restoration. In 1862 the T'ung-wen kuan was established in Peking for the purpose of training selected young Bannermen in foreign languages. In 1863 Li Hung-chang established the Kuang fang-yen kuan in Shanghai on precisely the same model, and in 1864 Jui-lin established a similar school in Canton. In 1866 Tso Tsung-t'ang founded the Ch'uan-cheng hsüeh-t'ang at Foochow for the study of English, French, navigation, and engineering. Each of these institutions grew rapidly from modest beginnings and rapidly expanded its functions.

It is worth noting that Chinese rather than foreign initiative was predominant in this first phase of educational reform, and that the emphasis was placed on creating schools in China rather than on sending students abroad. As early as 1860 S. Wells Williams had suggested that the $200,000 remaining from the Chinese indemnity might be used

> as a fund for establishing a school of a high rank in China where the natives of that Empire can be taught the lan-

guages and science of Western countries, under the tuition of competent men, with the object of making them service- able to their own countrymen and government.

Nothing came of this proposal—contrast the importance of the Boxer indemnity in the development of Chinese education forty years later. In 1865 American Presbyterians founded at Tengchow the institution that later became Cheeloo University, and in 1871 American Episcopalians established the future Hua-chung University at Wuchang, but these and similar in- stitutions became important only under the altered circum- stances of a later era. During the Restoration Protestant mis- sionaries concerned themselves more with translating religious texts than with introducing Western knowledge in general. Catholic missionaries, who had earlier devoted their main at- tention to scholarly work in China, withdrew from the educa- tional field during the Restoration.

The outstanding example of the Chinese effort to modern- ize Chinese education in the 1860s was the T'ung-wen kuan. By its establishment, Restoration officials hoped to incorporate the new learning into the old system, thereby ultimately strength- ening that system against Western expansion and its Chinese shock troops, the Cantonese compradores. Feng Kuei-fen argued that the new subjects should become recognized and esteemed fields of learning and should be included in the examination system. Since the compradores were also a new element in the traditional class structure, Feng's opposition to their advance represented a fusion of the class and cultural interests of the bureaucracy.

The Tsungli-yamen had originally hoped to use Chinese teachers in the T'ung-wen kuan, but soon discovered that even in Shanghai and Canton no qualified teachers of foreign lan- guages were available. The decision in 1862 to use foreigners to teach China's future officials seemed hazardous; anxiety over ideological penetration was overcome only when Wade reassured the yamen that foreigners could be found who would not teach Christianity.

The Tsungli-yamen was determined that the new school should provide effective training and should avoid the weaknesses of the old Russian-language school, which during its long career had yielded no results whatever. The original plan called for between ten and twenty-four students of about fifteen years of age, but their number expanded rapidly. Their progress was tested by regular examinations, and they were expected, after the first year's diligent study, to gain additional practice by translating incoming dispatches.

The schools established at Shanghai and Canton followed the Peking pattern. Li Hung-chang, like the Tsungli-yamen earlier, pointed out that foreigners had been studying Chinese for more than twenty years and that a number of them could read the Chinese Classics, Histories, and official documents. In contrast, very few members of the Chinese bureaucracy or gentry could read foreign languages; most of them were forced to rely on interpreters who might not be trustworthy. Moreover, it was necessary for Chinese officials to study the subjects that foreigners considered important, with a view to understanding the foreigners' intentions. Hence a good foreign language school was urgently required. With their great native ability, Chinese could easily learn new subjects.

As long as only languages were taught, there was routine progress. But the implications of the T'ung-wen kuan were far from routine, and as this became clear to the extreme conservative faction, there was a vociferous (if temporarily unsuccessful) protest. The Tsungli-yamen's successful defense of its stand on education exemplifies the degree to which the conduct of foreign affairs had been modernized within the old order.

On January 28, 1867, the Tsungli-yamen proposed that an additional school be established to teach engineering, astronomy, and mathematics to students training for government service. The yamen argued that science was the basis of Western technology, and that *fundamental* knowledge was essential to China's program of self-strengthening. Foreign instructors were to be selected, and the whole scheme had Hart's approval. The

North China Herald took the announcement as a sign that Chinese exclusiveness was at last really giving way and conceded the possibility that the Chinese, if trained in Western science, might develop "real intelligence" in addition to their admittedly excellent memories. On February 25, 1867, Hsü Chi-yü was appointed director of the expanded school.

When the new plan became known, the extreme conservative opposition under the leadership of Wo-jen mobilized immediately. A Shantung censor, Chang Sheng-tsao, speaking for Wo-jen, stated the literati's case: the examination system was based on literature, not on technical subjects; astronomy and mathematics were the proper concern of the Observatory and the Board of Works and should not be introduced into the education of officials; officials should be trained in the classic principles of government and their application; science was a technical skill, the concern of subordinates if of anybody, and should not be elevated to a recognized position within the sphere of true learning.

The Throne backed the so-called liberal faction, and in an edict of March 5, 1867, laid down the principle that astronomy and mathematics now were a proper part of the education of a Chinese scholar, that science was more than "cleverness," that students could learn to use Western methods without abandoning the way of the sages. This was the very essence of the T'ung-chih Restoration: radical innovation within the old order.

The opposition did not yield easily, and in March 1867, the Grand Secretary Wo-jen himself began the major attack. As early as 1850 Wo-jen had written a famous memorial contrasting fundamental ethical teaching with this same "cleverness." In the intervening years he had been president of several boards, a tutor to the Emperor, president of the Censorate, and chancellor of the Hanlin Academy. He was an authority on the prevailing Confucian orthodoxy and the recognized leader of the opposition to Prince Kung and Wen-hsiang; for some time the Tsungli-yamen had been trying to neutralize his opposition by getting him appointed to its own ranks. Rumors spread rapidly. Couplets were hung in the city bemoaning the loss of state policy and the abandonment of respect for the philosophers when alien breeds became teachers. In Imperial audience Wo-jen remained bitter and intractable.

Thus the apparently minor issue of teaching science brought to a head the whole latent conflict between Restoration leaders and the majority of the literati. It illustrated the magnitude of the change that had almost imperceptibly taken place in the thinking of the leaders in the course of a few years. The issue was clearly defined, and the highest officials in the Empire were involved.

In a memorial of March 20, Wo-jen attacked the teaching of mathematics and astronomy on principle: good government came not from men of specialized training but from men of character. The Tsungli-yamen countered by sending Wo-jen copies of the views of Tseng Kuo-fan and others in support of the T'ung-wen kuan. Wo-jen then shifted his ground and suggested that if Western subjects must be taught, they might at least be taught by Chinese instructors. The Tsungli-yamen replied that few Chinese had the necessary competence. When an edict ordered Wo-jen himself to nominate qualified Chinese, he replied that he had no acquaintances in the scientific field.

At the end of April the Tsungli-yamen summarized its case and repeated its refutation of Wo-jen's basic principle. The yamen's position was approved by the Throne, which instructed the T'ung-wen kuan to proceed with the enrollment of students who could pass the qualifying examination for the scientific courses. Once more Wo-jen himself was ordered to serve in the Tsungli-yamen, and again he refused on the ground that he would make mistakes. His refusal was not at first accepted, but somehow he avoided appearing at his new post. Eventually a face-saving formula was worked out; owing to his "illness," Wo-jen was relieved of all his duties except those of Grand Secretary. This automatically excused him from the Tsungli-yamen.

The drought of 1867 offered Wo-jen's party a chance to renew the battle. In traditional Chinese political theory a natural calamity was interpreted as the result of some error in policy, and it was the Emperor's duty to correct the error so as to restore the harmony of the universe. The extreme conservatives seized the occasion to claim that the Tsungli-yamen's action had disturbed the natural harmony and caused the drought. On these grounds a chou magistrate-designate, one Yang T'ing-hsi, proposed the closing of the T'ung-wen kuan in order to bring rain. Yang claimed that the Tsungli-yamen had usurped power and had influenced the Emperor to ignore his proper advisers, the censors. He then proceeded to the main point, the inadaptability of Western civilization to China's needs.

Yang's argument was ridiculed in the edict in reply, but the Throne expressed concern over the powerful clique (*tang*) that might be behind him. Wo-jen was warned by name to remember the obligations of an official. The edict went on to reaffirm in positive language the government's determination to support the Tsungli-yamen's policy, citing the careers of Tseng Kuo-fan and Li Hung-chang to prove that Confucian learning could be combined with Western learning. The edict concluded that there was no need for the Hanlin Academy to restrict itself to literary subjects.

Once the principle was made clear, the blow was softened. The Tsungli-yamen offered to resign, but the resignation was refused. Yang for his part was not reprimanded, on the ground that the Emperor did not wish to discourage officials from offering advice. Instead Yang was invited to draw up a memorandum on self-strengthening. When Chung P'ei-hsien, a reader of the Grand Secretariat, suggested that Wo-jen and his party had been reprimanded for pointing out errors in government, an edict in reply denied this and stated that Wo-jen, although misinformed, had been genuinely and properly concerned with the public welfare.

In spite of these efforts to preserve the dignity of the opposition, official policy was made perfectly clear in an extraordinary series of vigorous Tsungli-yamen memorials and equally vigorous edicts. Translations of many of the documents were printed by the Maritime Customs and reproduced in the press and in Western documentary compilations. The importance of the episode was widely recognized. Burlingame reported developments to Washington, where the State Department admired both the strategy and tactics employed by the Tsungli-yamen. There is no foundation for the charge that Burlingame forwarded to Washington only the edicts that were critical of Wo-jen, without the alleged final decree that reversed the government's position. There was no such final reversal.

At the height of the Restoration, in 1867–68, there appeared to be good reason for the nearly universal optimism concerning the future of the T'ung-wen kuan. W. A. P. Martin wrote: "It was no small triumph for the college to survive an attack led on by the champion of the literati aided by such portents as they were able to evoke from the discord of the elements." According to the *London and China Express:*

> The whole civilized world has a stake in its [the T'ung-wen kuan's] success. . . . Why not educate Chinese in China, combine native with foreign learning, and endeavour to turn out men versed in modern science, but also fitted by literary attainments to fill magisterial offices, to become provincial governors, and perhaps eventually Presidents of Boards?

The *North China Herald* found throughout the documents on the case a "spirit which it is a positive refreshment to perceive."

After the defeat of the Wo-jen faction, the affairs of the T'ung-wen kuan appeared to be proceeding smoothly as far as the Chinese were concerned, and not to have been greatly affected by the confusion among the foreign staff caused by a suit for fraud against Hart in connection with the school. The distinguished mathematician Li Shan-lan joined the teaching staff in 1868. A colleague wrote of Li: "His faith, if he had any, was a compound of West and East. Professing to be a Confucian, he was an eclectic, grafting ideas alike from India and the Occident on the doctrines of the Chinese sage." Examinations in mathematics and science became a matter of routine, and both the number of students and the status of the school increased.

And yet the T'ung-wen kuan was in the end a failure, a

failure for which contemporary foreign explanations were wide of the mark. Some found fault with the school's avoidance of religious instruction, but this circumstance favored its success as a Chinese institution. Others argued that the foreign instructors spent too much time studying Chinese subjects: "The Peking College for the instruction of the Chinese in English literature has become the Peking College for the instruction of the English in Chinese literature." Here again, the instructors' interest in China, if it had had any effect at all on the school, would have contributed to its stability and served to allay Chinese hostility.

Chang Chih-tung, who had just begun his distinguished official career at the time of the T'ung-wen kuan episode, wrote thirty years later that the school had been sabotaged by a whispering campaign conducted by narrow-minded and conservative literati. It withered in a hostile climate of opinion, as Restoration leaders were succeeded by lesser men, and there were no further innovations in Chinese education until after 1895.

Until recently, Chinese historians have generally referred to the founding of the T'ung-wen kuan as an important step in the modernization of China but have not seriously considered the causes of its failure. Chinese Communist historians, who have lately inquired into the matter, have concluded that the school was an anti-Chinese imperialistic tool serving the interests of Manchus and foreigners. According to Fan Wen-lan, the aim of the Tsungli-yamen clique was to build up a body of translators and compradores and to keep the control of foreign affairs in Manchu hands. In Fan's (and Wo-jen's) view, the school encouraged worship of foreigners and contempt for Chinese; it failed because Li Hung-chang and other strong dissidents broke away from this Manchu-Western imperialist axis.

The optimists of the sixties who thought they were witnessing a profound and fundamental change in Chinese culture were not so wrong as this. The T'ung-wen kuan failed, like so many innovations of its time, because as it grew it came to challenge the basis of the Confucian state. Jui-lin, Grand Secre-

tary and Governor-General of Kwangtung and Kwangsi, pointed
to the fundamental obstacle: the students of the new schools
were neglecting their Western studies and were attending mainly
to traditional studies, which remained the qualification for
provincial office. Jui-lin urged that some means of changing
this situation be found, but no means could possibly be found
short of revolutionary change in the character of the Chinese
state and its officials. High officials could try their hand at
innovation, but they lacked the power to coerce the literati and
gentry. Even if they had had this power, they could not, as
Confucian statesmen, have chosen to use it.

The Restoration success in modernizing foreign relations
was noteworthy. In writing a formal preface to the collection of
Chinese documents on foreign relations for this period, the
Grand Secretary Pao-yün wrote: "The thirteen-year reign was
bright and glorious. This book [the *I-wu shih-mo*] offers a
golden mirror of it." The *I-wu shih-mo* certainly does in fact
record not the customary easy reassertion of China's traditional
pretensions in foreign affairs, but something far more important:
the labored working-out, with many setbacks, of a modern
foreign policy. By necessity and by choice, the main lines of
the policy were civil, but the long-term importance of military
strength was not forgotten.

At the end of the 1860s China's international position was
stronger than it had been at any time since 1840, stronger also
than it was to be again for nearly a century. Direct foreign
military intervention had virtually ceased; the forward movement of Western commercial enterprise had come to a halt;
there was some talk of the rendition of extraterritoriality; and
the beginnings of nationalism were not supplanting but reinforcing traditional ethnocentric culturalism.

Restoration foreign policy had succeeded in protecting
Chinese interests without damage to legitimate foreign interests.
The groups that had looked forward to the early and complete
incorporation of China into the world of nineteenth-century
commerce were bitter, as were those who had thought of con-

quest and annexation. Yet if imperialist dreams were shattered, the actual position of the typical foreign resident was greatly improved. Fifteen ports, and in addition Peking, were open to him for residence. Nearly everywhere he found safe conditions of travel and courteous treatment. The physical plant for the conduct of trade was improving each year with the construction of docks, the increased use of steamers, the firm establishment of an efficient Maritime Customs service, and various procedural innovations. The officials with whom he had to deal were becoming better informed; if he had a legitimate grievance and stated it reasonably, he would probably receive a fair hearing. The French, never easily satisfied with the performance of Asian governments, conceded that the signs of the times were encouraging. Harry Parkes characterized the new look in Sino-foreign relations very fairly as "a sort of husband and wife arrangement, with slight incompatibilities of temper on both sides."

During the Restoration both Chinese and foreign officials were convinced that China's domestic problems were paramount and that if these could be solved, foreign relations would present no serious difficulties. By this, Alcock and his colleagues meant that foreign interests depended on peace, order, effective central control, and domestic economic prosperity. Prince Kung, Tseng Kuo-fan, Tso Tsung-t'ang, and others meant that whereas domestic weakness and disorder invited foreign intervention, domestic strength commanded foreign circumspection.

Two events of the summer of 1870 marked the end of Restoration foreign policy: the British rejection of the Alcock Convention, and the Tientsin Massacre. Although these disasters may appear at first glance to be failures of the new Chinese diplomacy, each was in fact the result of developments outside the sphere of Chinese foreign policy. The reluctant decision of the British government to withhold ratification of the Alcock Convention was the result of direct pressure by British merchants on the British home government. The Tientsin Massacre was an explosion of local xenophobia, ignited by literati and local officials whose status was threatened by the Western intrusion. Such accidents apart, the Tsungli-yamen had devised ways of dealing satisfactorily with the conventional subject matter of international relations. It was helpless where the immediate requirements of foreign policy ran counter to the fundamental requirements of the Confucian order. . . .

🕉 A Great Statesman Advocates
Self-Strengthening

CHINA'S PATH to modernization was slow and tortuous. Unlike
the culturally flexible Japanese, who quickly realized that the
only alternative to modernization was foreign domination, the
Chinese feared that Western techniques would poison their
traditional culture. What they did not understand was that
foreign invasion was an even greater threat to that culture.

In China, winning the acceptance of Chinese officialdom
for even minor reforms was a difficult task, for it was the
Chinese scholar-official class which retained the largest vested
interest in the old Confucian order. They were not amenable
to any alteration of the *status quo,* lest their positions be
threatened, and they clung tenaciously to tradition, vilifying
any attempts at reform as a betrayal of the sacred national
credo, Confucianism.

But there were some who struggled against the conservatives—practical men who, though still deeply wedded to the
Confucian traditions, saw the necessity to study the barbarians'
technology in order to control them.

Li Hung-chang was such a man. A veteran of the Taiping
Rebellion, in which he had fought with Tseng Kuo-fan and
become intimately acquainted with Western armaments, he
came to the conclusion that if China wished to be strong and
defend herself against intruders, she must build a powerful
industrial base of her own. The only way to do this was to
study the West. Li's critics were quick to take up the cry
against him and accuse him of heresy.

The following selection is from a memorial to the Emperor written by Li Hung-chang in 1872 in defense of a faltering steamship-building program. Reading the memorial today, it is easy to see his impeccable logic, but unfortunately, this logic was far from obvious to many of Li's conservative contemporaries.

LI HUNG-CHANG *
Problems of Industrialization

We have seen with admiration the Sacred Emperor's vigorous striving for self-strengthening and for laying down broad far-reaching plans. Our admiration is beyond telling. Your minister has been thinking that the various European countries in the last several decades have advanced from India to the southern oceans, from the southern oceans to the northeast, and have invaded China's frontiers and interior land. Peoples never recorded in previous histories, who have had no contact with us since ancient times, have come to our points of entry to ask for trade relations. Our Emperors have been as generous as the sky and have made treaties with all of them for international trade in order to control them. People from a distance of ninety thousand *li,* from the cardinal points of the globe, are gathering together in China; this is the greatest change during the last three millennia and more!

The Westerners particularly rely upon the excellence and efficacy of their guns, cannon, and steamships, and so they can overrun China. The bow and spear, small guns, and native-made cannon which have hitherto been used by China cannot resist their rifles, which have their bullets fed from the rear opening. The sailing boats, rowboats, and the gunboats which

---

* Li Hung-chang in Teng Ssu-yü and John K. Fairbank, *China's Response to the West* (Cambridge, Mass.: Harvard University Press, 1954), pp. 108–110.

have been hitherto employed cannot oppose their steam-engined warships. Therefore, we are controlled by the Westerners.

To live today and still say "reject the barbarians" and "drive them out of our territory" is certainly superficial and absurd talk. Even though we wish to preserve the peace and to protect our territory, we cannot preserve and protect them unless we have the right weapons. They are daily producing their weapons to strive with us for supremacy and victory, pitting their superior techniques against our inadequacies, to wrangle with and to affront us. Then how can we get along for one day without weapons and techniques?

The method of self-strengthening lies in learning what they can do, and in taking over what they rely upon. Moreover, their possession of guns, cannon, and steamships began only within the last hundred years or so, and their progress has been so fast that their influence has spread into China. If we can really and thoroughly understand their methods—and the more we learn, the more improve—and promote them further and further, can we not expect that after a century or so we can reject the barbarians and stand on our own feet? Japan is just a small nation. Recently she has begun to trade with Europe; she has instituted iron factories and built many steamships. She has changed to the use of Western weapons. Does she have the ambition to plot to invade the Western nations? Perhaps she is merely planning for self-protection. But if Japan seeks only self-protection, she is nevertheless oppressing and looking down on our China. Should not China plan for herself? Our scholars and officials have confined themselves to the study of stanzas and sentences and are ignorant of the greatest change of the last several thousand years; they are accustomed to the temporary security of the present, and so they forget why we received the heavy blow and deep suffering of twenty or thirty years ago [the Opium War], and how we can obtain domestic security and control the foreigners within several centuries. That is how this talk of stopping steamship construction has originated.

Your minister humbly thinks that all other expenditures of

our nation can be economized, but the expenses for supporting the army, establishing defense measures, drilling in guns and cannon, and building warships should by all means never be economized. If we try to save funds, then we shall be obliged to neglect all these defense measures, the nation will never have anything to stand upon, and we shall never be strong. . . . The amount which has already been spent will, in turn, become a sheer waste. Not only will we be a laughingstock to foreigners, but we will also strengthen their aggressive ambitions. . . .

🐾 *A Practical Scholar-Official on*
New Methods of Reform

CHANG CHIH-TUNG (1837–1909), like Li Hung-chang, was one
of China's "self-strengtheners." Chang made famous the slogan
"Chinese learning for substance, Western learning for function"
(*"Chung-hsüeh wei t'i, Hsi-hsüeh wei yung"*). Chang, a brilliant
scholar and official trained in the classical tradition, coupled
a strong Neo-Confucian background and loyal defense of the
dynasty to a belief in moderate reform. His goal was to create
a modern Chinese military apparatus and graft it to China's
traditional Confucian society. His reform efforts included building arsenals, iron foundries, military academies, and technical
schools.

But as is evident from the following passage written in
1898, Chang was by no means an advocate of radical reform
or tampering with traditional Chinese institutions, and he was
certainly not a constitutionalist. He states emphatically, "The
doctrine of people's rights will not bring us a single benefit but
a hundred evils." Chang calls only for limited reform. But his
cautiousness cannot hide his deep concern over the fact that
China was no longer either "powerful or impressive." China's
weakness became a great source of distress to Chang, and he
proposed to make China strong and to preserve Chinese values
by studying Western knowledge. One is tempted to ask: How
can one defend Chinese ways by adopting Western ways? Was
it realistic for Chang to think that he could build modern
arsenals and train officers at Western-style military academies
and still expect the men involved to behave and act as Con-

fucian gentlemen? Were Chang's suggested reforms not tanta-mount to letting the fox into the henhouse, and then naïvely assuming that he would not eat the chickens? As Yen Fu (see pp. 283–292) later pointed out, "Chinese learning has its own substance and function; Western learning also has its own substance and function." To assume that the two could co-exist without any interaction was pure fantasy, and this was the main fallacy in Chang's argument; techniques do affect values, and means do determine ends. Modern factories, armies, and schools bring with them a way of life. The Chinese were slow to realize this, thus not until the old order lay in ruin at their feet did the idea of moderate reform within the perimeter of Chinese tradition finally yield to the idea of revolution.

CHANG CHIH-TUNG *
From *Exhortation to Study*

Nowadays scholars who hate the customs of the times are angry at the foreigners for cheating and encroaching upon us, at the generals for being unable to fight, at the great officials for not carrying out reforms, at the directors of education for not de-veloping schools, and at numerous officials for not investigating industry and commerce. Therefore they promote discussion of the people's rights [*min-ch'üan*, the term used above by Wang K'ang-nien and later used by Sun Yat-sen: "democracy"] in order to get the people to unite and exert themselves. Alas, why use such words that incite disorder!

The doctrine of people's rights will bring us not a single benefit but a hundred evils. Are we going to establish a parlia-ment? Among the Chinese scholars and people there are still many even today who are content to be vulgar and rustic. They

* Chang Chih-tung in *ibid.*, pp. 166–173.

are ignorant of the general situation of the world, they do not understand the basic system of the state. They have not the most rudimentary ideas about foreign countries—about the schools, the political systems, military training, and manufacture of armaments. Even supposing the confused and clamorous people are assembled in one house, for every one of them who is clearsighted, there will be a hundred others whose vision is beclouded; they will converse at random and talk as if in a dream—what use will it be?

Moreover in foreign countries, in such affairs as raising funds [levying taxes] and other financial matters, the emphasis is on the lower house; in other (important) legislation the emphasis is on the upper house. In general one must have moderate wealth in his family to get to be a member of parliament. Nowadays Chinese merchants rarely have much capital; the Chinese people, moreover, are lacking in farsighted long-range ambitions. When an important proposal for raising funds is to be discussed, all of them make excuses and keep silent. So their discussion is tantamount to nondiscussion. This is the first reason why there is no use (in having a parliament). . . .

Nowadays China is indeed neither impressive nor powerful. Nevertheless, the populace are still content with their daily work because the laws of the dynasty hold them together. Once the doctrine of people's rights is advocated, foolish people will assuredly be delighted; unruly people will rise up; the laws will not be carried out; great disorder will arise on all sides. . . .

Furthermore, the towns will certainly be plundered and churches burned or destroyed. I am afraid that certain foreign countries will be sure to take the protection of their nationals and properties as a pretext and send their gunboats with land forces to penetrate deeply and occupy our territories. The whole country then will belong to others with our acquiescence. Thus the doctrine of people's rights is just what our enemies will like to hear about. . . .

FOLLOWING THE PROPER ORDER

Now if we wish to make China strong and to preserve Chinese knowledge, we must study Western knowledge. Nevertheless, if we do not use Chinese knowledge to consolidate the foundation first and get straight in our minds what our interests and purposes are, then the strong will become rebellious leaders and the weak will become slaves of others [*i.e.*, of the foreigners]. . . .

Scholars today must master the classics first, in order to understand the purpose underlying the establishment of education by our ancient Chinese sages and teachers. They must study history, in order to learn the rise and fall of succeeding dynasties of China, and the customs of the empire. They must glance over the philosophical works and belles-lettres in order to become thoroughly familiar with Chinese academic ideas and exquisite writings. And then they can select and make use of that Western knowledge which can make up our shortcomings, and adopt those Western methods of government which can cure our illnesses. These, then, will be beneficial and harmless. As one who is recuperating must first get some energy from rice, and then be offered all sorts of delicacies . . . so the acquisition of Western knowledge must follow after Chinese knowledge.

In all schools in foreign countries the Bible of Jesus Christ must be read every day to illustrate their religion. In grade schools Latin must be learned first to insure the preservation of antiquity. The map of their own country must be familiar first, before the map of the whole globe is examined, to show that there is a proper order. . . . A Chinese scholar not versed in Chinese knowledge resembles a man who does not know his own surname, or a riding horse without a bridle, or a boat without a rudder; the more profound his Western knowledge the more severe will be his contempt for China. Even though there are such scholars, who have a broad knowledge of things and are equipped with many abilities, how can the country make use of them? . . .

ON REFORM

Reform [*pien-fa,* lit., a change of statutes] is the duty of the court. Why should it be discussed with scholars and the people? . . . The decision as to whether our system should be changed rests with the state, but actually it is determined by the wishes and discussions of scholars and the people.

Let us review events: when Tseng Kuo-fan was a vice-minister, he once submitted a memorial pointing out the defects of examining the Hanlin scholars in small-model writing and in the composition of poetry and the *fu* verse. After he was successful and became a state minister, if he had kept up [and taken action on] this criticism, he would have produced many men of ability in the Hanlin Academy during the last thirty years. Yet nothing more was heard about the matter. Why? Because after the great rebellion had been suppressed, he became fearful lest he be vilified by the contemporary scholars.

Wen-hsiang once opened the T'ung-wen kuan (see pp. 225–233) and published various books on international law and the natural sciences. If he had kept on promoting these things, he would have been able to obtain many men qualified to be sent to distant countries and thoroughly familiar with current affairs. Nevertheless, those who are careful about trifles and feel self-conscious warned one another against entering the T'ung-wen kuan or taking the examinations for secretaries of the Tsungli-yamen. Among the capital and court officials those who can discuss new knowledge are silent and unheard. Why? Because they were impeded by the erroneous ideas of all the absurd and narrow-minded scholars. Thus, even a meritorious minister [Tseng] and a venerable statesman [Wen-hsiang], though celebrated for their virtue and great authority, still cannot avoid being hindered by the criticism of those who are accustomed to using the wrong to overcome the right, and so no good effect can be seen. This is pitiful and lamentable!

Again, Tso Tsung-t'ang established a shipyard near Foochow and an arsenal and a woolen mill in Kansu; Shen Pao-chen set up the shipyard administration, opened schools, and consulted with Li Hung-chang in establishing the China Merchants' Steam Navigation Company; Ting Pao-chen instituted arsenals to make foreign guns and bullets in both Shantung and Szechwan—these were famous ministers who were known at the time to be honest, upright, and orthodox Confucians. Nevertheless, the things they undertook were all this kind of enterprise. At that time it was in the middle of the T'ung-chih period [1862–1874] and the first years of the Kuang-hsü period [1875–1908], when the nation was quiet and at ease. Unfortunately, current opinion caviled at many points, and those who followed (the men mentioned above) were again lacking in knowledge. They either let their establishments go to waste or operated them in a reduced form. None of them could achieve any expansion. Therefore the effect was not great.

In general, that which should not be changed is our human relationships and fundamental principles, not the system of laws; it is our sage's way, not instruments; it is the principle of the mind, not technology. Let us find evidence from the classics.

When all alternatives are exhausted, one has to make a change—change and accommodation to make the most of an advantage; change and accommodation to suit the time. The method of diminution and increase [of the statutes] should be used to keep abreast of the times. That is the idea of the *Book of Changes.*

"In instruments we do not seek old ones but new." That is the idea in the *Book of History.* "Knowledge exists among the four barbarians." That is the idea in the *Commentary on the Ch'un-ch'iu.* The Five Emperors did not follow the old music and the Three Kings did not copy the old ceremony. "The timely ceremony is the most important." That is the idea of the *Book of Rites.*

"He cherishes his old knowledge and is continually acquiring new. . . . When I walk with two persons, they may serve as my teachers; I select their good qualities and follow them." That is the idea of the Confucian *Analects.*

"When he employs (these virtues) they will be in accordance with right." That is the idea of *The Doctrine of the Mean*.
"When one has no sense of shame for not being equal to others,
what will he have with which to be an equal of them?"; that
is the idea of Mencius.

Let us find evidence from the histories. . . . In the successive dynasties the most conspicuous reforms are these four:
King Wu-ling of Chao [*ca.* 300 B.C.] reformed the traditional
military system (from footsoldiers) to mounted archers, and
by means of this the Chao frontier was made secure. King
Hsiao-wen [A.D. 467–499] of Northern Wei reformed the traditional system toward a more civilized one, by means of which
the Wei kingdom was well governed. These were gains from
reform. . . . Shang Yang reformed the traditional system
[359 B.C.], casting off filial piety, younger brotherhood, benevolence and righteousness. The Ch'in state remained strong for a
time and then fell into distress. Wang An-shih (1021–1086)
conducted a reform by devoting himself to harassing the people.
The Sung Dynasty was thereby involved in disorder. These
were losses from reform. The error of Lord Shang and of Wang
lay in the cruelty of harassing the people. It was not because
the reform should not have been made, but because these
particular reforms were improper. (Note: In Western political
systems two things, the elimination of punishments and the
feeding of the people, are matters of priority.). . . There
have been many changes (in the Ch'ing Dynasty). Even when
steamships and telegraph wires were first introduced, there was
much criticism. But at the present time, if anyone wished to
discard them, would there not be people who would bare their
arms and fight against the proposal?

Now those who reject reforms generally belong to three
categories. One consists of the narrow-minded scholars who
are ultra-conservative; the defects of ultra-conservatism are
easy to understand. Another consists of the vulgar officials who
like to take improper ease. For reform we must tax our thinking,
must collect funds, must select people, and must do actual
work. These are all inconvenient to the selfish plans of those

who are confused and lazy, and who like to shirk work, to be influenced by favoritism, or to take the easiest tasks. Therefore, under the cover of bookish and conservative talk, they gloss over the subterfuges of slippery officials who take improper ease. Such are their true feelings. When asked about their academic ideas and the governmental principles of the Chinese traditional system, all is revealed to have been neglect and sham on their part. They have not done a single thing. This is what they [the critics] mean by "follow the ancients." Is this sound? The third kind consists of the talkative scholars who like to be captious. Actually, in recent years there have been some imitations of Western methods which bore no fruit.

There are, however, four reasons for this. The first is, all people care for their selfish purposes, and so they plan only for themselves and no progress is made—for example, the various officials in charge of factories and the various people who went abroad. This is a defect of the people, not the defect of the reform. The second is the inadequacy of funds. From this comes a deficiency of money on all sides which prevents superior products, such as the shipyards. This is a defect of the times, not the defect of reform. Third, there is no fixed policy at Court. A new thing may be suddenly taken up and then suddenly suspended, with nothing accomplished, such as the sending of students abroad and of officials from the capital to travel in foreign countries. This is the defect of unfounded reports [as to their behavior], not the defect of reform. Fourth, there are instruments but no personnel to handle them. When we had not yet learned mechanical engineering, we bought machines; when we had not yet trained captains or admirals, we purchased a fleet—such were our navy and the various factories. This is the defect of having the wrong sequence in what should go first or later, not the defect of reform. Nevertheless, there is the idle talk of people not on the scene, who do not trace the causes of the [following] unfortunate results: the fluctuations of national policy, the carelessness in employing people, the decentralization of responsibilities, the insufficiency of funds, and the half-hearted effort in our studies. But they cavil at trifles and reproach us for producing little result. They are even worse than the person who "looks at a crossbow and immediately expects a roast dove before him; or who sees an egg, and immediately expects to hear it crow." When schoolhouses are just being built, they demand accomplished men of ability. When a mine has not yet been opened, they demand that it pay a profit. There is no fixed standard in handling matters and no fixed aim in personnel. When some state affair is urgent, then everything is taken up; and when things have slowed down, then everything is again put aside. One digs a grave, the other fills it up. How could we expect any success?

III. Collapse and Despair:
The Late Nineteenth and Early Twentieth Centuries

Japan's slashing victory over lumbering China in 1895 pushed the Chinese over the dividing line which separated hope from despair and decline from collapse. A small island nation of Eastern barbarians—who in the distant past had borrowed again and again from China and since 1870 had been rapidly building a modern nation—easily defeated the superior forces of China. China's much heralded navy turned out to be a paper tiger. The defeat accomplished, other imperialist nations quickly joined the scramble to cut chunks of territory and concessions out of China. Now finally stripped of her splendor, confidence, and pride, China stood dumbly aside, acquiescing to whatever the barbarians wanted of her.

Attempts at reform continued. Progressive scholar-officials agitated for a modern-type government, and a constitutional monarchy was belatedly proclaimed in 1906. In Eastern China business thrived, due in no small measure to the stimulating effect of foreign investment. Nevertheless, the intellectuals, who had traditionally given China her consciousness, no longer tried to hide their sense of helplessness and growing pessimism. The days of the world's oldest empire were numbered.

The period around the turn of the century was characterized by an uncertainty and a searching, everywhere apparent in the writings of the intellectuals. Historians have significantly failed to give this interim period between China's death and rebirth any specific name. There were few consistent currents. It was a decade and a half of intellectual turmoil, apparent in the writings of Yen Fu and Liang Ch'i-ch'ao. Famine, suffering, and inept government marked this period. China's future leaders, deep in thought, read voraciously and tried to understand the new concepts and isms the modern world was offering China. Great numbers of students were studying abroad, where they were exposed not only to Western ideas but to the new Western image of China. It was shameful to realize that China, once the center of the universe, was now a pariah among nations.

Among the younger students despair turned into hatred, not so much against the West and Japan, but against China's antiquated rulers. The Manchus were attacked as an alien race oppressing the true greatness of the Chinese people. From these anti-Manchu feelings modern Chinese nationalism evolved. In older times, secure in their identity, the Chinese did not call themselves Chinese—they were men of the T'ang Dynasty (as the Cantonese still call themselves today) or men of the Ch'ing. Now, as had happened in the Europe of post-Napoleonic times, young intellectuals, living abroad and steeped in Western learning, said proudly, "We are Chinese." Nationalism is the modern search for racial identity in a changing world, yet that identity often develops through hatred of an alien race: "They oppress our true selves; we are not what they are." And so China experienced her first great race hatred, not so much against the foreigners but against Manchus who looked and acted like Chinese yet were so different.

An American-educated Cantonese doctor started an anti-dynastic secret society in Kwangtung, and then went around the world plotting and agitating against the Manchus, channeling the currents of hatred into a wave which finally destroyed the dynasty. We shall deal with his movement in the following section, but here we must focus on the intellectual and political climate which made that movement possible. Intellectually it was a period of despair and growing hatred; politically it was a time of impotence.

China's present-day rulers were youths at that time. They remember the China of the turn of the century as a country where lawlessness spread, foreigners finally secured their privileges, long-gowned officials prayed that disaster would pass. They felt the deepest shame for their country. On the other hand, they became aware of a world forging ahead because of its ideas, science, and power. They worshiped Japan and respected the West. They read and talked and dreamt of the day they could save their country. Two thousand years of empire had made the Chinese into political men, and the devotion of one's life to the cause of the nation and the people came naturally. But at that time no one yet knew how to save China except by sweeping away the crumbling heritage of the past.

❧ Japan's Modern Sword Cuts into China's Body

THE Sino-Japanese War erupted in 1894 because of China's claim to suzerainty over Korea. The hostilities which followed were a dramatic test of the degree to which each country had succeeded in modernizing. On paper, Li Hung-chang's Peiyang fleet was an impressive force of some sixty-five warships. But in reality the Japanese navy's thirty-two ships were far superior because their crews were better trained and they carried more modern armaments.

In September 1894, when the two fleets met and clashed off the mouth of the Yalu River, the Chinese were quickly beaten in a tragic and humiliating defeat. China—the Middle Kingdom, the center of the tribute system, the elder statesman of East Asia—was humbled before her former vassal Japan. If defeat and humiliation from the West was painful, it was unbearable from the East. A drubbing from England or France could be explained away as victimization of crass material superiority. And what difference did it make as long as China and the East held spiritual superiority? But China could not apply this rationalization to Japan. Had not the Japanese borrowed their culture from China during the early Nara and Heian periods? Did not the Japanese look and write like the Chinese? What had happened? What had gone wrong?

For the first time in history the Chinese began to take a long look at themselves and to question the whole Confucian system. Their confidence in the efficacy of their old traditions seasoned with moderate reforms was shattered. What good was the past if it could not even protect them against Japan? Obviously the situation called for radical measures. Li Hung-chang aptly described China when confronted by Ito Hirobumi during peace negotiations at Shimonoseki after the war. Ito said to him, "Ten years ago at Tientsin I talked to you about reform. Why is it that up to now not a single thing has been changed or reformed?" Li replied, "Affairs in my country have been so confined by tradition."

China's defeat, however, was not without its saving grace. News of the defeat hit half-slumbering China like a bucket of cold water: the brief Reform Movement which followed was in no small measure a response to the Japanese victory.

The first selection below is Japan's declaration of war against China, in which the Japanese Emperor explains his country's position vis-à-vis Korea. One must not be deceived by the behavior which Sir Robert Hart describes as being "a mixture of civilized grace and Asiatic slyness." Japanese intentions were clear: Japan was beginning to expand outward; Korea was only the first step in her long march across Asia which culminated in World War II.

The second selection is the Kuang-hsü Emperor's highly confident decree to the Chinese people in which he tries to explain the reasons for the war. He makes no attempt to hide his contempt for the Japanese by referring to them as *Wojen* (a highly pejorative name, literally, "dwarf"): he says that Li Hung-chang is "to hasten to root the *Wojen* out of their lairs. He is to send successive armies of valiant men to Korea in order to save the Koreans from the dust of bondage." Such confidence was unwarranted, but it took the Sino-Japanese War to prove it to the Chinese.

The third selection is a short passage by Sir Robert Hart, Inspector General of the Chinese Imperial Customs, who was renowned as "a friend of China." He poignantly expresses the comic tragedy of proud China's defeat.

THE JAPANESE EMPEROR *
Declaration of War Against China

We, by the grace of Heaven, Emperor of Japan, seated on a Throne occupied by the same dynasty from time immemorial, do hereby make proclamation to all our loyal and brave subjects, as follows:—

We hereby declare war against China, and we command each and all our competent authorities, in obedience to our wish and with a view to the attainment of the national aim, to carry on hostilities by sea and by land against China, with all the means at their disposal, consistently with the Law of Nations.

During the past three decades of our reign our constant aim has been to further the peaceful progress of the country in civilization; and, being sensible of the evils inseparable from complications with foreign states, it has always been our pleasure to instruct our Minister of State to labor for the promotion of friendly relations with our Treaty Powers. We are gratified to know that the relations of our Empire with those Powers have yearly increased in good will and in friendship. Under the circumstances, we were unprepared for such a conspicuous want of amity and of good faith as has been manifested by China in her conduct towards this country in connection with the Korean affair.

Korea is an independent state. She was first introduced into the family of nations by the advice and guidance of Japan. It has, however, been China's habit to designate Korea as her dependency, and both openly and secretly to interfere with her

* The Japanese Emperor in MacNair, *Modern Chinese History, op. cit.,* pp. 530–532.

domestic affairs. At the time of the recent insurrection in Korea, China despatched troops thither, alleging that her purpose was to afford a succor to her dependent state. We, in virtue of the treaty concluded with Korea in 1882, and looking to possible emergencies, caused a military force to be sent to that country.

Wishing to procure for Korea freedom from the calamity of perpetual disturbance, and thereby to maintain the peace of the East in general, Japan invited China's co-operation for the accomplishment of the object. But China, advancing various pretexts, declined Japan's proposal. Thereupon Japan advised Korea to reform her administration so that order and tranquility might be preserved at home, and so that the country might be able to discharge the responsibilities and duties of an independent state abroad. Korea has already consented to undertake the task. But China has secretly and insidiously endeavored to circumvent and to thwart Japan's purpose. She has further procrastinated and endeavored to make warlike preparations both on land and at sea. When those preparations were completed she not only sent large reinforcements to Korea, with a view to the forcible attainment of her ambitious designs, but even carried her arbitrariness and insolence to the extent of opening fire upon our ships in Korean waters. China's plain object is to make it uncertain where the responsibility resides of preserving peace and order in Korea, and not only to weaken the position of that state in the family of nations—a position obtained for Korea through Japan's efforts—but also to obscure the significance of the treaties recognizing and confirming that position. Such conduct on the part of China is not only a direct injury to the rights and interests of this Empire, but also a menace to the permanent peace and tranquility of the Orient. Judging from her actions, it must be concluded that China from the beginning has been bent upon sacrificing peace to the attainment of her sinister object. In this situation, ardent as our wish is to promote the prestige of the country abroad by strictly peaceful methods, we find it impossible to avoid a formal declaration of war against China. It is our earnest wish that, by the loyalty and valor of our faithful subjects, peace may soon be permanently restored and the glory of the Empire be augmented and completed.

Given this 1st day of the eighth month of the 27th year of Meiji. . . .

THE CHINESE EMPEROR *
Declaration of War Against Japan

Korea has been our tributary for the past two hundred odd years. She has given us tribute all this time, which is a matter known to the world. For the past dozen years or so Korea has been troubled by repeated insurrections and we, in sympathy with our small tributary, have as repeatedly sent succor to her aid, eventually placing a Resident in her capital to protect Korea's interests. In the fourth moon (May) of this year another rebellion was begun in Korea, and the King repeatedly asked again for aid from us to put down the rebellion. We then ordered Li Hung-chang to send troops to Korea; and they having barely reached Yashan the rebels immediately scattered. But the *Wojen,* without any cause whatever, suddenly sent their troops to Korea, and entered Seoul, the capital of Korea, reinforcing them constantly until they have exceeded ten thousand men. In the meantime the Japanese forced the Korean king to change his system of government, showing a disposition every way of bullying the Koreans.

It was found a difficult matter to reason with the *Wojen.* Although we have been in the habit of assisting our tributaries, we have never interfered with their internal government. Japan's treaty with Korea was as one country with another; there is no law for sending large armies to bully a country in this way, and compel it to change its system of government. The various powers are united in condemning the conduct of the Japanese,

* The Chinese Emperor in *ibid.,* pp. 532–534.

and can give no reasonable name to the army she now has in Korea. Nor has Japan been amenable to reason, nor would she listen to the exhortation to withdraw her troops and confer amicably upon what should be done in Korea. On the contrary, Japan has shown herself bellicose without regard to appearances, and has been increasing her forces there. Her conduct alarmed the people of Korea as well as our merchants there, and so we sent more troops over to protect them. Judge of our surprise then when, halfway to Korea, a number of the *Wojen* ships suddenly appeared, and taking advantage of our unpreparedness, opened fire upon our transports at a spot on the seacoast near Yashan, and damaged them, thus causing us to suffer from their treacherous conduct, which could not be foretold by us. As Japan has violated the treaties and not observed international laws, and is now running rampant with her false and treacherous actions commencing hostilities herself, and laying herself open to condemnation by the various powers at large, we therefore desire to make it known to the world that we have always followed the paths of philanthropy and perfect justice throughout the whole complications, while the *Wojen,* on the other hand, have broken all the laws of nations and treaties which it passes our patience to bear with. Hence we commanded Li Hung-chang to give strict orders to our various armies to hasten with all speed to root the *Wojen* out of their lairs. He is to send successive armies of valiant men to Korea in order to save the Koreans from the dust of bondage. We also command the Manchu generals, viceroys, and governors of the maritime provinces, as well as the commanders-in-chief of the various armies, to prepare for war and to make every effort to fire on the *Wojen* ships if they come into our ports, and utterly destroy them. We exhort our generals to refrain from the least laxity in obeying our commands in order to avoid severe punishment at our hands. Let all know this edict as if addressed to themselves individually.

Respect this!

SIR ROBERT HART *
The Tragedy of China's Defeat

China's collapse has been terrible, and the comical and tragical have dovetailed all along the frontier of incident in the most heartbreaking, side-bursting fashion. Even today those who can try to make their own game out of any *sycee* issued for expenditure and the heart of the country knows nothing of the war, and will not make allowances for defeat: thus the government will have its own difficulties in getting the people at large to believe in sacrifices made for peace, and internal trouble may appear just as the external war ends. But in fact, although it is only at a minute spot along the fringe of this big empire that the Chinese have received thrashing after thrashing, it is the shell of the egg that is cracked, and—it seems to me a bad case of Humpty Dumpty. The conditions were terrible, and those wily Japanese have played their cards—even in framing conditions—with such a mixture of civilized grace and Asiatic slyness that all the world will be on their side and applaud, and all China will wince from North to South and for a whole cycle! I am trying to get rid of an innocent impossibility which might any day become a breach of treaty and a new *casus belli* and also of a pound of flesh plus blood stipulation which would be hard to stagger under, as well as to round off a few corners to a shape that will be easier: but I find the other party is too clever and knows both what it wants, and how to get it, too well, to allow me to hope for success. Japan wants to lead the East in war, in commerce, and in manufactures, and next century will be a hard one for the West! Everything that China should have yielded gracefully to others when asked for will now have to be yielded to Japan's hectoring. Japan will then pose and say to all creation—"That's the way to do it, you see, and it's I that did it!"

* Sir Robert Hart in *ibid.*, pp. 543–544.

🏵 Suffering and Starvation Among
the Chinese People

"FAMINE AND FLOOD are China's sorrow. From time out of mind Chinese chronicles have recorded these recurrent disasters with the beating, persistent note of doom." So wrote Theodore H. White of the great Honan famine of 1943.

Famine was as much a part of the Chinese peasant's life as the rising and the setting of the sun. Floods, droughts, and pestilence swept China from time immemorial, killing millions in a single year. No government since the dawn of Chinese history was able effectively to control the periodic rampages of the Yellow River or check the hordes of locusts which frequently descended on the fields, blocking out the sun and devouring all crops before them.

As Walter Mallory, former Secretary of the China International Famine Relief Commission, points out in the selection below, famine will endure and the peasant will be at its mercy until China learns to control the ravages of nature. Mr. Mallory writes almost prophetically when he says, "The chronic famine situation in China cannot be adequately relieved without a stable and effective government." What China needed was a strong government able to control nature: to build dams and dikes, dig out reservoirs, open up new irrigation channels, organize men and mobilize materials to kill pests, and perhaps most important, to develop a capability for moving food from surplus to deficit regions.

No Chinese government has been as powerful as the present Communist government in China. Though great dynasties of the past undertook waterwork programs on a remarkable scale, none can match the present government for the scope of its efforts. Communist waterwork programs have been criticized within and without China for disregarding nature's ecological balance. Yet, if famine control be considered a measure of success and failure, then the success of the Communist government in preventing wholesale starvation during the severe food crisis of 1960–1962 suggests that a way may have been found finally to eradicate China's eternal curse of famine.

WALTER H. MALLORY *
From *China, Land of Famine*

Food is the most urgent problem of the Chinese. This fact is reflected even in the speech of the people. In China the polite salutation on meeting a friend is "Have you eaten?" instead of the customary inquiry as to one's health or well-being usually employed in other tongues. This form of greeting is a creation of the rural community, and the implication is that if the person so saluted has not eaten, the inquirer will see that his needs are quickly met. Foreigners who study the language with a Chinese teacher find that almost the first words and phrases given to them have to do with food, eating, and money (with which to buy food). "The rich man has food to eat, the poor man has none," forms the basis of one of the first lessons. Beggars are referred to in the colloquial idiom as "food wanters"; and they all provide themselves with pails or bowls in which they can receive the refuse from the tables of the well-to-do.

The food problem is an ancient one in China: from the earliest times famines have been an ever recurring scourge. A study recently completed by the Student Agricultural Society

* Walter H. Mallory, *China, Land of Famine* (New York: American Geographical Society, 1926), pp. 1–4, 189–191.

of the University of Nanking brought to light the surprising and significant fact that between the years 108 B.C. and A.D. 1911 there were 1,828 famines, or one nearly every year in some one of the provinces. Untold millions have died of starvation. In fact the normal death rate may be said to contain a constant famine factor. Depleted vitality following years of want also tends to increase the death rate. Chinese history is filled with the details of past disasters and not only recounts at great length the nature of the calamity and its causes but names the officials under whom relief work was administered and describes the methods pursued in bringing succor to the unfortunate victims.

The Emperor Yü, who lived four thousand years ago, achieved great renown and is still regarded by the Chinese people as a national sage, for the wisdom displayed in his flood prevention work on the Yellow River. Since his time officials have repeatedly endeavored to follow his example, and fame has been more readily achieved by devising methods to relieve and prevent famine emergencies than in almost any other way.

The great drought that occurred in North China in 1920–1921, during which, according to the best obtainable information, five hundred thousand of the natives perished, is still fresh in the minds of the public. Mr. Dwight W. Edwards, in his comprehensive report, estimates that at the height of the distress nearly twenty million people were destitute. In some of the worst affected districts not only was the entire reserve of food consumed but also all other vegetation. A house-to-house canvass revealed the following bills of fare: *k'ang,* mixed with wheat blades, flour made of ground leaves, Fuller's earth, flowerseed, poplar buds, corncobs, *hung ching tsai* (steamed balls of some wild herb), sawdust thistles, leaf dust, poisonous tree bean, *kaoliang* husks, cottonseed, elm bark, bean cakes (very unpalatable), peanut hulls, sweet potato vines ground (considered a great delicacy), roots, stone ground up into flour to piece out the ground leaves. Some of the food was so unpalatable that the children starved, refusing to eat it.

Everything of any intrinsic value was sold by the poorer people, even including the roof timbers; and interest rates rose until even 100 per cent was considered not unreasonable in some places. There was extensive migration of the people from the dry regions, in some localities whole villages moving out. The sale of women and children, particularly young girls, reached such proportions that a special committee was organized for the protection of children. Prices ranged from $3.00 to $150.00, Chinese currency (one dollar in United States currency equals approximately two Chinese dollars), and thus the sacrifice of one or two of the younger members of the family served to provide the wherewithal to purchase food for the rest. Parents were not ready to give up their children but did so rather than see them starve.

Mr. Edwards estimates that more than $37,000,000, Chinese currency, was made available to meet the needs of the sufferers. Of this more than half was administered under international auspices; and this included large sums from abroad, particularly America. At the height of their operations the international committees alone were feeding more than 7,700,000 individuals.

A notable work was accomplished. But what of the future? Has a starving population today been saved simply to die during the next famine a few years hence unless further aid is forthcoming? Is there no means by which these great disasters can be prevented?

Well-wishers of China who have studied her famine problem have brought forward many schemes for improving conditions. They reflect the particular interest with which their authors are identified, ranging all the way from the fundamentalist missionary's faith that if the Chinese masses will become Christians, "the Lord will provide" to the machinery salesman's idea that China's only hope is the early adoption of industrialism.

Conservancy engineers tell us that the most urgent need is the control of China's rivers to prevent devastating floods, the carrying-out of irrigation, land reclamation, and similar projects to increase the cultivable land. Economists propose the introduction of better banking methods which will lower the interest rates and make possible the application of the surplus capital in the cities to the rural sections of the country. Or, again, they advance the proposal to relieve the pressure of population in the thickly settled regions by colonization of the vast areas of Manchuria and Mongolia. Provision of better transportation facilities is also urged so that the abundant crops of a prosperous district may be quickly and cheaply moved to a section where flood or drought may have created a condition of want.

The educator advocates the teaching of agriculture in the schools and colleges and the advanced training of foresters. He traces China's ills, particularly of the northern provinces of the country, to deforestation—a process which has been under way for centuries.

Many of those who give their thought to the social aspects of the situation point to the phenomenally high birth rate and insist, quite justly in the author's opinion, that no permanent solution of the problem of famines in China is possible until the people are content to regulate the size of their families according to their resources.

All agree that the present unusually bad conditions are in a measure traceable to the political disorganization of the country. However, there is no more appropriate time than the present to consider by what means better conditions can be brought about; and indeed there are many remedial measures that can be initiated even in these disordered days.

The question is one of such magnitude that, if any appreciable progress is to be made, all of the plans mentioned above must be followed. But there are certain types of work that will yield results more quickly than others, and it is the author's purpose not only to present plans but to examine them in some detail and endeavor to point out the relative importance of each.

The chronic famine situation in China cannot be adequately relieved without a stable and effective government. This does not mean, however, that no amelioration can be achieved during these disordered times. Any doubt on that score has been removed by the operations during the past six years of the China International Famine Relief Commission and its constituent committees.

There are some lines of work that will yield results more quickly than others. In order of importance they are:

(1) Flood control, irrigation, land reclamation.
(2) Economic improvement, rural credits, colonization, home and village industry.
(3) Improved agriculture and forestation.
(4) Development of transportation.
(5) Education.

Several of these might be undertaken at once. In fact all of them should be pressed as vigorously as possible, and it should be noted that some progress is actually being made day by day in several of these directions. But on account of the limited funds at the disposal of cooperative enterprise, the undertakings that would be most quickly productive should be put in the forefront.

Many persons will not agree with the writer as to this arrangement. For instance, some will doubt the wisdom of putting education last when the reduction of the birth rate is so vital to the prosperity of the people of China and hence to the famine problem of the future. But even the most sanguine will agree that modification of the fundamental concepts of the people will be a very slow and expensive process. What is needed is the immediate release of the masses from the constant threat of starvation. This will in itself create conditions where education can be appreciated and where more thought can be devoted to the larger social aspects of life.

The greatest immediate benefit to the nation will come from insurance of the crops against flood and drought and provision of means to increase the area of cultivable land and the yield on the fields already worked. This can be done by flood control, irrigation, land reclamation, and other similar projects which modern engineering has made possible. The cost of such work in China, where human labor is plentiful and cheap, is relatively small compared with the benefits which result; and the effect is at once apparent, even minor projects bringing prosperity almost immediately to thousands of people. Although the largest schemes must wait for better political conditions, there are almost unlimited fields for work on problems of small dimensions.

Next to conservancy, the most quickly productive work is the economic improvement of the rural population by the provision of better credit facilities, by the introduction of home and village industries, by colonization, and similar enterprises. Most of these, except colonization, can be undertaken at once and carried forward even under present conditions in China. Improved agriculture and forestation might also be included in this category; but they are more difficult to bring about, and their benefits are not so quickly apparent.

The development of transportation is important, but in its effects on the famine problem it is put fourth. There are already existing trunk lines which serve the provinces that are most susceptible to distress, and the cost of extending the system is at present almost prohibitive. Quicker results can be effected by using funds for conservancy or rural improvement.

Education, in its broader sense, is the fundamental cure for the ills not only of China but of the world. It goes hand in hand with the projects of improvement listed above—in fact it may even be considered an integral part of every one of them. Education is used here not in its broad sense but in the commonly accepted meaning of the acquisition of knowledge from books, and hence is put at the end of the list.

And now for a final word about the population problem. In the writer's opinion it is overpopulation that constitutes the fundamental reason for the recent famines in China. Furthermore, overpopulation is now a matter of world concern. What has occurred in China will, if the human race lets nature take her course, most certainly occur in other lands which are now prosperous. If a pair of rabbits are shut in an enclosure which has a limited area of good grass they will be comfortably pro-

vided for; but their numerous progeny will have very hard
scratching unless some altruistic person throws in fodder from
outside. There are optimists among us who ascribe to Provi-
dence this role of benefactor to the ever increasing human race,
but they fail to take cognizance of the fact that no bountiful
showers of manna have fallen in China. And who will say that
there is no need?

🌀 The Western Missionary: Sympathy, Contempt, and Preaching

THE POPULAR image of turn-of-the-century China was formed by the Chinatowns of American cities and contact with American missionaries in China. The "Chinaman" in America was truly a being from another planet. The Chinese remained aloof from the communities in which they lived thereby arousing much suspicion and misunderstanding. This image of an exotic and unintelligible people was reinforced by missionary writings and letters back to their congregations from their posts in China.

The missionary was America's hot line to China. Thus it is not surprising to find that the American people judged China in the same moral terms as the missionaries in the field. The missionary, who had sacrificed all in order to go forth among the heathen and preach the gospel of Jesus Christ, was deeply respected by the folks back home. As Paul Varg said in *Missionaries, Chinese, and Diplomats* (p. 121), "To leave America and go anyplace was sacrifice; but to go to China was tantamount to offering life itself, the last measure of full devotion." Although the missionary often spoke with great bias, he spoke as an on-the-spot observer, and his word was Gospel to those who read it in America's small towns.

Missionaries, with some notable exceptions, approached China with almost unbounded self-righteousness. The picture they painted of China portrayed the Chinese as quaint pagans misled from the path of eternal salvation by their own false religions. The Chinese were proclaimed as men lacking in all "character" and "conscience" who had systematized corruption and deceit; their inefficiency and backwardness were ridiculed as the natural products of a misbegotten culture. Gone were the days when Western men like Voltaire and Quesnay (see pp. 114–120) looked enviously to the East. China was the quintessence of incompetence among nations. Her only salvation lay in "God" and the "West."

Although missionaries tended to disparage China, they held a strong sentimental attachment to the country and her people. China became the arena for a group of deeply religious Americans who wished to proclaim themselves charitable decent Christians. China's weakness and helplessness offered a perfect object toward which this reformist zeal and Christian enthusiasm could be directed. But all these well-intentioned motives were prefaced by one unalterable assumption: superiority. Missionaries were rewarded with a feeling of great dedication and sacrifice in knowing that they were helping people who could not help themselves. But this paternalism was a dead-end street, and it made it very difficult for Americans to accept China and the "Chinaman" as equals. It was with a sense of bewilderment and betrayal that Americans watched Chinese nationalism and hostility toward the West develop during the last half century. Weren't we China's faithful friend? Wasn't it ungrateful of them to throw us out after we had built schools, hospitals, and churches, after we had spent endless painful hours trying to bring them the Gospel, and after all the years of physical privation we had spent away from home?

The following selection is taken from the writings of Arthur H. Smith, a missionary of thirty years' residence in China and highly popular as a lecturer on China around the turn of the century. His first statement—"What the Chinese lack is not intellectual ability . . . [but] Character and Conscience"—reveals the core of the missionary attitude toward the Chinese. The missionaries had discovered that the Chinese were as intelligent as any foreigner, if not more so. But in the absence of moral conviction which could come only from true religion, this intelligence was wasted and corrupted. China needed God and Christianity to make her great, and it was the missionary's sacred duty to bring about her moral rebirth. After all, the missionaries argued passionately, it was for China's own good, her own salvation.

The Chinese felt indignant at these Westerners, many of whom were their cultural inferiors, acting as schoolmasters toward children who had to be trained to become adults. Yet one may wonder whether something of the missionary message did actually affect the Chinese. From the latter decades of the nineteenth century, missionary stations were found throughout China, even in the remotest regions. Missionaries everywhere preached religion, character, and conscience. Though few Chinese converted, many attended Christian schools.

Today we see a new China in which moral character, spirit, individual conviction, and devotion to the higher cause is exalted over crass materialism and individualism. Much of the "Thought of Mao Tse-tung," save for its Marxist content, could have come out of missionary schools. Chinese Communism's moral and emotional content has roots in China's tradition of rebellion and in the revolutionary cries that came from Russia. Yet with its thought reform, intensive self-analysis, puritanism, and its obsession with changing the individual, Chinese Communism has traits not generally found in other Communist Parties. Arnold Toynbee has called Communism a Christian heresy. Perhaps the missionaries' incessant preaching had its effect. While few were convinced that character and conscience could come from Christianity, millions believed that individual regeneration was necessary for China's salvation. Not Christianity with religious beliefs that came out of the hoary past and struck many Chinese as not so different from what they had known in Buddhism and Taoism, but Communism with its rational-scientific conception of the world and its historical inevitability became the source of regeneration. The Chinese desired moral regeneration, not from religion, which they regarded as "feudal superstition," but from science, reason, and the new *Tao* of the forces of world history.

ARTHUR H. SMITH *
From *Chinese Characteristics*

What the Chinese lack is not intellectual ability. It is not patience, practicality, nor cheerfulness, for in all these qualities they greatly excel. What they do lack is Character and Conscience. Some Chinese officials cannot be tempted by any bribe, and refuse to commit a wrong that will never be found out, because "Heaven knows, earth knows, you know, and I know." But how many Chinese could be found who would resist the pressure brought upon them to recommend for employment a relative who was known to be incompetent? Imagine for a moment the *domestic consequences* of such resistance, and is it strange that any Chinese should dread to face them? But what Chinese would ever think of carrying theoretical morals into such a region as that? When it is seen what a part parasitism and nepotism play in the administration of China, civil, military, and commercial, is it any wonder that Chinese gatekeepers and constables are not to be depended upon for the honest performance of their duties? . . .

Chinese society resembles some of the scenery in China. At a little distance it appears fair and attractive. Upon a nearer approach, however, there is invariably much that is shabby and repulsive, and the air is full of odors which are not fragrant. No photograph does justice to Chinese scenery, for though photography has been described as "justice without mercy," this is not true of Chinese photography, in which the dirt and the smells are omitted.

There is no country in the world where the symbol denoting happiness is so constantly before the eye as in China.

* Arthur H. Smith, *Chinese Characteristics* (New York: Fleming H. Revell Co., 1894), pp. 316–330.

But it requires no long experience to discover that it is a true observation that Chinese happiness is all on the outside. We believe it to be a criticism substantially just that there are no homes in Asia. . . .

That many of the evils in Chinese society the existence of which we have pointed out are also to be found in Western "nominally Christian lands," we are perfectly aware. Perhaps the reader may have been disappointed not to find a more definite recognition of this fact, and some systematic attempt at comparison and contrast. Such a procedure was in contemplation, but it had to be given up. The writer's acquaintance with any Western country except his own is of an altogether too limited and inadequate character to justify the undertaking, which must for other reasons have failed. Let each reader make his own running comparisons as he proceeds, freeing himself as far as he may be able from "the bias of patriotism," and always giving the Chinese the benefit of the doubt. After such a comparison shall have been made, the very lowest result which we should expect would be the ascertained fact that the face of every Western land is towards the dawning morning of the future, while the face of China is always and everywhere towards the darkness of the remote past. A most pregnant fact, if it is a fact, and one which we beg the reader to ponder well; for how came it about?

The needs of China, let us repeat, are few. They are only Character and Conscience. Nay, they are but one, for Conscience *is* Character. It was said of a famous maker of pianos that he was "like his own instruments—square, upright, and grand." Does one ever meet any such characters in China?

At the close of the biography of one of the literary men of England, who died but a few years ago, occurs the following passage, written by his wife: "The outside world must judge him as an author, a preacher, a member of society; but they only who lived with him in the intimacy of everyday life at home can tell what he was as a man. Over the real romance of his life, and over the tenderest, loveliest passages in his private letters, a veil must be thrown; but it will not be lifting it too far to say, that if in the highest, closest of earthly relationships, a love that never failed—pure, passionate, for six-and-thirty years—a love which never stooped from its own lofty level to a hasty word, an impatient gesture, or a selfish act, in sickness or in health, in sunshine or in storm, by day or by night could prove that the age of chivalry has not passed away forever, Charles Kingsley fulfilled the ideal of a most true and perfect knight to the one woman blest with that love in time and to eternity."

The fairest fruit of Christian civilization is in the beautiful lives which it produces. They are not rare. Hundreds of records of such lives have been produced within the present generation, and there are thousands upon thousands of such lives of which no public record ever appears. Every reader must have known of at least one such life of single-hearted devotion to the good of others, and some have been privileged to know many such, within the range of their own experience. How are these lives to be accounted for, and whence do they draw their inspiration? We have no wish to be unduly skeptical, but after repeated and prolonged consideration of the subject, it is our deliberate conviction that if the forces which make the lives of the Chinese what they are were to produce one such character as Mrs. Kingsley represents her husband to have been, that would be a moral miracle greater than any or all that are recorded in the books of Taoist fables. No human institution can escape from the law, inexorable because divine: "By their fruits ye shall know them." The forces of Confucianism have had an abundant time in which to work out their ultimate results. We believe that they have long since done all that they are capable of doing, and that from them there is no further fruit to be expected. They have achieved all that man alone can do, and more than he has done in any other land, under any other conditions. And after a patient survey of all that China has to offer, the most friendly critic is compelled, reluctantly and sadly, to coincide in the verdict, "The answer to Confucianism is China."

Three mutually inconsistent theories are held in regard to reform in China. First, that it is unnecessary. This is no doubt the view of some of the Chinese themselves, though by no means of all Chinese. It is also the opinion adopted by certain foreigners, who look at China and the Chinese through the mirage of distance. Second, that reform is impossible. This pessimistic conclusion is arrived at by many who have had too much occasion to know the tremendous obstacles which any permanent and real reform must encounter, before it can even be tried. To such persons, the thorough reformation of so vast a body as the Chinese people appears to be a task as hopeless as the galvanizing into life of an Egyptian mummy. To us, the second of these views appears only less unreasonable than the first; but if what has been already said fails to make this evident, nothing that could here be added would be sufficient to do so.

To those who are agreed that reform in China is both necessary and possible, the question by what agency that reform is to be brought about is an important one, and it is not surprising that there are several different and inharmonious replies.

At the very outset, we have to face the inquiry, Can China be reformed from within herself? That she can be thus reformed is taken for granted by those of her statesmen who are able to perceive the vital need of reformation. An instance of this assumption occurred in a recent memorial in the *Peking Gazette,* in which the writer complained of the inhabitants of one of the central provinces as turbulent, and stated that a certain number of competent persons had been appointed to go through the province, to explain to the people the maxims of the Sacred Edicts of K'ang Hsi, by which vigorous measure it was apparently expected that the character of the population would in time be ameliorated. This explanation of moral maxims to the people (originally an imitation of Christian preaching) is a favorite prescription for the amendment of the morals of the time, in spite of the barrenness of results. When it fails, as it always does, there is nothing to be done but to try it over again. That it must fail, is shown by the longest experience, with every modification of circumstances except in the results, which are as nearly as possible uniformly nil. This has been sufficiently shown already in the instructive allegory of the eloquent old man whose limbs were stone.

But if mere precept is inert, it might be expected that example would be more efficient. This topic has also been previously discussed, and we need recur to it only to point out the reason why in the end the best examples always fail to produce the intended results. It is because they have no power to propagate the impulse which gave them life. Take, for instance, the case of Chang Chih-tung, formerly Governor of Shansi (see pp. 240–248), where he is reported to have made the most vigorous efforts to put a stop to the practice of opium smoking among the officials, and opium raising among the people. How many of his subordinates would honestly cooperate in his effort, and what could possibly be effected without such cooperation? Every foreigner is compelled to recognize his own comparative helplessness in Chinese matters when the intermediaries through whom alone he can act are not in sympathy with his plans for reform. But if a foreigner is comparatively helpless, a Chinese, no matter what his rank, is not less so. The utmost that can be expected is that when his purpose is seen to be inflexibly fixed, the incorruptible official will carry everything before him (so far as external appearances go), as a cat clears an attic of rats, while the cat is there. But the moment the official is removed, almost before he has fairly gone, the rats are back at their work, and everything goes on as before.

That a Chinese statesman should cherish hopes of personally reforming his country is not only creditable to him, but perfectly natural, for he is cognizant of no other way than the one which we have described. An intelligent British official, who knows "the terrible *vis inertiæ* of Oriental apathy and fatalism—that dumb stupidity against which Schiller says even the gods are powerless"—and who knows what is involved in permanent "reform," would have been able to predict the result with infallible precision. In referring to certain abuses in southwest China, connected with the production of copper, Mr. Baber remarks: "Before the mines can be adequately worked, Yunnan must be peopled, the Lolos must be fairly treated, roads must be constructed, the facilities offered for navigation by the upper Yangtze must be improved—in short, China must be civilized. A thousand years would be too short a period to allow of such a consummation, unless some force from without should accelerate the impulse." To attempt to reform China without "some force from without," is like trying to build a ship in the sea; all the laws of air and water conspire to make it impossible. It is a principle of mechanics that a force that begins and ends in a machine has no power to move it.

Between Tientsin and Peking there is a bend in the Peiho, where the traveler sees half of a ruined temple standing on the brink of the bank. The other half has been washed away. Just below is an elaborate barrier against the water, composed of bundles of reeds tied to stakes. Half of this has been carried away by the floods. The gods stand exposed to the storms, the land lies exposed to inundation, the river is half silted up, a melancholy type of the condition of the Empire. There is classical authority for the dictum that "rotten wood cannot be carved." It must be wholly cut away, and new material grafted upon the old stock. China can never be reformed from within.

It is not long since the idea was widely entertained in the lands of the West that China was to be regenerated by being brought into "the sisterhood of nations." The process by which she was introduced into that "sisterhood" was not indeed such as to give rise to any well-founded hopes of national regeneration as a consequence. And now that the leading nations have had their several representatives at Peking for more than thirty years, what beneficial effect has their presence had upon the evils from which China suffers? The melancholy truth is that the international relations of the great powers are precisely those in which they appear to the least advantage. The Chinese are keen observers; what have they perceived in the conduct of any one of the states of the West to lead to the conviction that those states are actuated by motives more elevated than those which actuate the Empire which they wish to "reform"? And now that China is herself becoming a "power," she has her hands fully occupied in playing off one set of foreign interests against another, without taking lessons of those who are much more concerned in "exploiting" China than in teaching her morals. If China is to be reformed, it will not be done by diplomacy.

There are not wanting those who are firmly persuaded that what is needed by China is not merely admission into the family of nations, but unrestricted intercourse, free trade, and the brotherhood of man. The gospel of commerce is the panacea for China's needs; more ports, more imports, a lower tariff, and no transit taxes. Perhaps we do not hear so much of this now as two or three decades ago, during which time the Chinese have penetrated more fully than before into Australia and the United States, with results not always most favorable to "unrestricted intercourse" and the "brotherhood of man." Have there not also been loud whispers that Chinese tea and Chinese straw-braid have been defective in some desirable qualities, and has not this lack been partly matched by defects in certain articles imported into China from the lands of the West?

As an auxiliary of civilization, commerce is invaluable, but it is not by itself an instrument of reform. Adam Smith, the great apostle of modern political economy, defined man as "a trading animal"; no two dogs, he says, exchange bones. But supposing they did so, and supposing that in every great city the canine population were to establish a bone exchange, what would be the inevitable effect upon the character of the dogs? The great trading nations of antiquity were not the best nations, but the worst. That the same is not true of their modern successors is certainly not due to their trade, but to wholly different causes. It has been well said that commerce, like Christianity, is cosmical in its aim; but commerce, like the rainbow, always bends towards the pot of gold.

It is sufficient to point to the continent of Africa, with its rum and its slave traffic, each introduced by trading and by Christian nations, and each an unspeakable curse, to show that, taken by itself, there is no reformatory influence in commerce.

There are many friends of China well acquainted with her condition, whose prescription is more comprehensive than any of those which we have named. In their view, China needs

Western culture, Western science, and what Mr. Meadows called "funded civilization." The Chinese have been a cultured nation for millenniums. They had already been civilized for ages when our ancestors were rooting in the primeval forests. In China, if anywhere on the globe, that recipe has been faithfully tried. There is in culture as such nothing of a reformatory nature. Culture is selfish. Its conscious or unconscious motto is, "I, rather than you." As we daily perceive in China, where our boasted culture is scouted, there is no scorn like intellectual scorn. If Chinese culture has been unable to exert a due restraining influence upon those who have been so thoroughly steeped in it, is it probable that this result will be attained by a foreign exotic?

Of science the Chinese are unquestionably in the greatest need. They need every modern science for the development of the still latent resources of their mighty Empire. This they are themselves beginning clearly to perceive, and will perceive still more clearly in the immediate future. But is it certain that an acquaintance with science will exert an advantageous moral influence over the Empire? What is the process by which this is to take place? No science lies nearer to our modern advancement than chemistry. Would the spread of a general knowledge of chemistry in China, therefore, be a moral agency for regenerating the people? Would it not rather introduce new and unthought-of possibilities of fraud and violence throughout every department of life? Would it be quite safe, Chinese character being what it is, to diffuse through the Empire, together with an unlimited supply of chemicals, an exact formula for the preparation of every variety of modern explosives?

By "funded civilization" are meant the material results of the vast development of Western progress. It includes the manifold marvels resulting from steam and electricity. This, we are told, is what China really needs, and it is all that she needs. Railways from every city to every other city, steam navigation on her inland waters, a complete postal system, national banks, coined silver, telegraphs and telephones as nerves of connection

—these are to be the visible signs of the new and happy day for China.

Perhaps this was the half-formed idea of Chang Chih-tung, when in his memorial on the subject of railways he affirmed that they will do away with many risks incidental to river transport, "such as stealing by the crew." Will the accumulation, then, of funded civilization diminish moral evils? Do railways ensure honesty in their employees, or even in their managers? Have we not read "A Chapter of Erie," showing how that great highway between states was stolen bodily, the stockholders helpless, and "nobody to blame"? And will they do these things better in China than it has as yet been possible to be sure of having them done in England or in America? Is funded civilization an original cause by itself, or is it the effect of a long train of complex causes, working in slow harmony for great periods of time? Would the introduction of the ballot box into China make the Chinese a democratic people, and fit them for republican rule? No more will funded civilization produce in the Chinese Empire those conditions which accompany it in the West, unless the causes which have produced the conditions in the West are set in motion to produce the like results in China. Those causes are not material, they are moral.

How is it that with the object-lessons of Hong Kong, of Shanghai and other treaty ports before them, the Chinese do not introduce "model settlements" into the native cities of China? Because they do not wish for such changes, and would not tolerate them if they were introduced. How is it that with the object-lesson of an honest administration of the Imperial Maritime Customs before their eyes for nearly a third of a century, the government does not adopt such methods elsewhere? Because, in the present condition of China, the adoption of such methods of taxation of Chinese by Chinese is an absolute moral impossibility. British character and conscience have been more than a thousand years in attaining their present development, and they cannot be suddenly taken up by the Chinese for their own, and set in operation, like a Krupp gun from Essen, mounted and ready to be discharged.

The forces which have developed character and conscience in the Anglo-Saxon race are as definite and as certain facts of history as the landing of Julius Caesar in Britain, or the invasion of William the Conqueror. These forces came with Christianity, and they grew with Christianity. In proportion as Christianity roots itself in the popular heart these products flourish, and not otherwise. . . .

In order to reform China the springs of character must be reached and purified, conscience must be practically enthroned and no longer imprisoned in its own palace like the long line of Japanese Mikados. It is a truth well stated by one of the leading exponents of modern philosophy, that "there is no alchemy by which to get golden conduct from leaden instincts." What China needs is righteousness, and in order to attain it, it is absolutely necessary that she have a knowledge of God and a new conception of man, as well as of the relation of man to God. She needs a new life in every individual soul, in the family, and in society. The manifold needs of China we find, then, to be a single imperative need. It will be met permanently, completely, only by Christian civilization.

🦋 A Chinese Scholar at the Crossroads Seeks to Uncover the Secrets of the West

THE PRECEDING selection has given us some idea how the West saw China during the turn of the century. How did the process work in reverse? What did the Chinese see when they looked to Europe? What was their estimation of Western culture?

The decades following the Opium War saw a pronounced increase of contacts with the West. But, as we shall subsequently see in the passages by Liang Ch'i-ch'ao (see pp. 293–305), it was not until after 1900 that Western ideas really began to permeate the ranks of the conservative scholar class. One of the first intellectuals to translate and popularize the works of Western liberal thinkers was Yen Fu (1854–1921), who had joined the Navy in the 1870s and gone to Europe, where he was able to observe the West first-hand. He concluded from his observations that the West's "wealth" and "power" resulted from the dynamism of Western liberal thought.

Yen Fu became a convert to Herbert Spencer's Social Darwinism. He admired the competitive spirit and energy he found in England, and when he turned to his own country, he found these qualities almost totally absent. As Benjamin Schwartz, Professor of History and Government at Harvard University, has pointed out in his book *In Search of Wealth and Power,* Yen Fu attributed China's backwardness to the lack of the "Faustian-Promethean character of the West." Like many other intellectuals, he became convinced that the "energies which account for the West's development are stored up in the individual and that these energies can be realized only in an environment favorable to individual interests." The problem was, how could these energies be released in China?

Yen Fu typified an age during which Chinese intellectuals were turning hopefully toward the West and testing the applicability of new ideas for China. They were asking the old question, Why is the West strong and China weak? But they were not getting the same answers as their predecessors. They began to look at reform in more total terms, and to see the inescapable organic link between thought and institutions. But frequently in their eagerness to adopt Western ideas as a life preserver to save sinking China, means were emphasized and ends ignored. Ultimate ends were obscured by short-term goals. Such ideas as liberalism were adopted because they appeared to help pave the way to "wealth" and "power." But as Schwartz brilliantly demonstrates, what does not always come through in such emulations of the West was "precisely that which is often considered to be the ultimate core of liberalism—the concept of the worth of persons within society as an end in itself, joined to the determination to shape social and political institutions to promote this value."

BENJAMIN SCHWARTZ *

From *In Search of Wealth and Power*

Turning back from the discouragements of old age to the vision of the younger Yen Fu (while noting that the discouragements themselves throw some light on the nature of the vision), we return to the central question. What does the West have which China lacks? Where does the crucial difference lie? The question is, of course, not raised in a spirit of disinterested inquiry. It is

* Benjamin Schwartz, *In Search of Wealth and Power* (Cambridge, Mass.: Harvard University Press, 1964), pp. 237–247.

thrust forward by an urgent, overriding concern with the woeful debility of the Chinese state—its lack of wealth and power. This does not mean that Yen Fu does not have perspectives which lie beyond this immediate preoccupation. Like Herbert Spencer himself, he discerns in the golden future a state in which struggle will have ceased (Taiping) and in which welfare, freedom, and every other value will prevail in a utopian equilibrium. I would urge again, however, that this "ultimate" perspective is by no means as significant in shaping the nature of his vision as the preoccupation which occupies the foreground.

While the preoccupation itself may seem narrowly political, in seeking out the ultimate sources of the West's power Yen Fu finds himself driven far beyond the domain of the political to an inquiry into the very essence of modern Western civilization. Unlike some of his more superficial successors he does not find the crucial difference in the conventional dichotomy between the materialist West and the spiritual East. He is too keenly aware of the role of the spiritual-intellectual component in the Promethean surge of the West. He is deeply conscious of the fact that the whole machinery of industrialism, of modern state bureaucracy, modern legal systems, and military organizations could not have been the creation of men exclusively interested in immediate material pleasures. As already indicated, he tends to find more "materialism" (in the ethical sense) among his Chinese contemporaries than in the modern West. The crucial difference is not a question of matter but a question of energy. The West has exalted human energy in all its manifestations—intellectual, moral, and physical. It has identified spirit not with passivity and withdrawal but with energy and assertion. The West has discovered the unlimited nature of human capacities and has fearlessly proceeded to actualize human potentialities undreamt-of in traditional Chinese culture. The terms which come to mind as key-value terms are dynamism, purposive action, energy, assertiveness, and the realization of all potentialities.

These are, after all, terms which are valued by the most diverse modern Western ideologies and which cut across all their divergencies. One is indeed tempted to describe that to which Yen Fu responds, in the first instance, as the Faustian character of Western civilization. Without necessarily endorsing Spengler's total treatment of this notion, or his effort to find its origins in the primeval forests of Germany, the term is useful as a designation of that quality of Western civilization which is probably primary in the perception of Yen Fu and of many others in the non-Western world. Like his master Herbert Spencer and unlike some romanticists, he sees in the increasingly complex machinery of modern Western civilization an embodiment of, not an impediment to, the West's Faustian energy. The Faustian nature of Western culture has led to the Promethean conquest of external nature and the enormous growth of social-political power within human society. It is obviously the Faustian-Promethean nature of Western civilization which has produced the West's enormous output of wealth and power.

Viewed in this light, Darwinism as interpreted by Spencer emerges not simply as a scientific hypothesis concerning the nature of biological evolution, but as a singularly appropriate cosmic myth epitomizing and supporting all the values of a Faustian civilization. Energy, action, assertiveness, struggle leading to the actualization of human potentialities on ever higher levels of heterogeneity, complexity, and organization—all these values are clearly realized in a Darwinian universe. In sharp contrast to many sensitive spirits in Victorian England, the younger Yen Fu accepts the Spencer-Darwin image of the universe because he ardently wishes it to be true.

If the Faustian character of the West is crucial, the strictly liberal aspects of Yen Fu's vision must be considered as a part of the whole—as a means to an end. Herbert Spencer, Adam Smith, and, to a certain extent, John Stuart Mill have convinced him that the energies which account for the West's development are stored up in the individual and that these energies can be realized only in an environment favorable to individual interests. Liberty, equality (above all, equality of opportunity), and democracy provide the environment within which the individual's "energy of faculty" is finally liberated. From the very outset, however, Yen Fu escapes some of the more rigid dogmatic antitheses of nineteenth-century European liberalism. Precisely because his gaze is ultimately focused not on the individual per se but on the presumed results of individualism, the sharp antitheses between the individual and society, individual initiative and social organization, and so on, do not penetrate to the heart of his perception. His more detached eye sees in the modern industrial corporation a triumph both of individual enterprise and of social organization. Prometheus is no more favorable to rugged individualism per se than to social organization per se, and will use whatever means are appropriate to the achievement of his ends. While the individual may be the ultimate source of energy, the consolidation of individual energies in bureaucratic organizations does not inhibit or diminish these energies. It rather enhances and channels them toward constructive goals.

If Yen Fu thus escapes the dogmatic features of Spencer's individualism, the real question which confronts us is, How profoundly rooted is his variety of liberalism? In the final analysis one may assert that what has *not* come through in Yen Fu's perception is precisely that which is often considered to be the ultimate spiritual core of liberalism—the concept of the worth of persons within society as an end in itself, joined to the determination to shape social and political institutions to promote this value. Yen Fu's concept of liberalism as a means to the end of state power is mortally vulnerable to the demonstration that there are shorter roads to that end. Spencer has given him the conception of the individual as a unit of energy, as well as the notion that this unit is valuable only in proportion to its efficiency. What if it can be demonstrated that these useful energies can be called forth in states which completely negate the values of liberty and political democracy? What if it can also be demonstrated that a social organization has been as essential to the enhancement of social energies as individual initiative? The positive authoritarianisms of the twentieth century have not inhibited the physical, moral, and intellectual (that is, technico-intellectual) energies of the energetic individual. These authoritarian states have in fact been deeply interested in enhancing these energies. Spencer's ideal "happy" man—"the healthy man of high powers, conscious of past successes, and by his energy, quickness, resource made confident of the future"—can function as well as a *Gauleiter,* commissar, or Soviet industrial manager as a capitalist tycoon, particularly if he is endowed with the requisite lack of moral imagination and reflectiveness.

Spencer's concept of individuality allied to a preoccupation with state power can only lead to a deformation of the values of liberalism. Even in its original "individualistic" form, this concept had little to do with the spiritual core of liberalism as defined above. What it involves is not the assertion of the intrinsic value of individuals but the exaltation of wealth and power on the individual rather than the collective plane. The cult of "the man of high powers" on the individual plane is likely to be just as contemptuous of the "ill-endowed" person as any totalitarian philosophy. It was, after all, this demonic strain in Spencer which aroused the profound antipathy of the elderly Huxley.

The possibility of this type of deformation is by no means confined to liberalism. The cluster of notions which hover about the word "socialism" are, if anything, even more vulnerable to deflection in the service of power goals. There is an element of surface paradox in Yen Fu's efforts to prove that the ethic of economic individualism can serve the collective interests of the state. On the surface, at least, the "ethic of socialism" seems much more directly available to the collective ends of state power. In the Stalinist development of Marxism-Leninism one has a classical instance of how socialism (defined in terms of state ownership and planning) can become a means to the end of power. The argument that socialism in this sense is superior because it leads to higher rates of economic growth, superior technology, and national might has become a central feature of current Soviet apologetics, although it would have seemed most strange to Marx and many other nineteenth-century socialists.

Yen Fu's English liberalism was not to prosper in China

after the May Fourth period. However, his preoccupation with wealth and power and his response to the Faustian element in Western civilization have remained fundamental features of the consciousness of the Chinese intelligentsia, underlying and becoming entangled with all the separate ideological currents which have since emerged, whether they have been labeled socialist, liberal, or even neo-traditionalist. This generalization does not, of course, apply to many individual thinkers, poets, and literary figures whose concerns have been quite unrelated to the goals of national power. But it remains, it seems to me, true in the aggregate.

One might indeed broaden the scope of this observation to include many of the emerging intelligentsia of the non-Western world at large. As in the case of Yen Fu, one discerns in their "response to the West" something which lies below all the explicit social, political, ideological commitments. On the one hand, they profoundly resent the failure of their own cultural traditions to reveal man's limitless Faustian capacities. On the other hand, they profoundly resent the West, which has used its Faustian power to humiliate those who lack this power. The latter *ressentiment* is, to be sure, not particularly present in Yen Fu. His special brand of Social Darwinism will not allow him to blame the "fittest" for asserting their powers. Yet in his essential concern with the crucial, humiliating difference between East and West, Yen Fu may well represent a universal, underlying element in the response to the West everywhere. It would nevertheless be quite wrong to dispose of Yen Fu's treatment of Western ideas as a distortion of modern Western thought in a non-Western mind. If Social Darwinism and liberalism are linked in his thought, it is because he already finds them entangled with each other, in a somewhat different way, in the writings of Herbert Spencer. The unsolved problems of nineteenth- and twentieth-century Western thought must themselves be brought into the arena of discussion. *De nobis fabula narratur.*

Broadly speaking, it seems to me that one can distinguish two strands of modern Western development in Yen Fu's writings: (1) the Faustian-Promethean strain—the exaltation of energy and power both over non-human nature and within human society, involving the "rationalization" (in the Weberian sense) of man's whole socioeconomic machinery; (2) what might loosely be called the stream of social-political idealism. The latter strand, represented by terms such as freedom, equality, democracy, and socialism, has been concerned with the nature of relations among men within the larger macroscopic structures of political and social life and with the shaping of those structures to promote these social-ethical ends. It represents one particular variety of ethical thought. Much of the ethical passion of Western man in recent centuries has been directed toward such social-ethical ends and has been involved in conflicts concerning the relations of these various ends to one another. Some, no doubt, would object violently to any effort to distinguish these strands even conceptually; it is indeed true that in "life" they are hopelessly intertwined. Historic simultaneity is not, however, a proof of immanent logical ("functional") relationship, and we may distinguish in analysis that which comes together in life.

The vast issues raised here can hardly be dealt with in the space of a few pages. Some questions may, however, be raised. The notion that the two strands are "functionally" related comes to the fore in many complex forms in the ideologies of the nineteenth and twentieth centuries. Before the nineteenth century, the relationship was by no means so obvious, and it is by no means certain that the two strands spring entirely from the same sources. Many serious historians have sought the roots of the concern for liberty, equality, democracy, and socialism in impulses rising, intentionally and unintentionally, out of the Reformation (combined with other strands of ancient and medieval thought), coming into confrontation with the concrete historic circumstances of the seventeenth and eighteenth centuries. On the other hand, some aspects of the Faustian growth of the West—the emergence of the modern bureaucratic, military, legal, and even industrial machinery—are clearly linked to the emergence of the absolute nation-states and the conflicts of these states. We are forcefully reminded that Jefferson, Rousseau, and many other patron saints of libertarian and democratic views during the latter half of the eighteenth century perceived no necessary functional relationship between liberty, equality, and democracy and the machinery of industrialism, let alone the machinery of power. Halévy makes a good case for the proposition that the democratic and utilitarian movements (the latter most clearly associated with Adam Smith's economic orientation) in England were in origin quite separate and only gradually became fused at the end of the century.

It is only in the early nineteenth century that close functional relations come to be perceived between the expanding machinery of wealth, in particular, and the social and political ideals, even though the question of the nature of the relationship remains a matter of dispute. One can find it argued, on the one hand, that the teachings of Locke made possible the industrial revolution, and on the other, that the industrial revolution brought liberty, equality, and democracy into being. For Karl Marx it was obvious that we are borne to socialism on the wings of the forces of production. Common to Spencer, Saint-Simon, and Marx is the belief that the machinery of industrialism will automatically realize their most cherished political and social ideals. Also common both to economic liberals (such as Spencer) and to Marxists is a tendency to think of the industrial age as marking the end of the age of the nation-state and of its power goals. There is a common assumption that while the expanding machinery of wealth is a functional prerequisite for the achievement of either liberal or socialist goals, the machinery of state and military power is either already obsolete or about to become so.

In fact, a candid, retrospective glance would indicate that at no time in the history of nineteenth-century Europe, even at the height of Manchester liberalism, was economic development ever completely divorced from the machinery and goals of state power, even though its immanent economic end may be defined as the ultimate achievement of general economic welfare. It can hardly be claimed that this "mercantilist" factor has diminished in the slightest in the middle of the twentieth century, when the two world superpowers confront each other in terms of the balance of terror. Here again, Yen Fu's old Chinese formula permits him to perceive more clearly than many Western thinkers confined by their ideological commitments the fact that the machinery of industrialism and the concerns of national (or supernational) power are never divided by an iron wall. If the values of liberalism and/or socialism are a by-product of the "rationalization" of modern society, then they must be related to this rationalization in all its aspects—political, military, and economic. The growth of state and military power is as relevant as the march of industrialization.

One need not deny all claims of positive relation between the political and social values mentioned above and the machinery of wealth and power. I would suggest, however, that the relationship between them is much more accidental, equivocal, haphazard, and mutable than is generally assumed in the bland religion of modernization. The more "liberal" state structure of eighteenth-century England may have provided a more favorable environment for the first breakthrough of industrial capitalism than the bureaucratized states of the Continent. The machinery of wealth and power does require the expansion of its ruling elite and—up to a point at least—a stress on achievement is inherent in the process of modernization. This does imply a growing area of equality of opportunity. One will thus find a growing equality of opportunity in societies as diverse as Meiji Japan, Nazi Germany, the Soviet Union, and the United States. The freedom to choose among career opportunities and to develop one's physical and intellectual powers (when these are safely technical in the broadest sense of that term) are equalities and freedoms which have been fostered within both democracies and the modern, positive authoritarian states. These authoritarian states have been quite able, however, to dispense with civil rights involving the physical inviolability of individuals, with spiritual liberty, with political democracy and social equality. If the word "socialism" involves a concern with human equality and not simply a "planned" and centrally organized society, it has been amply demonstrated that the machinery of wealth and power is inherently hierarchic and authoritarian. There are those who assure us that the happy day when the processes of modernization will spontaneously realize all social and political ideals is just over the horizon. As of the present, however, it should be noted that in those societies where these values have been realized to any extent and with any degree of solidity there have been conscious historic movements expressly devoted to their achievement and not merely a blind reliance on the "forces of modernization."

One can hardly stand in judgment on Yen Fu or the modern Chinese intelligentsia for concerning themselves with the question of state power. China has indeed been deeply humiliated, and no society can survive in the modern world without state power. However, the fact remains that where values are judged as means toward the attainment of power these values are likely to be rendered precarious, weak, and deformed.

In becoming involved with these problems, Yen Fu and China have already entered the uncharted sea of the modern world in which we all are afloat. The problem of the relation between the Faustian religion of the limitless pursuit of wealth and power and the achievement of social-political values—and even more fundamental human values—remains a problem for us as much as for them.

❷ A Modern Intellectual Becomes Conscious of China's Degradation

THE REFORM movement swept across China in waves, each wave advancing farther and superseding the last. What was radical for Li Hung-chang was the point of departure for K'ang Yu-wei. What was radical for K'ang Yu-wei proved too conservative for Liang Ch'i-ch'ao. Slowly the face of China was being changed as successive generations brought her farther and farther down the path toward a repudiation of her past.

In many ways the thought of Liang Ch'i-ch'ao represents the transition between the old idea of reform, namely reform within the bounds of Confucian tradition or sanctioned by Confucian canon, and the new ideas of revolution which led to the overthrow of the dynasty in 1911. Liang was the first Chinese intellectual to put Chinese problems in the context of world history. He abandoned attempts of his predecessor K'ang Yu-wei to justify all change by the teachings of Confucius, and instead of trying to interpret Confucius as a revolutionary, he turned quietly to Social Darwinism. If the world really was based on the principle of the survival of the fittest, it was obvious to Liang that China must compete on her adversaries' terms, which meant that it would no longer do to borrow Western technology and keep Chinese thought and institutions. Liang says, "As we have gradually thought back, in our disappointment, we realize that a social culture is a whole unit, and as such, it definitely cannot make use of new institutions with an old psychology." China needed a stiffer dose of reform or she would have continued to falter in the world community.

In time, however, even Liang's prescription for China's

ills became outdated. A member of China's gentry elite, Liang had always refrained from harsh attacks on the Manchu Dynasty, believing that his people were unprepared for a truly democratic government. Talk of revolution of any kind made him uneasy, and he remained a gradualist until his death, by which time China's youth had moved on and become absorbed in new ideas such as those of Dr. Sun Yat-sen.

The first selection is a plea against the return of monarchy under Yüan Shih-k'ai. It was ironic that Liang, who had earlier opposed the Republican Revolution, should be writing a polemic for republican government. Behind this apparent change of heart lay Liang's basic conservatism, which rendered him distrustful of all violent change regardless of its nature. He says, "The path to progress leads to further progress, but the path to revolution leads to further revolution. . . . Therefore a man who has any love of his country is afraid to mention revolution; as for myself, I am always opposed to revolution." Despite his distaste for violent change, Liang Ch'i-ch'ao was a key figure in the intellectual revolution which played a major part in the transformation of China.

The second selection is a survey of China since the T'ung-chih Restoration (see pp. 205–235) written by Liang Ch'i-ch'ao for a Shanghai newspaper in 1922. In it Liang outlines the three phases of reform through which China had passed. One senses, despite the forced optimism at the end, a note of despair and disillusionment with China's progress. It is important to remember that at the time this was written China had already passed through revolution into chaos.

All of China's efforts at reform seemed to have been in vain. The dynasty had been overthrown, but the experiment in republican government had proved to be a disaster. Imperial China's splendor and pride had vanished. China was humiliated and divided; her leaders and intellectuals searched desperately for some new credo to restore her from her fallen position.

LIANG CH'I-CH'AO *
A Polemic for Republican Government

No form of government is ideal. Its reason of existence can only be judged by what it has achieved. It is the height of folly to rely on theoretical conclusions as a basis for artificial arbitration as to what should be accepted and what discarded. Mere folly, however, is not to be seriously condemned. But the danger and harm to the country will be unmeasurable if a person has prejudiced views respecting a certain form of government and in order to prove the correctness of his prejudiced views, creates artificially a situation all by himself. For this reason my view has always been not to oppose any form of government. But I am always opposed to any one who engages in a propaganda in favor of a form of government other than the one under which we actually live. In the past I opposed those who tried to spread the republican form of government while the country was under monarchical government. . . .

I do not say that the merits or otherwise of the republican system should not be discussed, but the time for such a discussion has passed. The most opportune time for such a discussion was in 1911 when the Revolution had just begun; but since then further discussions should not be tolerated. . . .

Do you not realize that the state is a thing of great importance and should not be disturbed carelessly? How can you then experiment with it and treat it as if you were putting a chest into a dead hole, saying "Let me place it here for the moment and I will see to it later.". . .

Can it be possible that those who are now holding up the constitutional principle as a shield for their monarchical

* Liang Ch'i-ch'ao in MacNair, *Modern Chinese History, op. cit.,* pp. 747–751.

views have a different definition for the term "constitution"? The Ch'ing (Manchu) Dynasty considered itself as possessing a constitution in its last days. Did we recognize it as such? Let me also ask the critics what guarantee they have to offer that the constitution will be put into effect without hindrance as soon as the form of state is changed. If they cannot give any definite guarantee, then what they advocate is merely an absolute monarchy and not a constitutional monarchy. As it is not likely to be a constitutional monarchy, we may safely assume that it will be an imperial autocracy. I cannot regard it as a wise plan if, owing to dislike of its defects, the Republic should be transformed into an imperial autocracy. Owing to various unavoidable reasons, it is excusable in spite of violent opposition to adopt temporarily autocratic methods in a republican country. But if the plan proposed by present-day critics be put into effect, that on the promise of a constitution we should agree to the adoption of a monarchy, then the promise must be definitely made to the country at the time of transition that a constitutional government will become an actuality. But if, after the promise is made, existing conditions are alleged to justify the continuance of autocratic methods, I am afraid the whole country will not be so tolerant towards the Chief Executive. To assume outwardly the role of constitutional government, but in reality to rule in an unconstitutional manner, was the cause of the downfall of the Ching Dynasty. The object lesson is not obscure. Let us take warning by it.

If, on the other hand, the present-day critics are really in earnest for a constitution, then I am unable to understand why they believe that this cannot be secured under the Republic but must be obtained in a roundabout way by means of a monarchy. In my view the real hindrances to the adoption of a constitution at the present day in China are the existing conditions, *viz.* the attitude of the officials and the traditions and intellectual standards of the people. But these hindrances have not resulted from the adoption of republicanism. Therefore they cannot be expected to disappear with the disappearance of the Republic. For instance, from the President down-

ward to the minor official of every official organ in the capital
or in the provinces, every one inclines to be independent of the
law, and considers it convenient to deal with affairs as he
pleases. This is the greatest obstacle to constitutional government. Now has that anything to do with the change or not of
the form of State? . . .

Now my friends, you have stated in a worthy manner the
reasons why the republican form of state cannot assist China
to maintain her existence; now let me state why it is impossible to restore the monarchical system. The maintenance of the
dignity of a monarch depends on a sort of mystical, historical,
traditional influence or belief. Such an influence was capable of
producing unconsciously and spontaneously a kind of effect
to assist or indirectly in maintaining order and imparting blessing to the country. In this lies the value of a monarchy. But
dignity is a thing not to be trifled with. Once it is trodden down
it can never rise again. . . . Ever since the days of monarchical
government the people have looked on the monarch with a
sort of divine reverence, and never dared to question or
criticize his position. After a period of republicanism, however,
this attitude on the part of the common people has been abruptly
terminated with no possibility of resurrection. A survey of all
the republics of the world will tell us that although a large
number of them suffered under republican rule, not a single
one succeeded in shaking itself free of the republican fetters.
Among the world republics only France has had her monarchical
system revived twice after the republic was first inaugurated.
The monarchy, however, disappeared almost immediately. Thus
we may well understand how difficult it is for a country to
return to its monarchical state after a republican regime. It
may be said that China has had only a short experience of the
republican regime; but it must also be remembered that the
situation has been developing for more than ten years and
in actual existence for about four years. During the period of
development the revolutionists denounced the monarch in most
extravagant terms and compared him to the devil. Their aim
was to kill the mystic belief of the people in the Emperor; for

only by diminishing the dignity of the monarch could the revolutionary cause make headway. And during and after the change all the official documents, school textbooks, press views and social gossip have always coupled the word monarch with reprobation. . . .

The Odes say, "The people are tired. Let them have a respite." In less than four years' time from the eighth moon of the year Hsin Hai we have had many changes. Like a bolt from the blue we had the Manchu Constitution, then "the Republic of Five Races," then the Provisional President, then the formal Presidency, then the Provisional Constitution was promulgated, then it was suddenly amended, suddenly the National Assembly was convoked, suddenly it was dissolved, suddenly we had a Cabinet system, suddenly it was changed to a Presidential system, suddenly it was a short-term Presidency, suddenly it was a life-term Presidency, suddenly the Provisional Constitution was temporarily placed in a legal position as a Permanent Constitution, suddenly the drafting of the Permanent Constitution was pressed. Generally speaking the average life of each new system has been less than six months, after which a new system quite contrary to the last succeeded it. Thus the whole country has been at a loss to know where it stood and how to act; and thus the dignity and credit of the government in the eyes of the people have been lowered down to the dust.

A copy of Yang Tu's pamphlet "Constitutional Monarchy or the Salvation of China" reached me after I had finished writing the above discussion. . . . Who would have thought that a man, who cares not for the question of the form of state like myself and who opposed you—Mr. Yang Tu—during your first campaign for the change in the form of state—you were a Republican then—would be opposing you again now that you are engaged in advocating another change in the form of state? A change in the form of government is a manifestation of progress while a change in the status of the state is a sign of revolution. The path of progress leads to further progress, but the path of revolution leads to more revolution. This is a fact proved by theory as well as actual experience. Therefore a man who has any love for his country is afraid to mention revolution; and as for myself I am always opposed to revolution. I am now opposing your theory of monarchical revolution, just as I once opposed your theory of republican revolution, in the same spirit, and I am doing the same duty. My belief is that since the country is now in a most weakened state, we may yet fail even if we do all we can at all times to nurse its wound and gather up its scattered strength. How can anyone devote his time and energy to the discussion of a question of no importance such as the form of state, and so obstruct the progress of the administration? . . .

. . . Once I wrote a piece of poetry containing the following lines:

> Ten years after you will think of me,
> The country is excited. To whom shall I speak?

I have spoken much in my life, and all my words have become subjects for meditation ten years after they were uttered. Never, however, have any of my words attracted the attention of my own countrymen before a decade has spent itself. Is it a misfortune for my words or a misfortune to the country? My hope is that there will be no occasion for the country to think of my present words ten years hence. . . .

LIANG CH'I-CH'AO *

From *A Review of China's Progress*

In the realm of learning and thought, we cannot but recognize that there has been considerable progress, and that actually a way of great progress has been opened for the future. In this the most vital turning point is the abolition of the civil-service

---

* Liang Ch'i-ch'ao in Teng and Fairbank, *China's Response to the West, op. cit.*, pp. 269–274.

examination system. This system has had more than one thousand years' history, and can really be regarded as deeply rooted and firmly based. Its greatest shortcoming was to make the minds of the scholars of the whole country hypocritical, traditional, and vague, and thus block all sources for the development of learning and thought. The movement for abolition of the civil-service examination had already begun nearly fifty years ago. Kuo Sung-tao, Feng Kuei-fen and others had all briefly expressed some ideas to this end. By the time of the 1898 Reform Movement, the so-called new party of that time, including K'ang Yu-wei, Liang Ch'i-ch'ao and their group, may be said to have used their whole energy in launching a general attack against the civil-service examination system. After about ten years from first to last, and after undergoing a great number of vicissitudes, this obstacle to civilization was finally broken down. Now these past events seem to be ordinary, but from the point of view of an historian of the last fifty years they must be counted as of great importance.

After these fifty years, what knowledge can we present to other people? It is embarrassing to say that there is practically nothing. But the minds of the scholars have been changed to a very large degree. I remember that in 1876 there was a minister to England, Kuo Sung-tao, who wrote a travel account in which there was a paragraph which said in effect, "The present barbarians are different from former barbarians; they also have two thousand years of civilization." Good Heavens, this was terrible! When this book reached Peking the public anger of all the officials and scholars in the government was aroused. Everybody denounced him; every day he was accused; the matter was not concluded until the printing blocks of the book were burned by Imperial decree. So little time has passed since then, yet the phrase "new cultural movement" has now become a habitual slogan of all learned societies. Ma-k'o-ssu [Marx] is almost competing for the seat of honor with Confucius, and I-pu-sheng [Ibsen] is nearly overthrowing Ch'ü Yuan [343–290 B.C.]. Whether this kind of psychology is correct or not is another question, but in general the radical change of thought of the last forty-odd years was indeed never dreamed of during the preceding four-thousand-odd years. . . .

An old proverb well says that "when one keeps on learning, then one realizes that one's knowledge is insufficient"; and during the last fifty years the Chinese gradually have realized their own insufficiency. This little consciousness, on the one hand, is the cause of the progress of learning; and, on the other, it may be counted as the result of the progress of learning.

In the first period our mechanical articles were first realized to be insufficient. This realization gradually started after the Opium War until in the period of T'ung-chih [1861–1874] foreign troops were borrowed to suppress the civil war. Hence people like Tseng Kuo-fan and Li Hung-chang acutely felt that the solidity of foreign ships and the effectiveness of foreign cannon were really superior to ours. . . . (see pp. 236–239). Therefore the shipyard and academy in Fukien and the arsenal at Shanghai and other institutions were gradually established. But during this period the world of thought was little influenced. During this time the most memorable things were the several science books translated by people in the arsenal. To us now these books may seem archaic and superficial, but among the groups of translators there were several who were quite loyal and devoted to knowledge. It was really a painstaking enterprise for them to produce such works then, because at that time no scholars could speak a foreign language, while those who could speak a foreign language did not read books. Therefore these translations really blazed a trail for "the experts in Western knowledge who did not understand foreign languages" in the second period.

In the second period there was a feeling of insufficiency concerning our [political and social] institutions. After the defeat by Japan (see pp. 254–260), people with good minds in the nation really seemed to have met a thunderbolt in a dream. Accordingly, they wondered why the great and grand China should have declined to such a degree, and discovered that all was due to her bad political system. Therefore they took *"pien-fa wei-hsin"* [*i.e.,* to change the statutes and to reform] as a big banner and launched a movement in society. The ardent leaders were the people like K'ang Yu-wei and Liang Ch'i-ch'ao. The people in this group were well trained in Chinese learning, but as for foreign languages they actually could not understand a single word. They could not tell others "what foreign knowledge consisted of and how to learn it." They could merely shout in loud voices every day, saying, "The old stuff of China is insufficient; many good points of the foreigners should be learned." Though these words sound general and undefined [lit., like swallowing a date whole], yet at that time they produced a tremendous effect. The political movement was a failure, with the exception of the above-mentioned abolition of the civil-service examination system. . . . This really opened a new phase for the future. During this period many schools were opened at home and many students went to study in foreign countries. . . . The most valuable productions in the academic field were the several works translated by Yen Fu, who introduced some of the main currents of nineteenth-century thought into China. It is regrettable, however, that too few people in the nation could understand them.

In the third period there was a feeling that the foundations of our culture were insufficient. The duration of the second period, comparatively speaking, had been very long—from the war of 1894 to 1917 or 1918—twenty years. Though great changes were wrought in the political arena, the realm of thought remained much the same. In brief, during this score of years we always felt that our government and laws, etc., were far inferior to those of others, and we were vexed at not being able to bring others' political organizations and forms one by one into our country. We took for granted that if this could only be done, myriads of other problems would be solved. It is almost ten years since the success of the [1911] revolution but all that we hoped for has proved vain, item by item. As we have gradually thought back, in our disappointment, we have realized that a social culture is a whole unit, and as such it definitely cannot make use of new institutions with an old psychology. By degrees there has grown up a demand for a reawakening of the whole psychology. At the conclusion of the great European war a great deal of active spirit was added to the tide of thinking of the whole world. Among the recently returned students there appeared quite a few able persons, who exerted their courage to promote a complete emancipation movement. Therefore during the last two or three years a new epoch has been demarcated.

The progress of thought in the three periods, if we try to measure between the people of the first and last periods, will be immediately very clear. In the first period [the pioneers] like Kuo Sung-tao, Chang P'ei-lun, Chang Chih-tung, and others, were regarded as very new monsters. When it came down to the second period, Sung-tao and P'ei-lun were dead, but Chih-tung was still living, and in the first half of this period Chih-tung was still regarded as a promoter of new things; but by the latter half he was considered simply an exponent of conservative, absurd ideas. In the second period K'ang Yu-wei, Liang Ch'i-ch'ao, Chang Ping-lin, Yen Fu, and others were all brave scholars of the world of thought, standing in the first line of battle. During the third period, when many new young men ran to the front lines, these people [of the second period] were pushed behind, one by one, and some have entirely withdrawn or retired from the ranks. This kind of phenomenon, the new replacing the old, may prove that the circulation of fresh blood in the world of thought during the last fifty years has been very rapid. It may prove that the body and spirit of the world of thought are gradually becoming healthy and strong.

If we take a number of fifty-year periods in our history to compare with the fifty years just past, great progress has indeed been made in this last half century. If, however, we take our last fifty years and compare them with the last fifty years in other countries, we shall be utterly ashamed. Let us take a look: What has the United States done in fifty years? What has Japan done in these fifty years? What has Germany done in these fifty years, and what has Russia done in these fifty years? Although politically their successes and failures are not the same, and their suffering and happiness are not equal, yet as to their academic and thinking elements, all may be considered to have advanced a thousand *li* a day. Even England, France, and other old nations—which one is not running forward as if flying? We have been talking noisily of new education for several decades. Let us ask our scientists, do we have one or two things which may be considered inventions of world importance? Ask our artists, do we have one or two productions which can be offered for world appreciation? And in our publication circles, do we have one or two books which are important works of the world? Alas, we had better wait until after the third period and see what it may bring. . . .

I dare say that once the signboard of the Republic has been hung up, hereafter in thousands and myriads of years it will never be taken down again. Regardless of whether you are as wise and sagacious as Yao and Shun, or as strong and tyrannical as the First Emperor of the Ch'in or the founder of the Ming, or as cunning as Ts'ao Ts'ao and Ssu-ma I, if you wish again to be the emperor of China, no one will ever allow you to do so. This fact should not be lightly regarded. . . .

In sum, during the most recent thirty years, of the tasks which have been accomplished by our nationals, the most important is the fundamental extermination of a government dominated by foreign people for more than one thousand years. . . . The second is the permanent destruction of the absolutist monarchical government of more than two thousand years. . . . And moreover, these two achievements are by no means unexpected coincidences; they have really been achieved by the fundamental awakening of the people, who have exerted the greatest effort before they could accomplish them. Seen from this point of view, the period can really fit the meaning of the word progress.

During the last ten-odd years since the establishment of the Republic, the political phenomena have indeed been disgusting; but I think we should not be too disappointed, because these phenomena have been caused by two special factors, and these factors are going to disappear soon. The first one is that, during the time of the Revolution, because the power of the people themselves had not yet become sufficient, they could not help relying on traditional influences.

The second factor is that it is normal for all matters in society to have their ups and downs. From 1894 and 1898 to 1911 benevolent people and scholars dedicated to a worthy cause have really been worked to the point of physical and mental exhaustion. The most regrettable thing is that many people who struggled for ideals died martyrs of the times. Their successors could not immediately take up the task. Therefore the interregnum has become a dark and colorless period; but I think this period will soon be over. The former leaders seem to have reawakened, caught their breath, and renewed their struggle. The fighting power in the rear has, furthermore, become stronger day by day. In these circumstances a new spirit and a new phase will naturally appear.

In summary, I am completely optimistic in regard to the political future of China. My optimism, however, has grown from the pessimism of ordinary people. I feel that China during the last fifty years has been like a silkworm becoming a moth, or a snake removing its skin. These are naturally very difficult and painful processes. How can they be accomplished easily? —only if biologically it is possible to function during the necessary change or removal, and if psychologically there is consciousness of the necessity for change and removal. Then, after we have undergone the unavoidably difficult and painful process, the future will be another world. Therefore, while everyone may consider that our political life is retrogressing, I feel that the possibility of its progress is very great. . . .

❧ *Chronology: 1644–1911*

1644: The Manchus conquer Peking and establish Ming Dynasty

1683: Taiwan falls to the Manchus

1670–1750: The Manchus conquer Turkestan and Tibet

1689, 1727: Border treaties with Russia concluded

1723: Christianity proscribed in China

1793: Lord Macartney leads a British delegation to China

1795: White Lotus Rebellion challenges the dynasty

1834: Lord Napier's mission skirmishes with the Chinese

1839: Opium War between China and Britain begins

1842: Treaty of Nanking concluded between China and Britain

1843: Hong Kong ceded to Britain; process of opening Treaty Ports begins

1850: Taiping Rebellion breaks out

1853: Taipings capture Nanking

1856: "Arrow" War, the second conflict with the West, begins

1857: British and French troops occupy Canton

1858: Treaties signed with Britain, France, Russia, and the United States, extending special foreign privileges

1860: Chinese renege on treaty terms; British and French troops occupy Peking; Russia gains concessions in Manchuria

1862: Beginning of T'ung-chih Restoration and the Self-Strengthening Movement

1864: Nanking retaken and Taipings crushed

1870: Tientsin Massacre

1871: Russian troops occupy Ili region in Sinkiang

1872: First Chinese students go abroad

1878: China sends first ambassadors abroad

1881: China recognizes Japanese occupation of Ryukyu Islands

1884: Sino-French War; Annam becomes a French protectorate

1887: Kowloon opened as port; Amoy formally ceded to Portugal

1888: Peiyang Army, China's first modern army, formed

1889: Kuang-hsü Emperor assumes power; Empress Dowager's regency abolished

1890: China's early industrialization: Li Hung-chang establishes China's first modern textile factory in Shanghai

1891: Anti-Christian movement spreads in Yangtze region

1892: Anti-foreign writings prohibited by Peking; floods, famines, natural disasters; Sun Yat-sen founds China Resurrection Society

1893: Chang Chih-tung establishes factories in Hankow region; China's first newspaper founded

1894: Sino-Japanese War breaks out

1895: China defeated; Japan obtains Taiwan and Liaotung Peninsula in Manchuria and other concessions in China

1896: China and Russia sign treaty for construction of jointly operated Central Manchurian Railway; railway concessions granted other powers; Sun Yat-sen arrested in London

1897: Russians occupy Dairen

1898: Abortive "Hundred Days" ends short period of liberal reform

1899: Boxer Rebellion begins; John Hay proclaims "Open Door Policy"

1900: Boxer-led anti-foreignism spreads; Allied nations occupy Peking; pace of industrial and business development quickens

1901: Li Hung-chang dies

1904: Russo-Japanese War breaks out; fighting in Manchuria; Japanese win

1905: Sun Yat-sen organizes anti-Manchu revolutionary movement in Japan
1906: Constitutional government proclaimed in Peking
1911: Manchu Dynasty overthrown

❧ Bibliography*

Empire and Splendor

Ch'ü, T'ung-tsu, *Local Government in China Under the Ch'ing* (Cambridge, 1962).

Fitzgerald, C. P., *China, A Short Cultural History* (New York, 1961).

Ho, Ping-ti, *The Ladder of Success in Imperial China* (New York, 1962).

Hsiao, Kung-chuan, *Rural China: Imperial Control in the Nineteenth Century* (Seattle, 1960).

Michael, Franz, *The Origin of Manchu Rule in China* (Baltimore, 1942).

Reischauer, Edwin, and Fairbank, John K., *East Asia, The Great Tradition* (Boston, 1960).

Decline

Chang, Hsin-pao, *Commissioner Lin and the Opium War* (Cambridge, 1964).

Fairbank, John K., *Trade and Diplomacy on the China Coast, The Opening of the Treaty Ports, 1842–1854* (Cambridge, 1953).

Fairbank, John K., and Reischauer, Edwin O., *East Asia, The Modern Transformation* (Cambridge, 1965).

Feuerwerker, Albert, *China's Early Industrialization: Sheng Hsuan-huai and Mandarin Enterprise* (Cambridge, 1958).

Hsü, Immanuel C., *China's Entry into the Family of Nations* (Cambridge, 1960).

---

* This bibliography does not include works cited in the text.

Michael, Franz, *The Taiping Rebellion* (Seattle, 1966).

Purcell, Victor, *The Boxer Uprising: A Background Study* (Cambridge, England, 1963).

Spector, Stanley, *Li Hung-chang and the Huai Army* (Seattle, 1964).

Collapse

Ch'en, Jerome, *Yüan Shih-k'ai, 1859–1916* (Stanford, 1961).

Hsueh Chun-tu, *Huang Hsing and the Chinese Revolution* (Stanford, 1961).

Jansen, Marius, *The Japanese and Sun Yat-sen* (Cambridge, 1954).

Levenson, Joseph R., *Liang Ch'i-ch'ao and the Mind of Modern China* (Cambridge, 1953); *The Problem of Monarchical Decay,* Vol. 2 of *Confucian China and Its Modern Fate* (Berkeley, 1964).

Index

✎ᠪ FRANZ SCHURMANN is Director of the Center for Chinese Studies at the University of California at Berkeley. Born in New York City, he received his Bachelor's degree from Trinity College and his Doctorate from Harvard University; he served in the United States Army during World War II. He is the author of *The Ideology and Organization of Communist China*, and co-author of *The Politics of Escalation in Vietnam*. Professor Schurmann writes frequently on Chinese History and Southeast Asian current affairs for both scholarly and popular periodicals. He makes his home in Oakland, California.

✎ᠪ ORVILLE SCHELL was also born in New York City. He has been educated at Harvard, Stanford, and Taiwan National Universities. He is presently a graduate assistant in Chinese Studies at the University of California at Berkeley. Mr. Schell has worked for the Ford Foundation Overseas Development Office in Indonesia and has been a newspaper correspondent in Southeast Asia.

03451

03451

DS
735
S43
V.1

Schurmann, Herbert Franz, *comp.*
The China reader, edited, annotated, and with introductions by Franz Schurmann and Orville Schell. New York, Random House [1967]

3 v. 22 cm.

CONTENTS.—**1.** Imperial China: the decline of the last dynasty and the origins of modern China; the 18th and 19th centuries.—**2.** Republic of China: nationalism, war, and the rise of Communism; 1911–1949.—**3.** Communist China: revolutionary reconstruction and international confrontation; 1949 to the present.

1. China—Hist. I. Schell, Orville, joint comp. II. Title.

DS735.S43 · 951 66–21489

Library of Congress [5]